THE
SOCIOLOGICAL
PERSPECTIVE

THE SOCIOLOGICAL PERSPECTIVE

A VALUE-COMMITTED INTRODUCTION

E·D·I·T·O·R·S

Michael R. Leming
Raymond G. DeVries
Brendan F. J. Furnish

Academie
Books Grand Rapids.
Michigan
Zondervan Publishing House

THE SOCIOLOGICAL PERSPECTIVE
Copyright © 1989 by Michael R. Leming, Raymond G. De Vries, and
Brendan F. J. Furnish

ACADEMIE BOOKS is an imprint of Zondervan Publishing House,
1415 Lake Drive, SE, Grand Rapids, Michigan 49506.

Library of Congress Cataloging in Publication Data

The Sociological perspective : a value-committed introduction /
  editors, Michael R. Leming, Raymond De Vries, and
  Brendan F. J. Furnish.
     p.   cm.
  Bibliography: p.
  Includes index.
  ISBN 0-310-21661-3
  1. Sociology, Christian.   I. Leming, Michael R.   II. De Vries,
Raymond.   III. Furnish, Brendan F. J.
BT738.S615 1989   88-27406
261.5–dc19   CIP

Printed in the United States of America

   89   90   91   92   93 / EP / 10 9 8 7 6 5 4 3 2 1

CONTENTS

JACK BALSWICK & JUDITH BALSWICK (FULLER
THEOLOGICAL SEMINARY)

ABOUT THE CONTRIBUTORS

Michael R. Leming is Associate Professor and Chairman of the Department of Sociology at St. Olaf College. He holds degrees from Westmont College (B.A.), Marquette University (M.A.), and the University of Utah (Ph.D.) and has done additional graduate study at the University of California in Santa Barbara. He is the author of *Understanding Dying, Death, and Bereavement* and *Understanding Families: Diversity, Continuity, and Change*. Dr. Leming is the founder and former director of the St. Olaf College Social Research Center, member of the board of directors of the Minnesota Coalition on Terminal Care, member of the steering committee of the Northfield AIDS Response, hospice educator, volunteer, grief counselor, and secretary-treasurer of the Christian Sociological Society.

Raymond G. DeVries is an Associate Professor of Sociology at St. Olaf College. Before coming to St. Olaf he taught at Westmont College and Gordon College. He holds degrees from Westmont College (B.A) and the University of California, Davis (M.A., Ph.D.). He is the author of *Regulating Birth: Midwives, Medicine, and the Law*.

Brendan F. J. Furnish is Professor of Sociology and Chairman of the Social Science Division at Westmont College. He holds degrees from California State University, San Francisco (B.A., M.A.) and the University of Southern California (Ph.D). Dr. Furnish has taught sociology at Westmont College for twenty-one years. He came into sociology from a background in physics and electronics and has published articles in a variety of different areas of sociology, but maintains a particular interest in the relationships among Christianity, science, and sociology.

Jack Balswick is Professor of Sociology and Family Development and Director of Research for Marriage and Family Studies at Fuller Theological Seminary. He holds advanced degrees from the

University of Iowa (M.A., Ph.D.) and has done postdoctoral study at Trinity Evangelical Divinity School. He has twice been appointed a Senior Fulbright Scholar—to Cyprus in 1972–73 and to Korea in 1982. He has authored over fifty professional articles and six books, the most recent being *The Inexpressive Male.* Forthcoming are *Marriage and the Family: A Christian Perspective* (with Judith Balswick) and *Social Problems: A Christian Perspective* (with J. Kenneth Morland).

Judith Balswick is Assistant Professor of Marriage and Family Therapy and Director of Clinical Training at Fuller Theological Seminary. She is a graduate of Augustana College (B.A.), the University of Iowa (M.A.), and the University of Georgia (Ed.D.). She has done postdoctoral study in Theology and Biblical Studies at Fuller Theological Seminary. She is the author of a number of articles, the most recent being "A Theological Basis for Family Relationships" and "A Maturity-Empowering Model of Christian Parenting." She has co-authored the forthcoming book *Marriage and the Family: A Christian Perspecitve* (with Jack Balswick).

Ronald J. Burwell is Professor of Sociology and Chairman of the Department of Behavioral Science at Messiah College. In addition to being a graduate of Wheaton College (B.A.), he holds degrees from Trinity Evangelical Divinity School (M.Div.) and New York University (M.A., Ph.D.). Prior to teaching at Messiah he taught sociology and anthropology at The King's College, New York, and served as Visiting Professor of Sociology at Wheaton College. He has authored many articles that have appeared in *Teaching Sociology, Review of Religious Research, Christian Scholar's Review,* and the *Journal of the American Scientific Affiliation.* In addition, he has contributed chapters to *Christian Perspectives on Sociology,* edited by Stephen Grunlan and Milton Reimer, and *The Reality of Christian Learning,* edited by Harold Heie and David Wolfe. Currently Dr. Burwell is conducting a longitudinal study of student outcomes in the area of social and moral development.

Robert A. Clark is Professor of Sociology at Whitworth College. He is a graduate of Whitworth College (B.A.) and Washington State University (Ph.D). He has published articles, delivered lectures, and taught courses in the following sociological areas: the sociology of knowledge, the relationship between Christian thought and sociology, marriage and the family, deviant behavior, and modern social criticism.

C. Stephen Evans is Professor of Philosophy and Curator of the Hong Kierkegaard Library at St. Olaf College. A graduate of Wheaton College (B.A.) and Yale University (Ph.D), Dr. Evans is the author of *Preserving the Person, Kierkegaard's Fragments and Postscript*, as well as four other books and numerous articles. He is also the editor of the series *Contours of Christian Philosophy*.

S. D. Gaede is Professor of Sociology and Chairman of the Department of Sociology at Gordon College. A graduate of Westmont College (B.A.) and Vanderbilt University (Ph.D), he is the author of numerous journal articles as well as two books, *Where Gods May Dwell: On Understanding the Human Condition* and *Belonging*. He has served as secretary to the Society for the Scientific Study of Religion and is currently the editor of the SSSR Monograph Series and member of the Zondervan Academic Books Editorial Board. Twice the recipient of the Excellence in Teaching Award at Gordon College, he speaks extensively and has served as a Staley Distinguished Christian Scholar Lecturer.

Richard B. Perkins is Professor of Sociology and Chairman of the Department of Sociology at Houghton College. A graduate of Wheaton College (B.A.) and the University of Massachusetts (Ph.D), Dr. Perkins has published articles in *The Journal for the Scientific Study of Religion*, *The Journal of the American Scientific Affiliation*, and *The Christian Scholar's Review*. He has contributed to Stephen Grunlan and Milton Reimer's *Perspectives in Sociology* and has authored *Looking Both Ways: Exploring the Interface Between Christianity and Sociology*.

Zondra G. Lindblade is Professor of Sociology at Wheaton College. She is a graduate of Wheaton College (B.A.), Michigan State University (M.A.), and Loyola University, Chicago (Ph.D). She has participated in social work with the Frontier Nursing Service (Wendover, Kentucky) and worked as Dean of Women at the Philadelphia College of Bible and at Wheaton College. Dr. Lindblade has been a board member of the Evangelical Child and Family Agency and is on the Advisory Council for Pioneer Ministries. She has authored articles, done research, and lectured on social relationships, the family, deviant behavior, and organizational management.

THE
SOCIOLOGICAL
PERSPECTIVE

INTRODUCTION—
CHRISTIAN SOCIOLOGY:
CONSCIOUSNESS WITH
CONSCIENCE

Raymond G. DeVries

Sociology and Christianity? Bringing these two things together is like trying to mix oil and water. Traditionally, sociologists have had as little use for Christianity ("Who needs that myth anyway? It is no different from any other myth about God, death and creation.") as Christians have had for sociology ("Isn't that the same thing as socialism? And don't all Socialists hate God?"). Living in the middle of this misunderstanding and malice are members of a faithful remnant—including the authors of the following chapters—who occasionally (when no one is listening) refer to themselves as "Christian sociologists."

Why is it so difficult to bring sociological thought and Christian faith together? The answer to this question lies in the one thing Christianity and sociology do have in common—they both regard themselves as disciplines. The dictionary tells us that *discipline* involves "instruction and exercise designed to train to proper conduct or action" and "subjection to rules of conduct or behavior." Both sociology and Christianity have a code of proper conduct, and each demands that its followers be subject to its code. The Christian sociologist is caught between two masters—each demanding complete loyalty. On one side the Christian says, "Of course you believe that the world was created and ordered by a loving God who sent his only son, Jesus Christ, to redeem fallen creation." On the other side stands the sociologist saying, "Of course all knowledge, including religious knowledge, is socially created. The Christian belief in God and Christ is just another product of society."

Imagine yourself to be a Christian sociologist walking into your church on a Sunday morning. If your primary allegiance is to Christianity, your response is to join in and worship your creator.

11

But if your first devotion is sociology, you will stop and analyze the situation, perhaps noting how religion—any religion—serves to promote social solidarity. You might go on to explore the mechanisms used in this situation to achieve that goal.

How can Christian sociologists be faithful to two disciplines? Typically they use one of three strategies: *compartmentalization, complementarity,* or *conspiracy.* All three of these strategies are visible in this volume.

Compartmentalization involves separating your Christian life from your sociological life. Although some Christian sociologists use the term *compartmentalist* pejoratively (as an insult), this strategy is not as bad as it sounds. In its worst form, compartmentalism is *not* good—that is in cases where the two worlds are kept so distant that the Christian sociologist is willing to do immoral things to advance sociological knowledge or carelessly disregards sociological knowledge in order to preserve Christian faith. But in those situations, Christianity and sociology are so remote that it is unfair to use the label "Christian sociologist." Christian sociologists who are compartmentalists proceed by doing the very best sociology they can do—adhering to all the rules of the sociological method—and then applying their findings in a way consistent with their faith. Although they are compartmentalists, their faith influences their sociology at two points. First, their faith leads them to do sociological work with integrity—work that is ethical and rigorous. Second, the results of this work are used for ends consistent with God's kingdom. They remain compartmentalists, however, because while they are doing their sociological work, the rules of sociology take priority. Their faith commitment is not allowed to influence their method.

A second strategy for bringing sociology and Christianity together is to see the two disciplines as *complementary.* The cliché that best expresses this approach is "All truth is God's truth." Those who believe that sociology and Christianity are complementary suggest that there are two ways to learn about God. The first is to explore the special revelation given in Scripture; the second is to investigate God's general revelation found in the world. Because all truth is God's truth, we can learn as much about God from a sociologist (or physicist, or biologist, or historian) as we can from a biblical scholar. The Christian sociologist need not be distinct in any way, because all good sociology—done by Christians or non-Christians—points us toward God. This strategy is perhaps best seen as a version of the compartmentalist approach; both believe the duty of the sociologist is to do rigorous sociology. But the approaches remain distinct because the compartmentalist would not necessarily claim that sociological truth reveals God's nature. In fact, the complementarity approach suffers from a fatal internal contradiction. The rules of sociology do not allow one to say "All truth is God's truth." The sociologist must say, "All truth is a *social* representation of God's truth"; hence we can never be *sure* of God's truth. If good sociology contradicts good Christianity, is it possible to be loyal to both?

A third strategy for bringing Christianity and sociology together is *conspiracy*. Although we associate conspiracy with unlawful acts, one of the definitions of the word is "any concurrence in action—combination in bringing about a given result." Conspiracy implies concurrence. Neither sociology nor Christianity can take precedence—each must be subject to the other. According to this approach, Christianity must discipline sociology, *and* sociology must discipline Christianity. For instance, the Christian belief that humans were created by God with the capacity for free will must temper the sociological belief in determinism. But this approach also holds that sociology must discipline Christianity—sociological knowledge causes us to reassess our faith, to rethink our doctrine, and to reject needless dogma.

The common feature of all three strategies, and of all the following articles, is the desire to put sociological knowledge to use to accomplish God's work in the world. All of the authors agree that it is better to be sociologically conscious than unconscious, and that the sociologically conscious Christian is better equipped to realize the goal of *shalom*, to implement love and justice in the world.

You will encounter all three strategies as you read the chapters of this book, and you will also discover the following as recurring themes in many of these chapters: conflicts between individualism and community, freedom and determinism, value-freedom and value-relevance, commitment and relativism; the need for praxis and Christian social action; the need to understand philosophical assumptions; and a concern for the sociological significance of individual and group sin. Christian sociology, regardless of the strategy used to bring these two disciplines together, is a step toward providing consciousness with conscience.

"BUT I WANT TO HELP PEOPLE!" NOTES ON THE NEED FOR A SOCIOLOGICAL IMAGINATION

Raymond G. DeVries

"How can I help?" Most people stumble into their first sociology class because they have a genuine desire to help others. They see friends suffering from the effects of broken homes, battling with anorexia and depression, using drugs, and abusing their bodies. Looking beyond their circle of friends, they see the pain others suffer as a result of unemployment, terrorism, poverty, and war. Faced with these problems, students turn to sociology hoping to become more effective helpers.

Our concern for others flows from our desire to be like Christ. As followers of Christ, we want to relieve the suffering we see around us. But we must remember that Christians have no corner on mercy—compassion is a common grace. Both the Christian and the non-Christian are moved as they watch an anorexic friend slowly starve. Both the "saved" and the "unsaved" are grieved when innocent children are maimed or killed by terrorists, or when poverty robs the motivation, health, and even the lives of their fellow human beings. It should not be troubling to learn that Christians do not have a monopoly on mercy. Certainly few of us would want to live in a world where only Christians are compassionate.

But compassion, Christian or non-Christian, is not enough. The compassion you feel when you see others suffer might help you—by confirming your self-image as a caring person or by reminding you of what is ultimately important in life—but "armchair compassion" does not help others or relieve suffering. Relief of suffering requires uncovering the causes of suffering. Of course knowledge of the roots of suffering is not needed to offer short-term relief to hurting people, but the systematic prevention of suffering cannot be accomplished without a thorough *under-standing* of its causes.

Students affirm their faith in sociology by enrolling in sociology courses—their act of enrolling demonstrates their faith that the sociological perspective will help them in their quest to uncover the causes of human suffering. And in fact, sociology can be a powerful tool for understanding the unique problems of life in the late twentieth century. But students often leave sociology courses feeling frustrated. There are two reasons for this, one is found in the nature of sociology, the other in the nature of the student.

Sociology is not what most students expect it to be. Students often come to sociology with a strong and immediate desire to help others. They are soon discouraged. They want to take meals to homeless families living in the local campground, but their sociology professor wants them to struggle through statistical tables that plot trends in unemployment and to grapple with the three or four different sociological paradigms that explain "social dislocation." Many of these discouraged students are expecting their *sociology* course to be a course in *social work*. But sociology is not social work. As Perkins (1987:42) puts it: "The goal of professional social work is to help people, whereas the goal of sociology is to. . .*explain human interaction.*" Sociology is nothing more (and nothing less) than the attempt to explain—and hence understand—human interaction. Because their first desire is *not* to explain but to *help*, the first question social workers ask about a given social situation is: "What is *wrong* here?" The notion is that: (1) something is wrong, (2) it needs to be changed, and (3) I am here to change it. Sociologists believe that the assumption "something is wrong" prevents accurate understanding. After all, what looks "wrong" to an outsider might actually be very right for those involved. Because their goal is to understand, sociologists ask a different question: "What is *going on* here?"

A second source of student frustration with sociology is found in the nature of the student. The peculiar biases that are the products of growing up in American society and of a Christian world view make it difficult for students to comprehend the sociological approach. Because of these biases, many students leave their sociology courses without ever understanding what it means to think sociologically. Although students come to sociology with a genuine desire to learn, they find it hard to shed their earlier understanding of human behavior. Let's consider some typical and nonsociological explanations for problems mentioned above: anorexia, terrorism, and poverty.

Anorexia. What causes a person to avoid one of the body's most basic needs—eating? Students note that their anorexic friends tend to be overachievers; hence the condition is understood as an obsessive sort of self-discipline. According to this explanation, the anorexic is looking for control in her life and chooses to tightly control the amount of food eaten. It is further noted that anorexics tend to be first-born children, leading to the conclusion that the anorexia is a response to overly ambitious, if not unreal, parental expectations.

Terrorism. Even though travelers are assured that the likelihood of being victimized by terrorists is minuscule, the threat seems very real when we see vivid pictures of gaping holes in the sides of passenger planes and the bleeding bodies of innocent women, men, and children. What leads a person to commit such hostile acts—acts that often require suicide? Our reference to terrorists as "madmen" hints at our explanation—terrorists are crazy people with pathological personalities. Psychologists trace terrorism to a variety of character flaws—a heightened need for the "aggrandizement of a sense of male potency," a way of dealing with guilt or, in the case of the assassin, a need for intimacy (*see* Beyette, 1986).

Poverty. Why are people poor? And why does it seem that the poor stay poor? Most students have little trouble with this question. Quick reading of the proverbs of Solomon leaves little doubt as to the cause of poverty:

> Go to the ant, O sluggard;
>   consider her ways, and be wise. . .
> How long will you lie there, O sluggard?
>   When will you arise from your sleep?
> A little sleep, a little slumber,
>   a little folding of the hands to rest,
> and poverty will come upon you like a vagabond,
>   and want like an armed man (Proverbs 6:6–11).

Clearly poverty is brought on by laziness.

Here we have some seemingly reasonable explanations of behavior—explanations that allegedly help us understand the causes of human suffering and enable us to be more effective helpers. These are the explanations students have little trouble accepting because they fit well with what they "know" to be true about people. But sociologists find these explanations unsatisfactory on two levels: (1) they are not grounded in good information, and (2) they suffer from a strong psychological bias.

To construct a sociological explanation for a certain event or behavior, one must begin by collecting reliable and valid information. Sociology is an empirical discipline, that is, it is based on thorough study of the subject at hand—not on hunches, intuitions, or what your Uncle Bob believes. Sociologists go out and observe people, interview them, and add up and sort out their responses. These seemingly simple actions often challenge common sense (what everyone "knows" to be true) and official explanations (what the authorities tell us is "true"). Sociologists are fond of pointing out that common sense is often contradictory. Which is true: "birds of a feather flock together," or "opposites attract" (Webster, 1987)? Common-sense explanations are often based on faulty information. Suppose I was reading the *Statistical Abstract of the United States* to you (sounds interesting, doesn't it?), and I said, "Hey, look at this. Blacks have a higher suicide rate than whites." You might respond, "Of course, that's obvious! Blacks kill themselves more often because of racial oppression." But then I notice that I read the table wrong. "Oops! In fact, *whites* kill themselves more often than blacks." "Of course, that's obvious," you say. "Whites suffer more stress!" I am left scratching my head. What *is* obvious? Sociologists recognize that conclusions about human behavior must be based on careful and disciplined research.

Because they challenge official explanations of events, the simple acts of observing, counting, and tabulating can be seen as subversive. Shliapentokh (1982) reports on the threat of sociology to Soviet leaders. In the 1960s several empirical studies by sociologists contradicted views of life in Russia offered by the Communist party. With the use of surveys, sociologists discovered that the Russian people, like those in non-Socialist nations, acted with the intent of satisfying personal needs, ignoring the "dominant social (i.e., Socialist) values," that the children of workers had much less chance of being admitted to the universities, and that Soviet readers were uninterested in publications filled with party ideology. These findings were threatening to the government, and so the authorities systematically dismantled the Institutes of Social Research.

The common-sense explanations of anorexia, terrorism, and poverty offered above suffer from a lack of empirical grounding, but they are also unacceptable to sociologists because they demonstrate a strong psychological bias. Americans prefer psychological explanations of behavior. When asked to explain some human characteristic, Americans will always start by looking at traits of the individual. Thus anorexia is explained by excessive self-discipline and the desire for control, terrorism is understood as the product of the need to enhance "male potency," and poverty is the inevitable result of laziness. Sociological explanations, which understand behavior as a social product, are not a part of the American imagination. *Psychology Today* is one of the most popular American periodicals. There is no *Sociology Today*. Peter Berger (1963:1) suggests that the endless number of jokes about psychologists is ample evidence of how firmly rooted psychology is in the American consciousness. Somewhat ironically, he laments that there are so few jokes about sociologists.

What does a sociological imagination look like? C. Wright Mills (1959) describes its essential elements. Those who possess a sociological imagination are able to distinguish between "private troubles" and "public issues"; they recognize that a given individual is the product not just of his or her own biography, but of the historical forces operating in society. Mills illustrates by considering the problem of unemployment. If in a city of 100,000 one man is unemployed, that is a "private trouble." In seeking to understand his unemployment, we rightly look to characteristics of the individual. But if in that same city 10,000 people are unemployed, we can no longer understand unemployment as a problem of individual character. Unemployment is a "public issue." If we are to understand why people are unemployed, we must look to society and the forces at work there. Mills applies this same reasoning to the problem of divorce. If only one out of every 50,000 marriages ends in divorce, we can explain that divorce in terms of the personalities of the individuals involved. But if 25,000 of every 50,000 marriages end in divorce, we are faced with a public issue. Understanding divorce requires examination of the ways in which individuals and the institution of marriage are placed under duress by the economy and society. Most social workers understand suffering as a private trouble. They seek "knowledge about 'maladapted *individuals*,' not 'malfunctioning *social systems*,' which often turns [them] toward psychological theories and remedies and away from those of sociology" (Perkins, 1987:42).

According to Mills (1959:6–7), the sociological imagination is driven by three categories of questions:

1. What is the structure of this particular society as a whole? What are its essential components and how are they related to one another? How does it differ from other varieties of social order? Within it, what is the meaning of any particular feature for its continuance and for its change?

2. Where does this society stand in human history? What are the mechanics by which it is changing? What is its place within and its meaning for the development of humanity as a whole? How does any particular feature we are explaining affect, and how is it affected by, the historical period in which it moves? And this period—what are its essential features? How does it differ from other periods? What are its characteristic ways of history-making?

3. What varieties of men and women now prevail in this society and in this period? And what varieties are coming to prevail? In what ways are they selected and formed, liberated and repressed, made sensitive and blunted? What kinds of "human nature" are revealed in the conduct and character we observe in this society in this period? And what

is the meaning for "human nature" of each and every
feature of the society we are examining?

How does one apply the sociological imagination to the
problems of anorexia, terrorism and poverty? Let's begin with
anorexia. The empirical bent of sociology leads the sociologist to
go out and tabulate the characteristics of anorexics. It is immediately apparent that anorexia is almost exclusively a problem for
women and girls. This simple observation suggests that to
understand the problem we must look at what it means to be a
female in today's society. An interview with Jacqueline Bisset
about her role as Josephine, the lover and wife of Napoleon
Bonaparte, gives us a picture of the expectations for females
(Deronda, 1987:9):

> While shooting in France, Bisset put on some weight. [Bisset
> comments:] "I didn't mind because I thought Josephine should
> be plump—as most women were in those days. Don't get me
> wrong. I'm not a heifer on the screen, but I look big. Actually I
> was at my natural weight." As soon as she returned to Beverly
> Hills, she began to slim down again. "Men can get portly and
> smell of cigars and still pull in the chicks. . .Women can't get
> away with that."

Chernin (1981) believes anorexia is to be expected in a society
that values young, attractive, independent women. If other types
of women are devalued, the attempt to stay young and attractive
is a supremely rational act. Physiological studies show anorexia
prevents maturation, delaying the onset of menstruation and
preventing the development of the large breasts and thighs
associated with mature women. Seen in this light, anorexia is not
a "private trouble"; it is a "public issue." The problem is best
solved not by training an army of counselors who can help women
recognize their personality flaws, but by changing the unjust roles
and unreal expectations that create these tensions in the lives of
women.

A student in my Introduction to Sociology class caught a
glimpse of the sociological imagination and used it to understand
her concern with her weight:

> I have this mental picture of how I "should" look: a couple of
> inches taller, quite a few pounds lighter, skin that is tanner, hair
> that is lighter. Where did this picture come from? Well, last
> week I read *Glamour* magazine and a 5' 10" model that weighed
> 115 pounds and had strawberry blonde hair was wearing a
> bright yellow bikini and she looked great! In [the movie] *Top
> Gun*, Kelley McGillis is tall, thin, and beautiful and look at the
> leading man she had! Even my own mother is 5' 8", wears a size
> four, teaches aerobics and eats alfalfa.

Admittedly, this student needs to develop her sociological imagination so that she can connect the images of women she sees in *Glamour* (and elsewhere) with economic change, the changing roles of women, the evolving arrangement between the sexes, and the fashion, diet, and exercise industries. But she has begun to broaden her vision, to understand that her view of herself is a product of the particular social forces at work in her society.

Similarly, terrorism must be understood as an act embedded in a social and political context, not as an act of a crazy individual. To understand why someone would walk into a hail of bullets or commit suicide by crashing a van loaded with explosives into an embassy building, we must know something of the characteristics of the society that created this person and the meaning that society gives to those actions. Religious institutions and other of society's socializing agents can develop individuals who gladly give their lives for others. Careful study will also reveal something of the political situations that spawn terrorism. As with anorexia, what seems irrational might in fact be a rational act when viewed from the context of the participants.

Using the sociological imagination to understand poverty requires reliable information on the extent and location of poverty. That is, how much poverty is there, and who is poor? Such information can be difficult to find. Statistics from government agencies are often arranged to show the effectiveness of government programs. Statistics from welfare rights groups and other advocates of the poor are arranged to show the failure of government programs. For instance, heated debates recently took place about the plight of the homeless in America. Most hotly debated was the *number* of homeless people—advocates for the homeless claimed that 3 million people were homeless, but the government insisted the number was under 500,000.

After sifting through the numbers, the next task is to explain what is found. Following the advice of Mills, the sociologist is not content to explain any social phenomenon with reference to characteristics of the person. For the sociologist, it is not enough to say that individual laziness causes poverty. The sociologist wants to discover the social circumstances that make people lazy, that rob them of their motivation. Using this sociological reasoning, William Ryan (1971) says that when we understand poverty to be the result of flaws in the individual, we are actually *blaming the victim*.

Imagine your feelings in the following situation: You return to your car after an afternoon of shopping at the mall only to discover someone has smashed through your window and stolen your car radio, cassette tapes, and some packages you placed in there earlier. You promptly call the police. When the patrol car arrives, the officer steps out and proceeds to write *you* a ticket.

You protest, "But, officer, *I* was the one who was robbed!" "I can see that," replies the officer, "but it is your fault. After all, if you didn't have a car, and if that car didn't have a radio, and if you hadn't parked your car here, you wouldn't be in this predicament!" This seems ridiculous, but Ryan says this is exactly what we do when we conclude poverty is the result of decisions by the poor.

Ryan uses a powerful illustration to support this sociological view. Convinced that poverty was the result of the unwillingness of the poor to work hard and save their money, a team of researchers went to an inner city school and a suburban school and asked the young students the following question: "Which would you rather have, *one* candy bar now, or *two* candy bars next week?" As expected, the majority of the poor children chose one candy bar now, and the middle-class kids "invested" their candy bar and waited to get two next week. The researchers patted themselves on their backs. "See," they concluded, "the poor are poor because they cannot defer gratification. If they get it, they spend it. They have no idea of the value of saving their money." Another team of researchers saw a problem with the study, and they decided to conduct a similar study of their own. They started the same way: an inner city school and a suburban school, same candy bar question, same results. But they added one new twist. They gave out candy bars to those who chose to take one that day, but they did not come back with two candy bars the following week. Those who decided to "invest" their candy bar lost it; they were cheated by the system. Six months later the researchers returned to the same classrooms with the same offer. What do you suppose happened? You are right. All the middle-class kids opted for one candy bar immediately. These researchers concluded that poverty is not created by poor decisions; it is created by unequal opportunity. People might make poor decisions, but those decisions are structured by the conditions under which they live.

Individuals who catch on to the sociological perspective and who are able to develop a sociological imagination find it a powerful tool for understanding their lives and the lives of those they seek to help. But most students never quite get the idea. In fact from the perspective of a teacher of sociology, it seems they *resist* sociology. Why the difficulty? I think the problem stems from growing up in Protestant America.

America is a land of heroes. From Davy Crockett (king of the wild frontier) to the self-made millionaires of the industrial era to the astronauts who died aboard the space shuttle, America celebrates the rugged individual who goes it alone. Pull yourself up by your bootstraps! Take charge of your destiny! America's emphasis on the individual and individual responsibility is deeply rooted in our history. In the 1830s Alexis de Tocqueville, a French sociologist, visited the United States and recorded his impressions in a book, *Democracy in America*. He was excited by the American experiment with democracy, but he was concerned with the destructive effects of something he termed *individualism*. He believed that the equality celebrated by Americans would produce an individualism that would separate every man from his neighbor. De Tocqueville feared that such a separation would open the door to tyranny.

In the 1950s David Riesman suggested that Americans were becoming "other-directed": conformists seeking affirmation by behaving like those around them. The cause of this change? American individualism, which cuts people off from the sense of identity provided by community and tradition. Most recently, several sociologists interested in the "habits of the heart" in the United States concluded that individualism is still the defining feature of American life (Bellah et al., 1985).

What does all this mean for students of sociology? In short, it means that America is a hostile environment for the sociological imagination. Growing up in this society makes it difficult to imagine that an individual is not the ultimate master of her own destiny. America is the "land of the free." If we are free, we must be responsible for our successes as well as our failures. Unemployment, divorce, anorexia, all of these are private troubles, the products of individual choice.

The sociological imagination is further thwarted by a Protestant world view. As Protestants, we learn from an early age that our faith, our relationship with God, and our salvation are matters of personal responsibility and personal choice. Sure, we get together with fellow believers once or twice a week, but what is the purpose of these meetings? To strengthen our *individual* commitments to God. For Protestants, the sociological imagination—which suggests that religious beliefs and styles of worship are shaped by social forces—is heresy.

But is this American and Protestant view of behavior a biblical model? I think not. The Bible is alive with illustrations of the sociological imagination. In both Old and New Testaments God judges his people corporately, not as individuals. He recognizes their various types of disobedience (worshiping idols, neglecting the poor) as public issues, not private troubles. Corporate punishment implies that evil emerges not just from individuals, but from the organizations they create. The minor prophets of the Old Testament speak God's judgment against Israel. Read Amos and notice that the entire *nation* is judged—men, women, even unborn children—not just the leaders of the nation. The church at Laodicea is in a similar situation; in Revelation we are told that *the church* will be rejected by God because of its lukewarm commitment.

Both Old and New Testaments emphasize the importance of society in shaping individual character and commitment. Biblical instructions for righteous living recognize the social influences on character. The writers of Proverbs were aware of the ability of the social environment to influence behavior, constantly reminding us to flee evil company. They did *not* say, "Go wherever you please and trust that the Holy Spirit will help you choose correctly." The ministry of Jesus was not an individualistic effort. The church of Christ has grown not because of the solo acts of "highly motivated" individuals who have "centered their personal energy." It has been a corporate effort. As Tarman (1987:51) notes, Jesus did *not* say ,"Go therefore, and maximize your own potential. Do not bother with Judea, Samaria, or the ends of the earth. They must take responsibility for their own growth. And lo, you are with yourself always, unto the close of your own life." The work of God in the world has always been accomplished through social organizations.

How far have you come with me? The ultimate test of your sociological imagination is your ability to conceive of social sin. Can a society, an organization, a church, be guilty of sin? How do you regard our current AIDS (Acquired Immune Deficiency Syndrome) epidemic? Those *not* exercising sociological imagination believe the spread of AIDS is the collective consequence of individual sin. Homosexuals and drug users are clearly sinful, and the spread of this dreadful disease is the result of their willful and freely chosen disobedience. It is their problem.

However, if we invoke our sociological imaginations, we find a different explanation—an explanation that shows how we share in their sin. Drug use and homosexuality are not isolated problems of a few individuals; they are public issues and behaviors tied to the structure of society. The sociological imagination presses us to discover those features related to our contemporary social environment that encourage people to use drugs and to seek alternative ways to exercise their sexuality. While not denying that AIDS is spread by drug users and homosexuals, we view their behavior as a consequence of social structure. We are implicated because we are a part of that social structure, we live in it, we help to create it, and even when we see its flaws, we do not resist.

Those who seek to develop and exercise the sociological imagination must remember that such an imagination is difficult to nurture in a society that prefers individualistic explanations. This recent exchange from one of our most popular sources of information about individual behavior—a "Dear Abby" column (Van Buren, 1987:2)—is typical:

> DEAR ABBY: As the father of a daughter returning to college for her second year, I am upset and angry. I realize that college

students are considered adults, but are they really ready for this enormous step? . . .it costs ($16,000-plus) for tuition. But the cost doesn't anger me as much as the lack of moral supervision these "adults" get at college. When I visited our daughter's campus last fall I was shocked to discover that the dorms and students' town houses reminded me of the brothels I have read about. I don't care how many talks parents have with their children, it's not fair to subject them to this kind of temptation. Instead of passing out condoms, the school should stop the cohabitation going on at our supposedly respectable campuses.

UPSET PARENT

DEAR UPSET: Most parents are very much concerned about the morals of their children, but when a grown child goes off to college, parents cannot expect the college authorities to assume guardianship of their children's sexual behavior. I think college students bring their moral values to college—they don't find them there. If young adults are inclined to fool around, they will find a way to do it on their lunch hour—living at home.

Clearly, our friend Abby lacks a biblical and sociological imagination. She implies that sexual ethics come solely from the individual. According to her analysis, a "grown child" will behave the same way—whether placed in a brothel or a convent. This conclusion is both unbiblical and nonsociological. The writer of Proverbs 7 would certainly disagree with Abby. Those with a sociological imagination would also disagree. The sociologist points out that sexual ethics are shaped by notions of childhood (what we consider a "grown child" today is much different from opinions in previous eras), changes in technology, the state of the economy, changed views of marriage, and threats of nuclear war.

You might be asking, "What happened to the question, How can I help? Can a sociological imagination help me help others?" Peter Berger (1963) offers an odd answer to that question. He says that sociology allows us to help others by "cheating" society. He advocates what he calls "sociological Machiavellianism." Machiavelli was a medieval Italian prince who wrote a guidebook for all who sought to get and keep political power. His book, *The Prince*, said the road to power requires rulers to lie, to cheat, and to manipulate others. Berger recognizes that the understanding provided by sociology allows us to be Machiavellians; it gives the knowledge we need to be very effective manipulators. But he encourages us to be Machiavellians with scruples—using what we learn about society to manipulate others in order to promote love and justice.

Let me give you an example. You are a personnel consultant hired by an automobile manufacturer to resolve the problem of absenteeism on the assembly line. In looking over the situation, you discover that absenteeism is not the only problem. The line workers are also abusing alcohol and other drugs. How do you respond? If you lack a sociological imagination (and many personnel consultants do), you might suggest creating an individual counseling center—bring in a team of industrial psychologists and require all workers displaying some pathology to spend one of two hours a week talking about their problem with a counselor.

If you exercise your sociological imagination, you will conclude that the problem is not the result of defective *workers*; it is the result of a defective *work situation*. What can be done? Instead of hiring a team of industrial psychologists, hire some engineers to redesign the assembly line. The manufacturers of Volvo automobiles in Sweden did just that. Faced with high absenteeism and drug abuse—problems typical in assembly line work—Volvo restructured its plant so that a team of workers built a car from start to finish. Workers had a new sense of accomplishment in their work, and both absenteeism and drug abuse declined sharply.

Note that the strategy used by Volvo treats workers as human beings with dignity. It is more cost effective to have one person spend all day screwing on right front fenders, but the effort to save money ignores the cost in human misery.

Unfortunately, you will see few job announcements that specify "sociological imagination required." In fact, most social service jobs require a psychological imagination. Social workers are trained to help people deal with problems individually. They get their clients enrolled in some program, or they smooth out problems with landlords, teachers, or employers. These efforts are satisfying because they bring immediate results, but they do little to change the social conditions creating those problems for individuals. Using the sociological imagination to help others does not bring the same immediate results and usually does not provide a steady income, but the long-term results can be astonishing.

Consider the case of Betty Friedan. You might not know who she is, but if it were not for her, many of you women reading this book would not be in college right now. Friedan is the author of *The Feminine Mystique* (1963), a book that was instrumental in changing the roles of American women—giving them the freedom to pursue a career other than that of housewife or secretary. In the 1950s, Friedan sought counseling to help her overcome frustration and depression. She soon realized that *she* was not the problem; the problem was a social structure that limited women. Her book was the result of this realization, and it became a rallying point for women experiencing the same problems. Had Friedan not used her sociological imagination (deciding instead to become a counselor to disgruntled housewives), women might still face the kind of oppression they did in the 1950s.

How can you help? You can help by exercising your sociological imagination, by recognizing the difference between private troubles and public issues, and by seeking to promote love and justice in the world by changing the social conditions that create human misery. The following chapters will help you develop your sociological imagination. As you read them, remember this is the first step toward helping others.

REFERENCES IN CHAPTER

Bellah, Robert, Richard Madsen, William Sullivan, Ann Swidler, and Steven Tipton. 1985. *Habits of the Heart*. Berkeley and Los Angeles, Calif.: University of California Press.

Berger, Peter L. 1963. *Invitation to Sociology*. Garden City, N.Y.: Doubleday/Anchor Books.

Beyette, Beverly. 1986. "A Timely Conference on Sigmund Freud." *Los Angeles Times*, April 17.

Chernin, Kim. 1981. *The Obsession*. New York: Harper & Row.

Deronda, Daniel. 1987. "Jacqueline Bisset is Josephine." *The Denver Post*, November 8.

Friedan, Betty. 1963. *The Feminine Mystique*. New York: Dell.

Mills, C. Wright. 1959. *The Sociological Imagination*. London: Oxford University Press.

Perkins, Richard. 1987. *Looking Both Ways: Exploring the Interface Between Christianity and Sociology*. Grand Rapids, Mich.: Baker Book House.

Riesman, David. 1950. *The Lonely Crowd*. New Haven, Conn.: Yale University Press.

Ryan, William. 1971. *Blaming The Victim*. New York: Random House.

Shliapentokh, Vladimir. 1982. "The Sociologist: There And Here." *The American Sociologist* 17:137–39.

Tarman, Bart. 1987. "Radical Individualism, The Society Of Jesus, And The American Liberal Arts College." *Faculty Dialogue* 8:51–55.

Tocqueville, Alexis de. 1835. *Democracy in America*. New York: Washington Square Press.

Van Buren, Abigail. 1987. "Campus Morals Rate an F in His Book." *Los Angeles Times*, November 4.

Webster, Edgar L. 1987. *Sociology An Introduction: Instructor's Manual*. New York: Macmillan.

SOCIOLOGICAL RESEARCH AND VALUE COMMITMENTS

Michael R. Leming

The director of personnel at a large church-affiliated hospital is surprised to discover that 52 percent of all American women with preschool children are in the work force. Because she is concerned that she might be contributing to this troublesome trend, she decides to conduct a study to determine the following: (1) What percentage of her female employees have preschool children? and (2) How does their employment influence the development of their children? She has on her staff two industrial sociologists who regularly do social research for the hospital. The first is a married woman with two preschool children; the second is a middle-aged single man. She is concerned that this be a fair and impartial study. Whom should she hire?

The dilemma faced by this personnel director is not unusual. Those who do social research have always been concerned with the way that values influence results. Can a black sociologist study the way in which professional sports influence the aspirations of black youths? Can an obese person do responsible field research on Overeaters Anonymous? Would an atheist be the best person to conduct a study of television evangelists? To answer these questions, we first need to understand the scientific nature of sociology.

SOCIOLOGY AS A SCIENTIFIC DISCIPLINE

George C. Homans (1967:7), in his book *The Nature of Social Science*, asserts that sociology is a science. He bases his claim on the fact that sociology does the two basic tasks of any science: discovery and explanation. The first task is to state and test more or less general relationships between empirical events of nature.

The second task is to explain these relationships within a theoretical context. A scientific explanation will tell us why, under a given set of conditions, a particular phenomenon will occur (Homans, 1967:22).

Even though the claim has often been made that the social sciences are different from the other sciences because they use a radically different technique of doing research, Richard Rudner (1966:5) would contend that the differences between the natural and the social sciences are much less fundamental than a difference in methodology. Both the natural and the social sciences use the same empirical methodology, which is based on observation and reasoning, not on supernatural revelation, intuition, appeals to authority, and personal speculation. This is the basis for the following statement by Homans, in which he argues that sociology is a science:

> What makes a science are its aims, not its results. If it aims at establishing more or less general relationships between properties of nature, when the test of the truth of a relationship lies finally in the data themselves, and the data are not wholly manufactured— when nature, however stretched out on the rack, still has a chance to say "No!"—then the subject is a science. By these standards all the social sciences qualify. (Homans, 1967:4)

In the process of discovery, the scientist is attempting to formulate general statements concerning empirical variables that can be verified by systematic observation. For example, Emile Durkheim (1951) hypothesized that suicide rates were strongly related to the intensity of social cohesiveness. He speculated that the character of social ties influences the likelihood that an individual would take his or her own life.

By studying the social characteristics of suicide victims, we discover a higher percentage of males, Protestants, unmarried and formerly married persons, unemployed persons, soldiers, officers, and older persons. Further investigation would tend to give empirical support to Durkheim's (1951) hypothesis that people who are less integrated into the social fabric of society are at greater risk of taking their own lives.

In the process of explanation, the scientist tries to explain the "why" of the relationships between the empirical variables. In Durkheim's (1951) study, he formulated three types of suicide— anomic suicide, egoistic suicide, and altruistic suicide. Each of these types of suicides attempts to explain why an individual might commit suicide under particular conditions related to social integration. The unemployed person or recently divorced person who commits suicide would be classified as anomic. In this type of suicide the value system of the group no longer has meaning for the individual, and he or she feels isolated, lonely, and confused. Any disruption of a way of life may lead to anomic suicide (Theodorson and Theodorson, 1969:427).

The suicide of a male Protestant might be classified as an egoistic suicide because the person may not be adequately supported by group ties. Women and members of the Jewish and Roman Catholic religious communities are more likely to find social support and less likely to become social isolates.

Altruistic suicide is the result of overly strong commitment to the group. The older person who has a terminal illness might commit suicide so as not to become a burden to his or her family. The soldier who throws himself on an enemy grenade in order to save his buddies' lives, and the captain who goes down with the ship after helping passengers into lifeboats are committing suicide because of their desire to serve the needs of the group. In each of these suicidal behaviors, the explanation of the behavior is given in terms of the social integration for the individual who commits the act.

Employing a systematic method for investigation based on sensory observation, sociology is concerned with the subject of human interaction. Sociologists, unlike psychologists, are less interested in the internal workings of the individual than in the relationships between individuals and groups of individuals. As a discipline, sociology is not concerned with the behavior of nonhuman animals. Although it might be interesting to develop hypotheses concerning human behavior from animal studies, the final test of these propositions must refer to data collected on human interaction. For example, a family sociologist may be interested in comparisons of baboon and human family structures, but would not make inferences to human interaction based on studies of baboon behavior. In medical and psychological research, scientists often make statements about human physiology based on data collected on other animals. This is necessary because of the ethical problems involved in experimentation on human subjects. Sociological studies tend to be less physically intrusive and harmful.

Sociology and the other social sciences share a commitment to the scientific method and to the jobs of describing and explaining human social interaction. Sociologists employ a number of research techniques—among them the historical and comparative approaches, qualitative methodologies involving field studies and unobtrusive techniques, survey, and experimental research designs. Their research interests will at various times overlap all of the other social sciences, but they are also uniquely interested in the relationships between these disciplines.

THE NATURE OF CAUSALITY

If we understand science as an attempt to make statements about relationships between empirical properties or events in nature, then it is imperative that we turn our attention to social scientific propositions. Scientific propositions are assertions concerning relationships between empirical variables. In both the natural and the social sciences these assertions usually take a cause-and-effect form. For example, crime rates are influenced by population density. According to Zetterberg (1966), for a relationship to be considered causal it must be irreversible (if X, then Y; but if Y, then no conclusion about X—this is an asymmetrical relationship), sufficient (if X, then Y, regardless of anything else), necessary (X, and only if X, then Y), and either deterministic (if X, then always Y) or probabilistic (if X, then probably Y).

With such stringent standards, it is not surprising that the term *cause* rarely, if ever, appears in sociological literature. Nevertheless, though the term may be absent, the idea for which it stands is widely used. In reading sociological research, we discover many other words with causal meanings. Some of the equivalents most often used are *varies directly, correlated,* or *associated with, produces* or *effects; significant relationship; interrelationship* or *interdependence among the variables; and explanation of the phenomena.*

No matter what term sociologists use, *causation* refers to the factors that make designated phenomena happen or change (Labovitz and Hagedorn, 1976). To illustrate a causal relationship in sociological research, we can consider the influence of socioeconomic status on career aspirations. In doing some systematic observation, we can discover that children who come from working-class families are more inclined to want to enter working-class occupations when "they grow up," and children from middle- and upper-class families express preferences for professional careers. We might do additional research and discover that 85 percent of all medical students and 10 percent of all barber college students have one or more parents employed in a professional career.

Does this evidence establish a causal relationship between socioeconomic status and career aspiration? Using Zetterberg's criteria for causality, we would have to say no because the relationship is neither *necessary* nor *sufficient*. Many factors affect career aspirations other than socioeconomic status, and some working-class children may have professional aspirations and some upper-class children may have nonprofessional career aspirations. However, using a less mechanistic or deterministic view of causal relationships, we are able to claim that there is a strong association between socioeconomic factors and career aspirations.

Sociology, as a science, produces propositions that are probabilistic in form. In making causal statements, the sociologist and the meteorologist have much in common. They both recognize that there are many variables (over which they have little or no control) influencing the outcomes they wish to describe, explain, and predict. It always amazes me to listen to a meteorologist say that there is a 60 percent chance of rain when I am looking out my window and observing the rain coming down in "buckets." Even I can improve upon this statement of scientific probability! The weather reporter is actually saying that given the present meteorological conditions in a particular geographic area, it will rain 60 percent of the time. I know that I am assisted by weather forecasts even though they do not always produce completely accurate predictions. I realize that these probabilistic explanations increase my understanding of an orderly and complex world. For the scientist, developing explanations that help us understand why variables influence each other is more important than being able to make accurate predictions without understanding the causal relationship.

What is true of the meteorologist is also true of the sociologist—just as Aunt Lucy with her bad knee claims that she can predict more accurately future thunderstorms, Jeane Dixon will make equally bold claims concerning the prediction of human social interaction using other nonscientific techniques. These persons will be correct at times, but they will not be able to explain the "why" of their predictions within the context of a body of empirical knowledge. In sociological research, the goal is to produce a body of knowledge consisting of a system of interrelated propositions that have been verified by sensory observation. These propositions provide an understanding of present circumstances and predict future events. (In chapter 3, while discussing social science and determinism, Evans raises some important issues related to scientific explanations, predictions, and notions of causality as they come to bear on human freedom.)

THE ROLE OF VALUES

The image I am providing of the sociologist, as scientist, is similar to that of a detective—one who discovers the causes of human behavior. However, included in this image one gets the impression that the scientist is interested in the facts—and *only* the facts. Yet, do the values of the scientist, and of those being studied, have any influence on the enterprise of scientific research?

There have been three leading points of view on this

question. The *first* position claims that the sociologist must be value-free; he or she must refrain from making any and all value judgments and must suspend all value commitments when taking on the role of scientist. Individuals who take the *second* point of view take a polar opposite position; they claim that it is impossible for any social researcher to be value-neutral. Therefore, they claim that the sociologist *must* choose a side and "get involved" in the social situation being studied. The *third* view is a synthesis of the other two, calling for social scientific research to be both value-relevant and value-free. Sociologists in this category agree that it is impossible for the social scientist to be completely ethically neutral; however, they feel that it is possible to be objective in performing social research.

Until the 1970s, mainstream sociology had been dominated by the point of view that the sociologist must not allow his or her personal values to intrude into the "objective" world being investigated. George Simpson (1954) articulates this perspective in the following description of social science: "Social science is a system of existential propositions (validated statements about what is) which would in no way, as a science, involve propositions of value (validated statements about what should be)."

Many other behavioral scientists who advocated value-freedom in their scientific endeavors based their value-neutrality on the writings of Max Weber. However, Weber's value-free stance was not as extreme as his followers. Weber's (1949) view was that two separate metaphysical spheres exist—the world of (scientific) facts and the world of (personal) values. Consequently, the scientist should be careful to distinguish between statements of fact and statements expressing evaluations. Michael Lessnoff (1974:131) summarizes Weber's value-free approach with the following words:

> Only the sphere of facts is the subject-matter of science, whether physical or social, for only facts, and not values, are ascertainable by the observational methods of science; science consists of statements of fact, not statements of value. Problems relating to the sphere of facts include: what phenomena exist in the world? what law-like relations hold between them? what explains them? By contrast, value-judgements are judgements of "the satisfactory or unsatisfactory character of phenomena," of the "desirability or undesirability." The sphere of values includes all problems as to what should be done in a given situation, and what states of affairs one should try to bring about—problems of rightness and goodness.

Weber's value-free principle should not be interpreted, as some have done, that the values of the scientist and those underlying human action are to be disregarded. Rather, Weber is saying that scientists should be careful to distinguish between scientifically warranted statements and personal convictions. The latter will always affect the research process, but the scientist has an obligation to distinguish between statements of evaluation and scientific findings.

A more appropriate sociologist to be cited as the extreme expositor of a value-free sociology is Emile Durkheim. In his treatise on the sociological method, Durkheim (1938) formulated the following rules for the observation of social facts:

1. All preconceptions of the scientist must be eradicated.

2. The subject matter of every sociological study should be comprised of phenomena defined in advance by certain common external characteristics—social facts.

3. Social facts must viewed as products of group experiences and not individual actions.

4. The cause of a given social fact must be sought in its preceding social facts.

These rules for objective observation of social facts must be seen as Durkheim's reaction to the German idealists who claimed that what one knows of the social world is largely an outcome of the process of knowing itself. According to Martindale (1960:53), "Durkheim restricts all explanation of phenomena purely to the phenomena themselves, preferring explanation strictly on the model of exact scientific procedure, and rejecting all tendencies, assumptions, preconceptions, values, and ideas which exceed the limits of scientific technique." Thus, in Durkheim's scheme, social facts have a reality of their own and are capable of being objectively studied independent of the scientist's value commitments.

The belief in value-neutrality has a tremendous appeal for most social scientists, especially those who desire the status accorded in the academic community to natural scientists. However, it is impossible for the scientist to totally exclude the consideration of values because values are always present in every research act. As early as 1939, Robert Lynd (1939:181) pointed out that sociology is itself part of the culture in which we live and, as part of culture, is value-laden. Cultural values have rubbed off on the sociologist and will affect the kinds of problems selected for investigation, research techniques employed, and even the way in which the data will be analyzed and interpreted. The same can be said of all the other social science and natural science disciplines.

Furthermore, Weber (cited by Lessnoff, 1974:147) has said that the social scientist's interest in the social world is different from the natural scientist's in the physical world because the phenomena under investigation are extremely relevant to the social scientist's values. And given the value pluralism found within the sociological community, various investigators will be interested in different aspects of the social phenomena and will conceptualize these phenomena differently. Consequently, this multiplicity of value concerns and perspectives may preclude any common language and/or consensus within the discipline.

For these reasons, Weber felt it was necessary to augment his value-freedom (*wertfreiheit*) perspective with a commitment to value-relevance (*wertbeziehung*). For Weber the value-relevance principle meant that it was appropriate for the social scientist to allow his or her values to determine the topic selected for investigation and the way in which research findings would be utilized. However, within the conduct of social research, the sociologist's values must be suspended for the sake of objectivity. To gain a fuller understanding of the relationship between these two perspectives, we must view the relationship within the context of Weber's biography, social context, and personal commitments.

When Weber was teaching in the German educational system, professors gained academic status on their "teaching abilities." Quality of teaching was determined by the number of students the professor was able to attract. As a result, the competition for students was considerable. Weber, and many others, felt that this system penalized good scholars and researchers while it favored instructors who pandered to students. Weber also noted that professors who expressed their values in class were more likely to attract students than those who did not.

Weber (1949:4) stated the problem like this: "Is it right for a scientist to take advantage of the prestige he has gained by purely scientific work to seek to impose his personal values and partisan views on others?" Given the comparatively exalted position of the professor in the lecture hall, Weber argued that it is unfair to subject the student to a pressure he or she is unable to evaluate or resist adequately. However, Weber did feel that it was appropriate for the professor to disseminate his or her ideals and values employing every means available to other private citizens: public meetings where disagreements are permitted, membership in organizations or groups, persuasive conversations within the context of everyday interaction, and other legitimate forms of social action (Freund, 1968:81).

From the writings of Weber, Freund (1968:82) abstracted the following set of "fair trade" rules to be followed by university professors:

1. Fulfill the task of teaching with simplicity.
2. Suppress one's personality in order to solely dispense instruction.
3. Only deal with topics within one field of expertise.

4. Value positions should be made explicit to one's students and to oneself.

5. Never ignore disagreeable facts—especially those which might be embarrassing for one's personal views.

6. Always distinguish between empirical observations and value judgments.

In the early part of the twentieth century Weber was passionately concerned with the course of German social and foreign policy. As an individual, he was a social and political activist. Gerth and Mills (1946:25), in a sort of biography on Weber, referred to him as the "last of the political professors." Yet, he always attempted to segregate his role as professor and scientist from that of activist.

For some, Max Weber's principles of *value-free* and *value-relevant* sociology may seem contradictory—how can one exclude values from the research act and still have them be relevant? Yet, Weber's point of view is that the sociologist must *distinguish* between (subjective) values and (objective) facts. This requires that the researcher be value-aware and value-explicit. According to Lessnoff (1974:148–49),

> Weber was careful to point out that his doctrine of value-relevance does not imply that social science concepts must pick out phenomena that are positively valued by the social scientist—their importance to him may be as evils rather than as goods (cf. criminology, conflict theory, etc.). And this doctrine in no way conflicts with, or detracts from, the doctrine of value freedom. While the investigator's values determine his concepts, and thus the subject-matter of his assertions, nevertheless these concepts must be definable in value-free terms, and what is asserted about this subject-matter must, to be scientific, exclude value-judgements. In assessing the truth of these (factual) assertions, value-judgements (other than methodological) remain irrelevant.

THE ROLE OF OBJECTIVITY

Is objectivity possible when scientists pursue research interests related to their value commitments? If positions of value and social policy development are relevant to sociological research, is the scientific status of the discipline compromised? The answer to these questions is a qualified no, provided that the scientist, in the conduct of inquiry, objectively evaluates facts with empirical data. If the sociologist has rejected all hope of being value-free and objective in the process of social research, and bases research conclusions on personal value commitments, it is impossible to produce anything scientifically significant. In the words of Howard Becker (1970:110): "We can never avoid taking sides. Our problem is to make sure that, whatever point of view we take, our research meets the standards of good scientific work, and that our unavoidable sympathies do not render our results invalid."

However, there is no conflict between trying to be objective in gathering and analyzing data and having firm convictions about the kind of social order one considers desirable. Individuals committed to social application of sociological research have an obligation to communicate effectively what they know as social scientists. They also have an obligation to clearly state where they stand in terms of value commitments. There is nothing wrong with stating one's values, as long as these values do not get in the way of objectivity. This requires that the scientist, *for the sake of objectivity*, be value-explicit to the scientific community and personally value-aware. When the scientist does this, Weber's value-free and value-relevant doctrine has a paradoxical potentiality—it enables the social scientist to make *better* value judgments rather than *none* (Gouldner, 1962:210).

Many students do not realize that agreement within the scientific community is a necessary requirement of science. This means that consensus must exist among scientists as to what is, or is not, verified knowledge. Consequently, scientific knowledge has the desirable characteristic of *intersubjectivity* —because persons with different values and assumptions agree concerning what is verified knowledge. Notice that with intersubjectivity we have transcended shared objectivity and have achieved a much more difficult form of consensus or agreement within the community of scholars.

For this reason, it is imperative for scientists to be aware of their own value commitments and assumptions and to explicitly state these positions to other members of the scientific community. Value-explicit research makes intersubjectivity a more likely outcome, and it adds to the honesty and integrity of the scientific enterprise.

APPLICATION OF WEBER'S PRINCIPLES

At this point we will consider two unpublished research case study examples that were written by C. Stephen Evans. In both research situations the values of the scientists have an influence on their research activities. After presenting the case studies, we will evaluate the appropriateness of the application of value commitments.

Example #1: Biblical Data

Sam Johnson is a Christian sociologist of the family who decided that the theories he learned in graduate school are permeated by faculty members' non-Christian assumptions. He is currently interested in research on childhood socialization, and runs across (in his daily Bible reading) Proverbs 22:15 which reads:

> Folly is bound up in the heart of a child,
> but the rod of discipline drives it far from him.

Using this as his evidence, he concludes that physical punishment is the true core of any sound method for bringing up children.

Example #2: Hypothesis Based on Religious Convictions

Rama Swamibar is a Buddhist sociologist who is interested in studying life-satisfaction as a sociological phenomena. As a Buddhist, he believes in the "no-self" theory—the individual self is an illusion and individual desires and cravings are part of what makes people unhappy. As he reviews the research literature, he is specially impressed by some studies which correlate unhappiness with individualistic cultures like the United States, and with other studies which correlated higher degrees of life-satisfaction with more traditional societies which emphasize larger social units such as the clan or village as the prime reality. He wonders if the cause of life-satisfaction in countries like the United States might be the preoccupation with the concept of the self, and develops a research hypothesis to see if life-satisfaction can be specifically correlated with socially induced beliefs about the self.

In each of these research case studies the sociologist should be commended for attempting to integrate his faith and sociological endeavors. Both sociologists are trying to allow their value commitments to influence the process of selecting a research topic. However, in the first research example, Sam Johnson is allowing the biblical statement to substitute for empirical observations. In contrast, Rama Swamibar begins with a faith assumption as a research hypothesis, but the truth or falsity of the hypothesis will be determined by the empirical evidence he gathers.

Swamibar's approach would be in keeping with Weber's value- free and value-relevant principles. He also makes it possible to affirm the empirical base of sociology as a social scientific discipline. On the other hand, Sam Johnson's approach would create a radical departure in the meaning of scientific data and would recast sociology as a subdiscipline within theology.

CRITIQUES OF WEBER'S VIEW

Thus far we have advocated Weber's "middle ground" position as an appropriate alternative to the extreme perspectives of "ethical neutrality" on the one side and "getting involved" on the other. For the sake of honesty, and to provide some balance to our discussion, the people who have advocated the latter point of view (which some have labeled "subjective sociologists") would have us consider five critiques of Weber's point of view.

First, facts and values may not be as distinct as Weber would have us believe. Many "facts" become facts because our values make them so. Value commitments and research assumptions help determine which data and empirical evidence are worthy of our consideration in the process of conducting social research.

Second, many important sociological concepts have value-implications enmeshed in their definitions. Consider the following list of concepts that sociologists routinely employ: marital adjustment, life satisfaction, religiosity, secularization, legitimate authority, role conflict, group cohesiveness, dysfunctional behavior, prejudice, and discrimination. The conceptual and operational definitions of each of these concepts will be influenced by the sociologist's values.

Third, it is inappropriate to assume that the natural and the social sciences should share the same empirical methodology. While the natural scientist does not need to take into consideration the intentions for the actions of physical agents, the social scientist has to recognize that the motivations of human beings do influence social behavior. For this reason, even Weber advocated the need for the *verstehen* (understanding) method in describing and explaining human behavior from the subject's perspective. Not to account for the subject's meaning for human actions is to miss the essence of the phenomena. When two people put their lips together, their intentions will differentiate many types of behavior— everyone knows that not all kissing is the same.

Fourth, scientific theories are always underdetermined by data or facts. When does one have enough data to conclude that the theory has been supported by empirical observation? The answers to this question will be determined by the value commitments, beliefs, and subjective feelings of the scientists involved. Furthermore, whenever two or more conflicting theories are equally compatible with the facts, we will always select the explanation that best comports with our values.

Finally, if we restrict ourselves to topics that can only be studied "objectively," some of the most interesting and important research will be excluded from sociological research. Consequently, the only roles left to the social researcher will be those of moral nihilist and the de facto defender of the status quo.

In response to these important critiques, one must ask the following question: If one is to adopt a value-committed and subjectivist orientation in the conduct of social inquiry, what is the role of objectivity and the residual meaning of "science" in the sociological enterprise? Until we can gain an acceptable answer to this question, I believe that we must conclude the following with regard to the relationship between value commitments and sociological research:

1. It is impossible for values to be totally excluded in the process of conducting social research.
2. It is imperative for the social scientist to be both value-aware and value-explicit.
3. It is mandatory for the social scientist to be objective in the tasks of classification and measurement, data collection, and statistical analysis.
4. The final test for scientific "truth" (or the validity of the research conclusions) is intersubjectivity within the scientific community. When many different scientists with differing value commitments can agree to the validity of the research findings, we are more confident in accepting the empirical support for the proposition.

IMPLICATIONS FOR THE CHRISTIAN SOCIOLOGIST

As a Christian sociologist, I have to ponder the following question: In what ways should my Christian commitments allow me to honor Christ in my roles as scholar, researcher, and teacher? My beliefs *will* influence my work. Personal integrity and honesty require that I ferret out the many ways in which these sociological endeavors are affected. In the remainder of this essay we will explore five areas where Christian commitments can, and should, affect the sociological enterprise.

The *first* area is concerned with assumptions one makes about the nature of truth and its relationship to empirically verifiable scientific knowledge. Science is concerned with only one type of knowledge—that which can be verified by sensory observation. This is only one type of knowledge, and it neither encompasses all that we know to be true nor is concerned with truth in an ultimate sense. (It would be ridiculous to employ the scientific method in determining whether or not you loved your intended spouse. We assume love is real, but realize that it is not empirically verifiable.) Actually, the method of science is falsification; the scientist attempts to prove that empirical propositions are false, and if it is not possible to find empirical evidence to demonstrate this to be the case, it is assumed that the propositions have been supported. Consequently, sociological knowledge consists of nonfalsified statements of relationships between empirical properties or events in the social world. It is possible that at some future date, what contemporary sociologists now assume to be true will be disproved. It is also the case that entire sociological theories (or explanations) will be reformulated by future research discoveries. This is what happened when Einstein discovered his theory of relativity thus making Newtonian physics obsolete.

The Christian sociologist can assume that God is the center of ultimate truth. As one seeks truth, God is not only honored in this quest, but will reveal himself in the process. However, the Christian sociologist must also remember the words of 1 Corinthians 13:12, "For now we see in a mirror dimly, but then face to face. Now I know in part; then I shall understand fully, even as I have been fully understood."

The *second* area in which Christian commitments will affect sociological research is in the assumptions we make about the social world and science. If I believe that humans are created in the image of God and that they possess some measure of freedom and autonomy; I cannot assume that causal statements—which preclude human choice and responsibility—accurately describe social relationships and human actions. If I believe that every person possesses inherent dignity and worth, then I must treat the subjects of my research with respect, being careful to guard their right to privacy and protecting them from physical and psychological harm.

Related to this point is Nicholas Wolterstorff's (1984:76) contention that the Christian scholar—seeking consistency, wholeness, and integrity in his or her beliefs and commitments— should allow Christian commitments to control the process of devising and weighing theories. According to Wolterstorff (1984:76-77),

> The Christian scholar ought to reject certain theories on the ground that they conflict or do not comport well with the belief-content of his authentic commitment. And he ought to devise theories which comport as well as possible with, or are at least consistent with, the belief-content of his authentic commitment. . . .For Christian scholars' beliefs ought to function as control over the sorts of theories which they are willing to accept.

The *third* way in which scholars' activities will be affected by their Christian commitments will be in the selection of research topics. The principle of elective affinities would suggest that it is impossible to commit oneself to every course of action. Furthermore, within the context of one's value-commitments, not all topics are judged to be equally worthy of investigation. Therefore, one must choose a limited number of topics for research consideration from among the many sociological concepts and areas.

I have invested my professional career in the following research areas: the sociology of religion, the family, and death and dying. It is not difficult for me to trace these research interests to the values of my parents and to my own Christian beliefs and commitments. This is my way of providing a sense of consistency and wholeness to my personal and professional commitments. For me, as one who has been called to be a Christ-follower, the Christian life involves a sense of "vocation"—or call to service. Being a sociologist of religion, a sociologist of the family, and a social thanatologist are ways in which I experience opportunities to serve others.

Closely related to this last point is the *fourth* way in which Christian commitments can affect one's role as sociologist—the application of sociological knowledge for the benefit of others. In their roles as applied sociologists, Christians utilize the findings of sociological research in the formulation and evaluation of social policy and in their efforts to create a more just and caring society. One can study penology, work within the criminal justice system for prison reform, and/or become involved in such organizations as Prison Fellowship. As a social thanatologist, I have conducted research on death anxiety, have been employed as evaluator and consultant to hospice programs, and have served dying patients and their families as a hospice volunteer. I have viewed each of these activities within the context of Matthew 25:34–40:

> Then the King will say to those at his right hand, "Come, O blessed of my Father, inherit the kingdom prepared for you from the foundation of the world; for I was hungry and you gave me food, I was thirsty and you gave me drink, I was a stranger and you welcomed me, I was naked and you clothed me, I was sick and you visited me, and I was in prison and you came to me.". . .*Truly, I say to you, as you did it to one of the least of these my brethren, you did it to me* (RSV italics added).

Finally, in a more general way, one can apply sociological knowledge in serving Christ's body—the church. Sociologists who are knowledgeable of organizational sociology, social psychology, and the sociology of the community can work within the local church helping to construct a social institution that is more able to meet human needs and encourage people in their Christian life and growth. Sociological knowledge can also be of value in maintaining programs of evangelism, in starting new churches, and in assisting the growth of older congregations. The possibilities for utilizing sociological research findings for the cause of Christ on earth can be limited only by our imaginations and commitments to service.

REFERENCES IN CHAPTER

Becker, Howard. 1970. "Whose Side Are We On." in *The Relevance of Sociology*, edited by Jack D. Douglas. New York: Appleton, Century, & Crofts.

Durkheim, Emile. 1938. *The Rules of the Sociological Method*. Translated by

Sarah A. Solovay and John H. Mueller and edited by George E. G. Catlin. New York: Free Press.

————. 1951. *Suicide*. New York: Free Press.

Freund, Julien. 1968. *The Sociology of Max Weber*. New York: Pantheon Books.

Gerth, H. H., and C. Wright Mills. 1946. *From Max Weber: Essays in Sociology*. New York: Oxford University Press.

Gouldner, Alvin. 1962. "Anti-Minotaur: The Myth of a Value-Free Sociology." *Social Problems* 9 (Winter): 199–213 Winger: 199-213.

Homans, George C. 1967. *The Nature of Social Science*. New York: Harcourt, Brace, & World.

Kaplan, Abraham. 1964. *The Conduct of Inquiry: Methodology for Behavioral Science*. San Francisco: Chandler.

Labovitz, Sanford, and Robert Hagedorn. 1976. *Introduction to Social Research*. 2d ed. New York: McGraw-Hill.

Lessnoff, Michael. 1974. *The Structure of Social Science: A Philosophical Introduction*. London: George Allen & Unwin.

Lynd, Robert S. 1939. *Knowledge for What*. Princeton: Princeton University Press.

Martindale, Donald. 1960. *The Nature and Types of Sociological Theory*. Boston: Houghton Mifflin.

Rudner, Richard S. 1966. *Philosophy of Social Science*. Englewood Cliffs, N. J.: Prentice Hall.

Simpson, George. 1954. *Man in Society*. New York: Random House.

Theodorson, George A., and Achilles G. Theodorson. 1969. *Modern Dictionary of Sociology*. New York: Thomas Y. Crowell.

Weber, Max. 1949. *The Methodology of the Social Sciences*. Translated and edited by Edward Shills and Henry A. Finch. New York: Free Press.

Wolterstorff, Nicholas. 1984. *Reason Within the Bounds of Religion*. 2d ed. Grand Rapids, Mich.: Eerdmans.

Zetterberg, Hans L. 1966. *On Theory and Verification in Sociology*. Totowa, N. J.: Bedminster Press.

MUST SOCIOLOGY PRESUPPOSE DETERMINISM?

C. Stephen Evans

Determinism is the claim that for every event there are prior causes, and that given the existence of those causes, no other events than those which occur are really possible. In this essay I wish to focus on human behavior, not subatomic particles, so I will define determinism as the claim that all human social behavior has causes which make any other behavior than that which in fact occurs impossible.

Many sociologists, especially those involved in doing empirical research, believe that determinism is true or that they must at least assume it is true in order to do good social research. Noted social research textbook author Earl Babbie (1986:43) says that "crudely put, social research assumes a deterministic paradigm that fundamentally denies the existence of free will." Though Babbie knows that determinism is not often discussed by sociologists, and he concedes that it is an "embarrassment for social scientists," he insists that its acceptance is fundamental to nearly all sociological research.

Surprisingly (at least to a nonsociologist), many Christian sociologists seem to agree with Babbie. Though they are less likely to embrace determinism wholeheartedly as a metaphysical conviction, they do agree that determinism is a necessary assumption they must make as social scientists. Stan Gaede (1985:129), for example, while careful not to embrace determinism, and in fact trying vigorously to avoid taking sides in the freedom-determinism debate at all, nevertheless says that sociologists who believe in free choice face a problem of "cognitive dissonance. All day long, as human scientists, they do nothing but try to demonstrate how perfectly predictable people are. How do they wed their deterministic, scientific minds with their freedom-loving hearts?"

That Christians should find determinism tempting is surprising because it seems to fit poorly with central Christian convictions. It is true that extreme Calvinists have sometimes embraced determinism because it fits their emphasis on the sovereignty of God. However, most Christians have believed that the doctrine of the sovereignty of God must be understood in a way that is consistent with affirming a degree of human freedom; they have been very concerned to put the responsibility for human sin squarely on human beings and to avoid any suggestion that God caused human beings to sin or did not allow them any choice in the matter. Christians see the God of the Bible as a God of justice, who holds people accountable for their deeds and who created human beings as the sort of creatures who can properly be held accountable. God is a God of mercy as well as justice, of course, but even his mercy seems to point to human freedom—God woos his often faithless people with long-suffering patience, but he allows them to spurn his overtures, even to the point of honoring the choice to permanently reject his love.

One might think that the best move for the Christian sociologist to make at this point would be to opt for methodological determinism and reject determinism as a true philosophical theory. That is, why not treat determinism as a working assumption that is made for the sake of empirical research, but one that is not believed to be true ultimately? I used to believe this was an adequate solution, but I no longer do. The temptation to convert methodological determinism to philosophical determinism seems overwhelming to me. If determinism works so well as a hypothesis, why not assume it is true? And if it is not true, why does it work so well as it is alleged to do?

I wish to show that the Christian sociologist does not have to make this deterministic assumption. Determinism is not necessary for doing social research or thinking sociologically; rather, it is an impediment to good sociology. The widespread opinions to the contrary are rooted in confusions. The confusions are very prevalent, and they are understandable confusions, but confusions nonetheless. The principal confusions concern the nature of freedom and determinism, the nature of causation, and the nature of explanations of human activity.

THE FREEDOM-DETERMINISM DEBATE: THREE POSITIONS

Over the centuries, three positions on the freedom- determinism debate have developed: hard determinism, soft determinism, and libertarianism. Understanding these three views and their differences is difficult, but it is essential if the debate is to be worthwhile.

Let us begin with hard and soft determinism. Many people assume that the difference here is one of degree, that hard determinists believe that all human behavior is determined and soft determinists hold that only some human behavior is determined. This is completely mistaken. Soft determinism, as originally defined by William James, and as defended by a long and venerable philosophical tradition, believes that all human behavior is causally determined. There is no difference on this point between hard and soft determinists.

The disagreement between hard and soft determinists concerns the implications of determinism, not determinism itself. Hard determinists believe that determinism excludes free will; since determinism is true, free will does not exist. Hard determinists thus embrace what philosophers call "incompatibilism". They believe that free will and determinism are not compatible.

Soft determinists deny incompatibilism. They believe that on the issue of freedom and determinism, you can eat your cake and have it, too. Determinism is just as true for them as for the hard determinists, but they believe that free will is also sometimes a reality for human beings because both free will and determinism are possible. Naturally, this view is called "compatibilism."

Libertarianism, which should not be confused with political libertarianism, is a belief that free will exists and that real freedom excludes determinism. So libertarians agree with hard determinists that compatibilism is false; they, too, are incompatibilists. They differ from hard determinists in claiming that determinism is false—people have free choices, at least sometimes.

It might appear that libertarians and soft determinists are very close in belief, since both claim that people are sometimes free and responsible for their actions. However, this agreement is an illusion. As we shall see, the agreement that people are sometimes free hides a profound disagreement on the nature of freedom and what is reasonably required to hold people responsible for their actions.

It is crucial to note that libertarianism does not claim that all human behavior is free or that human behavior is exempt from causal influences. Determinism makes a universal claim—it says that all human behavior is causally determined. Someone who denies determinism, as libertarians must do, is not therefore committed to the contrary universal claim. The libertarian is only claiming that not all human behavior is determined. How much behavior is determined is still an open question on which libertarians disagree, the contrary opinions ranging from "none" to "nearly all." The view that most but not all human behavior is determined is not, as some think, soft determinism; rather, it is a form of libertarianism. We shall see that many of the arguments

for determinism and many of the difficulties sociologists have with
libertarianism stem from lack of clarity about this point.

PROBLEMS WITH SOFT DETERMINISM

Before we attempt to defend libertarianism to see if it is
capable of supporting serious social science, it is well to see if it is
necessary to do so. After all, the soft determinist says that we can
have determinism and free will, too. So we need to determine
whether compatibilism is true.

The soft determinist believes that the key to resolving the
problem of freedom and determinism is to define the terms very
carefully. If we have a correct understanding of what we mean by
freedom and determinism, we can see that they are compatible.
From the soft determinist's viewpoint, genuine freedom is not lack
of determination; rather, it is being determined by one's inner
states. Freedom is self-determination. Lack of freedom is not lack
of causal determination; it is being determined by a certain type of
cause, an external cause.

A simple example may clarify the view. Suppose I am
watching television, and I see an appeal to help starving children
in Ethiopia. I want very much to help, so I pick up the phone and
pledge a donation. Is this act free? Certainly, says the soft
determinist. It is free because I am acting in accordance with my
inner wishes and desires. No outside force coerced me or
constrained me to make the donation; it is what I wanted to do.

Now it is true that my desire to help the starving children is
itself caused, and therefore my action is causally determined.
However, that is irrelevant, according to soft determinism, if the
question is whether the act is free. The situation would be
different if I had gotten a phone call from a blackmailer saying that
unless I made a donation to him, he would make public some dark
secret from my past. In this case I may also make a "donation,"
and the act is also causally determined. But now I am being
constrained or forced to do what I do not really wish to do. True
freedom is not lack of determination, but lack of coercion. The soft
determinist says that this is the only kind of freedom possible for
humans, and that it is the only kind of freedom really worth
having. An act that is not causally determined at all would merely
be a chance or random event, not a free action.

The soft determinist view is appealing, but I do not think it is
ultimately acceptable. The libertarian will claim that the kind of
freedom the soft determinist defends is not the kind necessary for
moral responsibility. The reason for this is that moral responsibility requires us to be able to say to a person who has performed an
act, "You had a real choice—you could have done otherwise."
Since the soft determinist believes that every act is causally

determined, there is a clear sense in which the person who did the act could *not* have done otherwise. Given my background and the television program I was watching, I could not help wanting to give money to the starving children and could not help doing so.

The soft determinist has a response to this charge. He or she will argue that there is a sense in which a person who acts freely "could have done otherwise." I could have done something other than give the money to the children, *if I had wanted to*. Of course it is true that I did not want to, and if determinism is true, there is a sense in which I could not have wanted to. Still, "I could have done otherwise" in the sense that nothing prevented me from doing just what I wanted to do, and nothing would have prevented me from doing something different if I had wanted to do that.

However, this response will not do. It is true that I could have done otherwise if I had wanted to, but that is irrelevant in cases where I could not have wanted anything else and my wants are viewed as causally determining my action. Saying that I am free because "I could have done otherwise" in this sense is like saying that a man in a coma in a hospital is free to leave the hospital because he could leave if he wanted to. Legally, perhaps, the patient is free to leave, but we would not say the patient is morally responsible for failing to leave the hospital because he has no real choice in the matter. He could leave if a certain condition were fulfilled, but that condition is not fulfilled, and the patient is powerless to fulfill it. Similarly, in every case of soft determinist–style freedom, the person could do something different if a certain condition were fulfilled, but that condition is not fulfilled, and the person is powerless to fulfill it since soft determinism is committed to determinism.

Soft determinism faces other severe difficulties. The soft determinist wants to say that I am not free in cases where I am coerced because I am not able to act as I want. However, this is not always true. In the case of the blackmailer mentioned above, I still have a choice as to how to respond to the blackmailer. If I choose to pay the money rather than call the police, there is a clear sense in which I am doing what I want to do, just as I do in the case of the appeal for famine victims. So even coerced actions may still be free. Granted, in a case of coercion a person's options are severely restricted, but human options are always restricted to some degree. This shows that our freedom is finite and limited, but it may still exist to some degree—even in extreme situations.

More seriously, the soft determinist is committed to viewing some actions as free, even if they arise from causes over which I have no control at all. Suppose that a mad scientist attaches electrodes to your brain that control your desires when activated by electrical signals he controls. (Of course this is not currently scientifically feasible, but it may be possible someday.) He controls your desires and gets you to act precisely as he wishes. Are you still free? According to the soft determinist theory, you would be, so long as you are able to do what you want to do.

Of course the soft determinist may object at this point that in this case your desires are no longer yours, since they are controlled by the mad scientist. But why aren't they your desires? Remember that in the soft determinist view, all your inner wants and desires are ultimately determined by external causes, and this is supposed to be irrelevant to the question of whether freedom really exists.

Suppose that instead of controlling your desires by electrical signals, the scientist had "programed" your brain at birth to have certain desires in certain circumstances, and then (with the help of a totalitarian government interested in the results of the experiment) he controlled the environment in which you functioned so that you had precisely the desires he wanted you to have and you acted precisely as he wished. Would this "slow" external causation make you any more free? If we replace the mad scientist with the impersonal forces of evolution and environmental conditioning, is your freedom increased? It seems to me that the answer to these questions is clearly "NO!" This argument demonstrates that you cannot eat your cake and have it, too, in the area of freedom and determinism. If we are strictly and totally determined, it is nonsense to think we are free in the sense required to be really morally responsible for our behavior.

OBJECTIONS TO FREEDOM

There are many arguments against believing in free will in the libertarian sense. Some are philosophical in nature; I will (for the most part) ignore these in this essay, not because they are unimportant, but because I am writing for sociology students. My gut conviction is that sociologists have rejected libertarian views of freedom, not for esoteric, philosophical reasons, but because they believe that accepting freedom would have unacceptable consequences for social science. It is those alleged consequences that I will address.

The main difficulties seem to me to be the following: (1) Social scientists fear that accepting free will would imply that human behavior would be disconnected from the past, random, and unpredictable. (2) They fear that free will would imply that human behavior is uncaused. (3) Finally, they fear that accepting free will would mean that no scientific explanations could be given for human behavior. I will try to allay each of these fears.

Objection #1: Unpredictable Behavior

Many sociologists do not see libertarianism as a viable alternative because they think that such a view would commit them to seeing human acts as disconnected from the past, completely uninfluenced by what has gone on before and what is currently going on around people. This would mean that human behavior is unpredictable, since we rely heavily on continuities between a person's past behavior and future behavior in making predictions.

If libertarianism did imply that human behavior was completely unpredictable and detached from the past, it would obviously be a false belief. We all know that people are heavily shaped by their pasts and that many reasonably accurate predictions can be made about a person if you know something about his or her history. If you are making predictions about the behavior of a group of people instead of an individual, the predictions can be even more accurate. For example, a social researcher can predict fairly accurately the number of Americans who will marry in the next year.

However, the libertarian does not have to view people as if they had no history or as if they were born anew every instant. It is true that the libertarian does not think that a person's past always makes a particular action inevitable. However, many acts may be inevitable, and many that are not inevitable may be highly probable.

Social researchers themselves often point out that an accurate prediction of the behavior of a group of people does not necessarily imply that an accurate prediction can be given for a specific individual. The research finding that blue-collar workers are more likely to vote Democratic is not disproved by Uncle Charley the plumber, who always votes Republican. This demonstrates that social research is a better predictor for group behavior than for any individual in the group.

In any case, for both individuals and groups, the predictions that social research makes possible are almost always probabilistic. But there is no reason for the libertarian to deny that people are usually heavily influenced by their past and that these influences make some behavior far more probable than other behavior. Libertarians know that human beings are historical, situated beings, not ahistorical angels.

In fact, a person's free choices are part of the history that must be considered. There are many cases where a person does not have a free choice about an issue, but is still morally responsible for his or her behavior. The reason for this is that the lack of freedom now may be due to the misuse of freedom in the past. An alcoholic may be unable to resist taking a drink today, but he may well have been able to resist the first time, the tenth time, even the hundredth time he imbibed. Real free choices have real consequences, and those consequences may include a loss or diminution of freedom in the future. For the libertarian, every free act leaves an imprint on the person's character and leads to effects in the world. Far from denying the person's historicity, the libertarian should insist on it. Without this property, free choices cannot have serious consequences.

The libertarian has no reason to deny that human behavior is predictable. As we shall see, when we look at the question of how actions are to be explained, even perfectly free actions may be regular and predictable. This is true because free beings, if they are reasonable, may well act in similar ways in similar circumstances. In any case, the actual probabilistic predictions social scientists make are compatible with a great deal of individual human freedom, even if one thinks that freedom does imply a degree of unpredictability.

Objection #2: Uncaused Behavior

Closely linked to the idea that free actions would be disconnected from the past of the agent is the idea that free actions are uncaused. The sociological researcher reasons as follows: "My job is to look for the causes of human behavior. The more causes I find, the more human behavior appears to be determined. To give up looking for causes is to put myself out of business. I must therefore, at least for professional purposes, assume that human behavior is determined."

A number of deep philosophical issues are buried here. First, I must make it clear immediately that it is *not* the libertarian view that free actions are uncaused. The libertarian position is that free choices are caused, at least in part, by the *self*. An uncaused event would just be an uncaused event, and we would have no ground to attribute it to the agent or hold the person responsible.

The libertarian view of the self, as part of the cause of an action, seems mysterious and puzzling to sociologists because it does not employ the concept of causation normally used in social science research. Science normally thinks of causation in terms of event-causation—a cause is one event or set of events that leads to another event or set of events. But the self is not an event or occurrence; it is a continuing entity. Consequently, there is a strong temptation to think of the causation that the self exerts in terms of events occurring within the self. For example, a determinist commonly thinks of an action (an event) as caused by a desire, construed as an event within the person.

The libertarian position is that event-causality is not the only kind of causality; there is also agent-causality—the kind of causality exerted by persons who have the power to act freely. I think it is somewhat understandable why scientists who do not believe in God should find agent-causality mysterious. However, I do not see why Christians should be reluctant to accept this as a reality. After all, Christians believe that God is a person and the supreme cause of all natural events. We surely do not think of God's creative causality as determined. It is hard to picture desires or other events occurring in God that compel him to do what he does. Since God is the creator of all the laws of nature, there are no natural laws regulating the connection of divine mental events to divine activity. God's actions may be regular and consistent, just as a free human being may act in regular and consistent (and therefore predictable) ways. But such regularity or consistency is not evidence of determinism. If agent-causality takes place when God acts, why is it not possible when those creatures act whom God created in his own image as responsible stewards over the rest of creation?

If determinists object at this point that they do not understand agent-causality, I would appeal to their own experience. It is true that the notion of causality is a mysterious one, but I do not think that the notion of agent-causality is any more mysterious than the notion of event-causality. In fact, I think we have a clearer grasp of agent-causality because our most primitive experience of the world is the experience of *doing*. We experience ourselves primarily as creatures who can make a difference in the world.

At this point, the sociologist may think that I have made the problem worse rather than better. To attribute an act to the agent (appealing perhaps to a primitive choice or an act of will on the part of the self) seems to be too easy and to preclude any search for the kinds of causes social scientists have tried to discover. It would seem that this point of view would put the sociologist out of work.

Here we must be careful about how we use the word *cause* . Many philosophers (and some scientists) use the word *cause* to mean "sufficient condition." That is, they think of a cause as a set of conditions sufficient to bring about a certain result and therefore guarantee that result when those conditions are present. In *this* sense of the word, the libertarian believes that free actions have no cause. There is no set of events, independent of the free choice brought about by the agent himself, sufficient to make the act inevitable—otherwise it would not be a free action.

However, this by no means implies that a free action is uncaused in other senses. In ordinary experience and in the writings of social scientists, the term *cause* is not normally used to mean "sufficient condition." Take the case of a young person who has died as a result of a drug overdose. What is the cause of the young person's action? One person might point to the easy availability of drugs in the young person's high school and the social acceptability of experimenting with drugs. Another individual might point out that the young person had no sense of purpose and meaning in life. Somebody else might note that the parents of the unfortunate young man had been unloving. Somebody else might point to a failure on the part of teachers or other responsible adults to heed some clear warning signs.

All these factors may be legitimate. If drugs were not available and acceptable, the young man might not have experimented with them. If the young man had had a sense that life was worth living, he might not have been tempted to try drugs. If his parents or teachers had acted differently, the tragedy might not have happened. The point is that each of the factors cited seems to be a necessary but not sufficient condition for the tragedy. Each may contribute and even be essential to the action, but not one of them is sufficient. Nor can one say with certainty that all of them together were sufficient to make the act inevitable. Still other factors may have played a part and one of these factors may well have been the individual's free choice.

If we think of a cause as a condition that contributes to an event, and may even be a necessary condition, then free choice in no way blocks the road of social inquiry into causes. To begin, as noted above, a libertarian does not necessarily think that all human acts are free; very few of them may be. So it is always legitimate to look for causes. But even when we have reason to suspect that the individual's freedom is a factor, we have no reason not to look for other causes. A free choice is never made in a vacuum; it is made in a concrete situation where many social forces are at work. The individual's free choice may at times enter into this play of causal forces, but even when it does, there is plenty for the sociologist to investigate. Many forces may make it more probable for the individual to behave in one way rather than another.

In reality this is the only type of cause social scientists ever discover. They may find that poverty is associated with juvenile crime and assume that poverty is a cause of juvenile crime. But obviously, many poor people never resort to crime as juveniles, so poverty is never more than one factor among others to be considered as part of the total social situation.

So if a cause can be a contributing factor to a result, I would conclude that free actions may be caused by a variety of outside factors. All the libertarian insists on is that in some cases the outside factors are not sufficient to make the act inevitable, even if they make it more probable.

Objection #3: No Explanations for Behavior

Another worry that social scientists have about allowing freedom into their bailiwick is that freedom shortcuts the search for explanations for human behavior. To say that a person performed an act because he or she chose to do it seems awfully easy, and it seems to preclude any scientifically verifiable explanation.

Our earlier discussion concerning causation should alleviate this fear to a great extent. Once we realize that free actions can have causes (contributing conditions) besides the free choice of the agent, then it is obvious that such actions can also have other explanations than "he or she chose to do it." It will be true that the explanations in terms of external causes will be incomplete in the case of genuine free actions, but incomplete explanations may still be useful. In fact, almost all scientific explanations are incomplete anyway.

However, there is more to be said about the notion of explanation. Many social scientists use the term *reason* synonymously with *cause*. Thus, to ask about a person's reasons for an action is to ask about the causes of the action. This is dangerous, because reasons are not causes in the ordinary scientific sense of the term. While I agree that *some* reasons are causes, not all of them are, and not all causes are reasons. A reason, when it is a cause, is a special type of cause.

Many social scientists are inclined to accept a particular view of explanation—called the "covering law model of explanation." According to this model, which owes its origins to the philosophy of logical positivism, explanation always requires a generalization—something that is at least similar to a law of nature. For example, if we know that water always freezes at thirty-two degrees Fahrenheit, and we know there is water around and the temperature is thirty-one degrees Fahrenheit, we know that the water will freeze. If someone asks why, we have a ready explanation. The water froze because water always freezes under these particular conditions, and the conditions were met. From this perspective, explanation and prediction are very similar. The same information prior to an event allows one to make a prediction; after the event, it provides an explanation.

Though it needs refinement, the covering law model is a powerful and attractive one for events in the natural world, and for some human behavior. However, it is not the only possible model for explaining human behavior, and it is not the model most people commonly use when they cite *reasons* for their behavior or the behavior of others. Many explanations of social scientists do not rely on the covering law model either— though this is not always noticed.

Let us take the case of a bank teller badly in need of money to finance an operation for his mother. He figures out a way to embezzle a little money each day and alter the books so as to make it unlikely that he will be caught (so he thinks). If we ask the reasons for the teller's behavior, an answer is near at hand. He needs the money badly, decides that he is unlikely to get caught, and (let us suppose) believes that his actions will not really hurt anyone—the bank's depositors are insured, and the owners of the bank are wealthy and will not miss a little extra profit.

The reasons given are perfectly plausible and understandable. But notice that the explanation given nowhere cites anything like a law of nature or even a plausible generalization. It is not true that bank tellers are likely to embezzle money if they can. It is not even true that bank tellers who need money badly are likely to do so. Even if we try to restrict the generalization to the teller in question, it is impossible to find a law necessary to the story. The teller may never have stolen anything in his life, so it is not necessarily true that he always or even usually does such things when he has the chance or when circumstances permit. Some generalizations may apply to the case, but the point is this: We do not know any laws, nor do we need to know any, to explain the behavior of the teller.

Why does the explanation work? It works because it cites a reason for the action. A reason is characteristically a set of desires and beliefs on the part of the agent. Given that the teller needs and wants money badly, believes he can get it this way, and believes that there is nothing wrong with the action, he has a reason for doing the action—a reason that at least to him looks like a good reason.

The connection between a reason and an action is not merely contingent and external, as is the case for causes in nature—where the explanation does depend on a law of nature. There is no reason (that we know) why gravity should operate to obtain the effects it does—that is just the way it operates. A reason, on the other hand, establishes an intelligible connection between a certain action and the goals and beliefs of an agent. If you have been looking for a certain book for a year, badly want it, find it in a bookstore, have the money to pay for it, and no reason not to buy it, it makes sense that you will buy it. If the agent is rational and has no powerful reasons to overrule his reason, we require no further explanation of a reasonable action. In particular, we do not need to know that other people would behave in a similar manner in other circumstances. If other people do not behave in such a manner, that means they are irrational, and *that* may call for an explanation, but it does not undermine the explanation of the rational action we normally accept.

I have taken some time to elaborate on the nature of a reason because I believe that social scientists frequently expend a great deal of effort exploring and learning about the reasons people have for their behavior. But it is very important to realize that a search for reasons is not necessarily a search for "covering laws."

The absence of covering laws is important because one mark of a genuinely determined natural phenomenon, such as the relationships between the planets in the solar system, is that behavior is describable by such laws. In looking for reasons, therefore, social scientists are not necessarily looking for determining causes. A reason seems to be the kind of cause that fits nicely into a libertarian explanation of human behavior or action.

We have already seen that in the libertarian view, free actions can be caused. Reasons seem to be just the sort of causes that could be part of the story of a free action without being the whole story. They contribute, in some cases decisively, without determining. This fits well with our ordinary experience. When asked if we had reasons for an action, we normally would say that we did, but we hardly think of those reasons as making the action unfree. Did I have reasons for agreeing to write this essay? Of course. Was my act unfree because I had those reasons? Of course not. I had good reasons for agreeing to do the essay, but I do not believe those reasons made the decision inevitable or precluded any free choice.

DEVELOPING A CHRISTIAN VIEW

If determinism is as unnecessary as I claim for sociology, why has a belief in determinism been so prevalent among sociologists? An obvious reason is simply that the confusions I have tried to clear up have been widespread, but this is not really an adequate answer. What one wants to know is why those confusions have been so widespread and so tenacious.

This is an important question. I believe that no simple answer will do, but at least part of the answer has to do with the religious orientation of social scientists. One of the findings of social science research is that religious commitments are stronger among natural scientists than among social scientists. The reasons for this are again complex, but I think Stan Gaede (1985) has revealed an important part of the puzzle by pointing out that the social sciences arose in the nineteenth century when Christianity had been dethroned from its role as the foundation of Western culture. The natural sciences, by contrast, developed when Christianity was the dominant world view, and the founding fathers—such as Galileo, Newton, and Copernicus—were all devout Christians.

If science is influenced by extrascientific assumptions, as most philosophers of science now agree, then it is plausible that the non-Christian assumptions of the founding fathers of the social sciences should have made an impact. I believe that this is just what happened. The idea that human beings were supernaturally created by a personal God in his image was not really taken seriously by men such as Comte, Durkheim, Weber, and Marx. Hence their basic perspective on human beings was that they were sophisticated animals, complex in their use of symbols, but without the real ability to transcend nature. Determinism fits such a worldview to a tee. Succeeding generations of sociologists have, by and large, been as relentlessly secular as their predecessors. The few Christians who have achieved prominence have generally been forced to conform to the reigning paradigm to maintain professional respectability. In such a professional context, a belief in determinism seemed not only legitimate, but the only possible perspective—given the prevailing confusions over the concepts of freedom, causation, and explanation.

I am convinced, however, that these confusions are not merely intellectual errors. They have, in sociological language, functional value for someone who wants to hold at bay the possibility that human beings are more than sophisticated animals. As a Christian, I believe that human beings have a fundamental need for God, but I also believe that human beings are sinful. As sinful creatures, they continually try to hide their own spiritual condition and destiny from themselves. It would be surprising if this sinful attempt to evade a confrontation with God did not affect social scientists when it can be seen so clearly in philosophers, writers, and artists.

Of course most sociologists are understandably reluctant to view their discipline as expressing prideful, sinful attitudes. They are excited about the value of their discipline and the potential of the knowledge gained therein to enrich the church, and this is entirely proper. They will, however, be more successful in convincing the church of the value of sociology if they can show clear evidence that their thinking about the social sciences is authentically Christian. They must remember that their task is not merely to disseminate the findings of an essentially secular social science to the church, but to represent the Christian church in a largely secular discipline. And they are also the social thinkers *of* the church—whose job is not merely to win respect from non-Christian colleagues, but to contribute to the church through their research efforts concerning human beings and social relationships. These endeavors can enrich and support the overall task of developing a Christian view of human nature and social relationships.

To do these things effectively, I think that Christian sociologists must not assume the truth of determinism. Rather, they must see human beings as historically situated, responsible agents, who sometimes have free choices. Even free choices may be largely predictable, and they are certainly partly caused by past influences and social forces. However, sometimes people act for reasons that are not rationalizations, and such reasons are not determining causes. Explaining human behavior means looking for causes, both nonrational, determining causes and rational causes that are compatible with freedom. Such explanations do not require us to reject the age-old view that human beings are responsible agents.

REFERENCES IN CHAPTER

Babbie, Earl. 1986. *Observing Ourselves: Essays in Social Research*. Belmont, Calif.: Wadsworth.
Gaede, S. D. 1985. *Where Gods May Dwell*. Grand Rapids, Mich.: Zondervan.

THINKING ABOUT CULTURE: THEIRS AND OURS

Robert A. Clark

Few concepts in sociology are as fascinating and important as the concept of culture. The sociological and anthropological study of culture reveals the uniqueness and richness of human experience. Unlike other species, humans are capable of creating, transmitting, and acting together in terms of elaborate systems of symbols. As creatures short on instincts that "program" us with specific ways of surviving and living together, we humans use culture as our primary way of adapting to our environment and working together in groups.

Culture is, in effect, a flexible and ever-changing "adaptive mechanism" for us as a species. Through language, norms,and a shared body of techniques, members of a human population can organize and govern their interaction, pool their learning,and transmit their mode of living to the next generation. Indeed, the study of culture points to the remarkable ingenuity of humans in successfully adapting to a wide array of living environments, from desert nomads and settled farmers to arctic fishing peoples and industrial urbanites.

In our examination of culture we also encounter the human quest for meaning, the development of religious and ethical traditions, the construction of world views and understandings of nature, time, our origins, and future. Through the window of culture, we see the magnificent ways in which humans express and display their beliefs, values, hopes, and shared experiences in art, drama, music, rituals, and celebrations.

Moreover, in all of these manifestations of culture, we witness the rich diversity of the human experience, the fascinating variety of ways in which humans adapt to their environment, manage their life together, and understand and express the meaning of human existence. Indeed, the study of culture is an ennobling process, causing us to reflect on the ingenuity, adaptability, intelligence, and moral consciousness of the human animal.

There is, however, a troubling side to the examination of culture, a side that can be especially problematic for Christians. To bring the issues into focus, let me briefly remind you of some themes in the standard sociological treatment of culture.

Sociology teaches us that though the capacity to create and use culture is part of our biological nature as humans, the content of any particular culture is not inborn. This is demonstrated by the fact that while we are one biological species, our cultures differ considerably, reflecting different environments and experiences. Each population builds its culture through processes of discovery and refinement, domination by powerful invaders, or borrowing from neighbors. Culture, then, is a human product, a "social construction." The language, values, beliefs, and norms of each culture have a human history of creation, conflict, and development. The culture of a people is then transmitted from generation to generation through the process of socialization. The young of any particular culture come to believe in and follow the culture surrounding them.

This sociological treatment of culture thereby introduces us to the problem of cultural relativism. Since what people believe to be true, good, and beautiful varies from culture to culture, no one of them can legitimately claim to have the only and final standards of truth, goodness, and beauty. Instead, customs, beliefs, and values must be seen as true or false, good or bad, only in relation to a particular cultural context. That is, customs, beliefs, and values are culturally relative.

When I first encountered these ideas in a sociology course at a Christian college, I was both attracted to and troubled by them. I enjoyed gaining broader horizons and learning about new and different cultures. I felt liberated from the narrow confines of my rather provincial, small-town background. And I took iconoclastic pleasure in pointing out the cultural relativity of claims made by chapel speakers, politicians, parents, and rule enforcers everywhere.

But I was troubled at the same time because I felt that many of my cultural beliefs and values were true. Not just "true for my culture," but true. Period. Indeed, I assumed that many of the beliefs and customs I adhered to were more or less ordained by God and ought to be accepted by everyone—regardless of their culture. I struggled with several questions: How should I think about culture? How should I think about my own cultural values, beliefs, and norms? How should I think about cultures quite different from my own? The issue pointed me in opposite directions. Part of me believed that my culture was grounded in transcendent truths—revealed by the God of all creation and, thus, a source of absolute standards of truth, goodness, and beauty. I could be confident in my beliefs, use them as the basis for my actions, and be equally confident that other cultures were simply wrong.

But my new sociological awareness suggested that my cultural beliefs were also merely human products—social constructions masquerading as a divinely inspired plan. Are my beliefs and values then true only in relation to my cultural context, but no more true than those of any other culture? Do I simply accept my culture's maxims because they have been jammed down my throat through processes of socialization and social control? Could I have grown up in a radically different culture and come to accept its beliefs just as strongly as I accept my current beliefs? How, then, should we think about culture, theirs and ours?

THE POLAR TEMPTATIONS OF CULTURE

It seems to me that we need to begin by getting past two tempting ways of thinking about culture that are fraught with difficulties: the absolutist and the relativistic. Before we explore a Christian sociological approach to culture, we must critique these popular but dead-end options.

Historically, humans have most commonly fallen prey to the temptation to view their own culture as absolute truth and to devalue the beliefs and customs of cultures that differ from their own. This is understandable, since giving in to this absolutizing temptation seems quite natural. Let me explain this through the experiences of a young man we will call Miguel Luis.

Miguel lives in a remote South American village on the shore of a great lake. The Lake People, as with all societies, have built up a way of life over the centuries through trial and error, conflict, and compromise. As they have dealt with property, work, governance, kinship, child rearing, health, and other matters of daily life, certain ways of behaving and thinking have become institutionalized—established as the way things are done among the Lake People. These "certified" ways of acting and thinking are more or less adaptive. The people of the fishing village have been able to survive, work, make collective decisions, maintain modest health, make sense of their experience in life, and enjoy beauty. To be sure, their way of life has its problems, but they cope reasonably well.

Miguel's people appreciate their culture. It works for them; it is the way of life given them by their revered ancestors. This way of life helps unify them. It gives the Lake People their identity, spelling out who they are and what they stand for. They celebrate and reaffirm this way of life through periodic festivals and rituals as well as in the songs and stories they share with one another. Moreover, their culture is reinforced through powerful processes of social control. Miguel has participated in celebrations and feasts given for heroes who embody the ideals of the Lake People. Power, respect, and privilege flow to those who honor the certified ways of thinking and acting. Miguel has also seen the ridicule, gossip, harassment, shame, shunning, and even death that have come to villagers who have challenged or dishonored their way of life. He knows it is dangerous to differ from the established ways.

But these rewards and punishments seem quite appropriate to Miguel, for he has been socialized into the Lake People's way of life by kin and other villagers. He has also been rewarded and punished for compliance and noncompliance with Lake People ways. As Miguel Luis grew up, he imitated the significant others around him; he learned by observing their words and behavior, their successes and failures. He learned the basic premises, assumptions, and categories of thought and value fundamental to his culture. He learned the many beliefs that justify and explain the customs and thoughtways of his people. He learned that the village way of life was given to his ancestors by powerful gods— gods who punish those who violate the sacred ways of the Lake People. And Miguel has learned to worship his ancestors who watch over the Lake People and bring good fortune to those who behave honorably.

Through these processes of socialization, Miguel has "internalized" the culture of the Lake People. He has taken on this culture as his own; he wants to act and think in the ways he is supposed to act and think. The patterns of his culture have become habitual; he almost "instinctively" thinks and behaves in appropriate ways. When Miguel is very hungry, he automatically dreams of fish from the lake cooked the way Lake People do. When things go well for him and his people, Miguel automatically thinks of thanking his ancestors.

So it is that, having come to see and experience life in terms of Lake People culture, Miguel Luis feels anger toward those who dishonor the ways of his culture—such evildoers deserve their punishment. Similarly, he enthusiastically joins in the praise of those who have diligently upheld Lake People virtues. Indeed, Miguel feels pride when he succeeds by Lake People standards, guilt and shame when he fails.

The important point about this discussion of processes of socialization, social control, celebration, and collective identity is to understand how Miguel Luis and his fellow villagers view their culture. To be sure, they see their customs, values, and beliefs as useful ways for people to survive and get along together. But it goes far beyond that. They view their way of life as the *natural* human way. It is taken for granted as the normal way humans live and think—a simple expression of human nature. Put differently, they have "absolutized" (made absolute) their customs, values, and beliefs. They assume that their customs are right, that their beliefs are true, that their understandings of goodness and beauty simply reflect the nature of reality—the given form of the universe. Acts that the Lake People view as evil are seen as *intrinsically* evil—going against the natural order of things. Their fish *by nature* taste good and make them brave, just as, *by nature*, their dead ancestors are active in watching over and shaping the fate of the Lake People. It is all self-evident and certain. Only a fool or an evil man would think otherwise.

The Lake People have little contact with outsiders. Indeed, their unfamiliarity with other ways of acting and thinking only reinforces conformity to Lake People culture, as do the processes of joking about, ridiculing, and criticizing foreign peoples. Moreover, their culture is a constraint that channels and focuses their thinking and experience. When Lake People do encounter the customs or ideas of other cultures, they experience and interpret these foreign ways through the screen of their own culture. It is thus not surprising that Lake People at best regard unfamiliar customs as strange and more typically consider them disgusting, threatening, and puzzling.

The process of absolutizing culture commonly manifests itself in *ethnocentrism*, which means viewing the ways of your culture or people as the correct and naturally superior standard by which you judge all other cultures. To the extent that the customs or thoughtways of another people differ from your own, they are inferior, immoral, ignorant, wrong, and/or weird. Directly or indirectly, the characteristics and contributions of other cultures are disvalued by being ignored, ridiculed, or loathed: "Only our ways are worthy."

We say, "America is number one"—a doubly ethnocentric phrase that takes the name of North, South, and Central America and applies it as if the United States were the only nation in the Americas that mattered. But we have a long heritage of such ethnocentrism. The European explorers and colonists of the seventeenth, eighteenth, and nineteenth centuries brought back stories of "primitives" and "ignorant savages" who needed to be "civilized"—a noble task termed the "white man's burden." More recently, given our Western ideas of progress and evolution, we speak of "backward" and "undeveloped" nations who are "developing" by becoming more like us—the "advanced" nations.

Christians are not immune to ethnocentrism. Paul struggled with Jewish Christians who viewed themselves as God's only chosen people and found it difficult to tolerate the lowly Gentiles in the church. They took their own cultural customs regarding gender roles, diet, and circumcision as absolutes that had to be practiced by everyone in the church, including the "heathen" Gentiles. What a cross-cultural challenge for Paul!

Well-intentioned missionaries in our own era have often succumbed to this same ethnocentrism. Western cultural patterns of dress, sexuality, marriage, worship, hymnody, and church governance have been imposed on people as if they were divinely ordained parts of the Christian gospel. In the words of Christian anthropologist Marvin Mayers (1987), these missionaries are "monocultural"—they are capable of operating out of the framework of only one culture, as if it were the final word.

The "Christian America" syndrome will serve as our final example of ethnocentrism in the church. In what sociologists call "civil religion," many people combine Christianity and "Americanism" in a curious mixture wherein the traditional customs and values of the United States are given divine approval. Free enterprise, capitalism, democracy, individualism, materialism, success, and traditional family forms become sacred. In effect, civil religious faith adapts to, celebrates, and justifies the major institutions and values of the culture. Religious symbols are sprinkled over the political landscape, from Presidential Prayer Breakfasts and enthusiastic renditions of "God Bless America" at political events to "In God We Trust" and "One Nation Under God." The history of "Christian America" is the story of God's chosen people who founded this nation on Christian principles to be a "city on a hill." We have a divinely given manifest destiny to carry our way of life far and wide. No one dare stand in our way, for in the battle against those who resist us, God is on our side! As the bumper sticker boldly declares, "God, guts, and guns."

To the sociologist, this process of absolutizing one's culture seems quite natural for humans. Indeed, cultural absolutism has many benefits for individuals and communities—as we observed with Miguel Luis and the Lake People. Their ethnocentrism gives them a sense of pride, of being special, and thereby promotes unity. Miguel has a clear identity; he knows who he is and what he stands for. With such a clear sense of right and wrong, individual and collective decision making is relatively easy. Miguel has a definiteness of purpose. He knows what he must strive for and is surrounded by others who share his goals. In other words, cultural absolutism helps generate the commitments and unity necessary for social life and meets the human needs for identity, meaning, and security.

But what a price is paid for these benefits! When a people are committed to beliefs and customs as absolutes, they are likely to be intolerant of criticism and unwilling to listen to new and contrary views. Such cultures become closed and relatively rigid systems. They may be shackled to institutions and ways of thinking that become maladaptive or obsolete in the face of social change. They may be unable to respond effectively to crises and emergencies that do not follow the usual routines to which the culture has been adapted.

Absolutist cultures may attempt to eliminate all internal dissent and criticism through processes of book burning, purges, and persecution or even eradication of dissenters. This is especially common when absolutist cultures invest total power in leaders who represent and promise to carry out the "unquestioned truth." Leaders who are convinced that they cannot be wrong, and followers who give them unquestioning obedience, have been the source of monstrous evils in the human experience—from the extermination of over 6 million Jews, to the total devotion to cult leaders such as Jim Jones.

When two or more cultures meet, ethnocentrism is especially problematic. For one thing, ethnocentric peoples simply cannot understand each other and work well together. They fail to understand the meanings and reactions of others; they also cannot appreciate the needs, concerns, strengths, and contributions of other peoples and traditions. Various trade, missionary, or humanitarian aid programs may fail or backfire because people are so monocultural that they cannot relate effectively with people from different cultures. But the problems are often even more serious.

Powerful absolutist cultures may require weaker cultures to submit to their political forms, technology, religion, or family customs. Such ethnocentrism has been manifested in colonialism, imperialism, white supremacy, militant nationalism, and countless wars. As Kovisto (cited by Herskovits, 1972) put it, "The wages of the sin of ethnocentrism is open conflict." In the "global village" of today's world, where different cultures have a high degree of contact and interdependence, where survival of the human race requires peaceful coexistence, we simply cannot afford ethnocentrism.

For Christians, the issue is even more pointed. When absolute allegiance to one's culture is reinforced by religious zeal, the results can be devastating. Historical examples include crusades, holy wars, inquisitions, and witch hunts; bloody battles between Muslims and Christians; and violent persecution of Anabaptists, Quakers, Catholics, and Mormons. As Pascal noted in *Lettres Provinciales*, "Men never do evil so completely and cheerfully as when they do it from religious conviction."

But it is not just a matter of ethnocentrism being dangerous. For the Christian, it is a spiritual evil. Ethnocentrism in Christian terms is cultural idolatry, giving an ultimate allegiance to culture that properly belongs only to God. Therefore, cultural absolutism is a social, physical, and spiritual dead end.

Recognizing the problems of cultural absolutism, sociologists have long championed a relativistic approach to culture. This second tempting view of culture is now dominant in universities, the media, the educated classes, and increasingly in the church. In thinking about morality, lifestyles, religions, the arts, and many other arenas of life, cultural relativism has become a major force to be reckoned with.

To understand the attractions and perils of this view of culture, we must return to the experience of Miguel Luis. When he was in his late teens, Miguel's family was killed in a devastating flood. Soon after that, Miguel met "Dr. Juanita." Dr. Juanita Alverez was a middle-aged agricultural development agent who had been sent by the national government to help the Lake People recover from the flood and rebuild a healthy, prosperous village. In her many weeks of working with the Lake People she had taken a special interest in the hard-working Miguel who was still grieving the loss of his family. In time she convinced Miguel to accompany her as an assistant and companion while she traveled among many villages to promote better agriculture. At first Miguel was terrified at the prospect. He had never been more than a day's walk from the lake—only rarely had he encountered an outsider. His knowledge of other peoples was largely confined to the stories his elders told of bizarre and sometimes silly customs and ideas to be found in other villages. To Miguel, the outside world was a mysterious and threatening realm to be avoided. But Dr. Juanita was an outsider, and he trusted her, so he decided to take the risk.

It didn't take long for his worst fears to be realized. In spite of Dr. Juanita's long talks in preparation for the trip, Miguel experienced culture shock soon after arriving among the Plains People. Having left the familiar world of his own culture to enter another, he felt like a fish out of water. All of the taken-for-granted customs, cues, and habits of his world were missing. The forms of politeness, the facial expressions and gestures, and the customs of the Plains People were so different. Some were disgusting! Miguel was confused and anxious. He would hear jokes, sometimes about himself, and not know why they were funny. Following his own culture's scripts, he would do things to please his hosts; instead, he offended them. They misread him, and he misread them. Miguel simply wanted to go home where things were done the "normal" way.

Dr. Juanita tried to explain to him that his problem was temporary, that soon he would discover the code, the deep cultural rules, categories, and premises that would make sense of the Plains People's actions. But Miguel was still too monocultural, trapped within the comforting confines of his culture. He could only react out of his ethnocentrism and think, How can they live like this? The Plains People actually ate pigs! A favorite treat for the kids was to catch and eat live grasshoppers. Miguel remembered the day when the sound of grasshoppers being crunched literally made him sick. Plains People speech sounded like grunts and squawks, and that was little better than their singing.

Through Dr. Juanita, Miguel learned that the Plains People mocked his ancestor worship, calling it "talking to ghosts." That offended him greatly, especially when he found out that they believed in reincarnation! These fools were certainly in no position to make fun of his ancestor worship. This contrast sparked a dialogue through Dr. Juanita between Miguel and the Plains People. The process fascinated Dr. Juanita and frustrated Miguel. She saw both sides offering a logic and an apologetic (complete with vivid examples) to explain their respective beliefs. Yet, without a shared frame of reference, neither side fully understood the other. They just seemed to talk past each other.

Miguel spent many hours working through these concerns with Dr. Juanita. He spent eight months with the Plains People, six months with the River People, and five months with the Mountain People. With each cultural experience he became less monocultural, less ethnocentric, and more capable of seeing the links between actions and their cultural context.

As he reflected on his travels, he saw various points of similarity among the cultures. But what stood out were the differences. Each culture was somewhat different in customs, values, and beliefs; yet each claimed to be *right*. Each had a sense of certainty about the truthfulness of its ways—a confidence in its superiority. But how could *all* these different customs and beliefs be absolutely true and right? How could an idea be absolutely true and sacred in one place, yet absolutely false and evil in another? It began to seem to Miguel as if there were no absolute and fixed truth and morality. There were no universal rules by which all cultures could be judged. Instead, each culture had its own customs and beliefs which the people mistakenly viewed as "natural" or "divine" standards by which all cultures were to be judged.

He saw that the Plains People had their own right and wrong, good and evil, truth and falsity. The customs of the River People only made sense relative to *their* culture. The ideas of the Mountain People were true in the context of *their* culture. And what of my own beliefs? Miguel wondered, Could it be true that the lake fish were not inherently tasty, but that instead he had learned to like their taste? Was it also the case, then, that worshiping his ancestors was not inherently true or right, but that he had only learned to think of ancestor worship as true because his people taught him so? He knew that the children of the Plains People were taught to believe in reincarnation and that they accepted it just as they had come to like crunching grasshoppers.

Miguel had many questions. Which culture is right? How do I judge between them? Are any of them right? Are my beliefs undependable, since they are merely the homemade concoction of my people—which they take to be absolutes? Is there any truth or morality beyond the relative truths and moralities of each people? Or is it all just a matter of taste—some like lake fish and some like grasshoppers?

Sociology and anthropology are indirect ways of understanding what Miguel learned through the experience of travel. Though relativism is an ancient concept, sociology and anthropology extended and popularized the idea in this century. Initially, the concern of sociology and anthropology was twofold. For one thing, they were trying to broaden the horizon of Westerners, to encourage respect and tolerance for other peoples of the world. Ethnocentric Westerners were involved in military, political, economic, and religious adventures overseas in ways that showed no understanding of the perspective and value of other ways of life and thought. By displaying the rich diversity of human cultures—the inner logic of a culture's customs and thoughtways; the adaptiveness of seemingly "bizarre" or "primitive" customs— sociology and anthropology sought to reduce ethnocentrism and promote cross-cultural tolerance.

A second goal of sociology and anthropology in developing the idea of relativism was more methodological. If the task of sociologists and anthropologists was to understand and explain the human social world and its components, then success required that they recognize and control their own cultural commitments when studying other peoples. How can we understand polygyny (one husband, several wives,) its development, its place, and its meaning in a people's way of life—if all we can see is "immorality" and "adultery"? That is, if we from a more or less monogamous culture are caught up in judging a custom by our own culture's standards, we are unlikely to fully understand that custom. To really understand a custom requires that we see it in its context, recognize the meaning and value it has for those who practice it, and become aware of its adaptiveness in its own setting. We may not personally accept the truthfulness of reincarnation and ancestor worship or the morality of polygyny, but as scientists (so the argument goes), our task is not to judge right and wrong but to understand and explain. This task requires that we set aside our personal cultural standards and think in terms of the relativity of customs, values, and beliefs.

It seems to me, however, that sociology and anthropology in recent decades have gone beyond these modest and worthy goals.

The kind of relativism that sociology has helped popularize, and that is typically represented in sociology textbooks and teaching, is not merely an academic, methodological notion, but an approach to living in a culturally diverse world. As a moral and ethical philosophy, sociological relativism encourages us to give up belief in universal, transcultural truths and moral standards and the possibility of making moral judgments across cultures. Let me briefly describe this sociological argument that serves as a shortcut to what Miguel learned through experience.

The human world is populated with many cultures—each reflecting the unique experiences, history, and setting of the respective people. Consequently, the customs of a people and what they take to be real, true, good, and beautiful exist alongside somewhat different customs and notions of truth, goodness, and beauty. Each culture holds its views with equal certainty as being obvious, natural, and superior to all contrary views. That is, each tends to judge others ethnocentrically.

But the claim that a particular culture is the "one true way" cannot legitimately be made. How can all of these contradictory claims of truth and morality be correct? The problem we are left with is how to judge which, if any, cultures are moral and true. We have no objective, culture-free way of judging one to be better than another. None of us can jump out of culture and history in order to objectively evaluate cultures by some neutral, universal standard. We cannot reliably know of any unconditionally valid, transcultural standards of right and wrong, truth and falsity.

The cultural relativist's solution to this problem is to abandon the notion of absolute standards and the process of evaluating different cultures in terms of such mythical standards. Instead, the argument goes, any custom or belief can only be legitimately evaluated contextually, relative to its cultural context. All judgments are relative to a judge's cultural framework. "Goodness" and "badness" are contextual matters. Is an apple better than a pear? Is monogamy better than polygyny? Truth, goodness, and beauty lie not "out there," but in the relationship between objects, ideas, or customs and the cultural communities who judge them. Each cultural system has its own means of judging and interpreting reality, and we have no supercultural way of ruling among them. We must learn to live *without* absolute and eternal truths.

Thus, the relativist implicitly claims that all cultures are equally valid and deserving of respect. The basic ground rule in a multicultural world is *tolerance*: Thou shalt not judge another culture by your culture's standards. And the second commandment is like unto it: Thou shalt not impose on others the ways of your culture.

This cultural relativism has great appeal in a culturally diverse world and some value that we should not ignore. But as with ethnocentrism, relativism has some serious flaws. Let me begin with a brief examination of some logical problems in Miguel's (and the relativist's) thinking.

Cultural relativism suffers from what has often been called the "self-referential fallacy." The relativist's statement that "all customs, values, and beliefs are relative to their cultural context" is treated as a universal truth claim. And yet the statement refers to itself. That is, cultural relativism is a belief, and if the relativist's statement quoted above is true, then the idea of cultural relativism is itself culturally relative—not absolute. As such, then, we can view cultural relativism as an idea carried by Western intellectuals in the modern era, an idea that is true in its particular context (Berger, 1969). Relativism thus becomes a limited perspective rather than an absolute and binding truth. The same holds for the claim that "there are no absolute truths." If that is so, then the claim itself cannot be absolutely true (Hasker, 1980). A way of thinking about culture that rests on such a logical contradiction is at best confused.

The second logical problem involves a false conclusion drawn about cultural relativity. The sociological concept of cultural relativism has largely come from the process of observing the diversity of human cultural patterns. The existence of many contradictory cultural systems of truth, goodness, and beauty becomes the basis for concluding that all cultural systems are arbitrary human constructions and that there is no absolute truth beyond these human constructs. That is, things are considered true, good, and beautiful only because some people agree to consider them true, good, and beautiful.

This relativistic conclusion, however, is based on a logical error. As Moberg (1962) has pointed out, one cannot legitimately infer from the fact of cultural diversity that there are not any absolute and ultimate values and standards. A difference of opinion among different peoples as to what is true "in no way proves that the object toward which the opinion refers does not exist" (Moberg, 1962:39). Cultural variety only demonstrates a difference in judgment regarding what is true, good, and beautiful. These judgments, which are culturally relative, can coexist with absolute and ultimate standards that transcend relativism and social construction.

Let me warn you about one other logical problem that may snare you. The strength of the idea of cultural relativism is that it encourages us as citizens and scientists to *understand* the customs and beliefs of other peoples by contextualizing them. We need to see how customs are adaptive for a people in their setting, how their beliefs make sense when seen in the framework of this culture. The temptation (sometimes encouraged by sociologists) is to assume that such understanding also means that you must *approve* of these customs and ideas, go along with them because they are "just as valid" as your own. Understanding by culturally contextualizing is not the same as approval, however. I can understand South African apartheid, United States' abortion clinics, and the Israeli treatment of Palestinians, yet profoundly disagree with and even seek to change these customs. Peter Berger (1974:134) sums this up well: "Cognitive respect means that one takes seriously the ways in which others define reality. But that does not mean that one makes no moral distinctions among these definitions and practices." It would be irresponsible for me as a human being to abandon my best judgments of what is true and right by approving or treating as "equally valid" any custom or idea I may encounter in another culture or subculture. A methodological tool that is useful in helping us understand other people is not the best ethical and political principle by which to live in a world of suffering, exploitation, and injustice. Understanding does not require approval.

Cultural relativism is plagued by logical problems, and it also creates some significant personal problems. As should be apparent by now, the idea of cultural relativism undermines individual attachment to collective beliefs, values, and customs. Through cultural relativism, sociologists debunk absolutism and reveal beliefs and values to be merely "local truth." As happened with Miguel, once we see the many cultural options (all of which claim to be true), we realize that each culture is only fooling itself. We recognize that we were socially programed to take as "given" and "obvious" the truths of our people.

Miguel saw his friends among the Lake People being programed to view ancestor worship as authentic, whereas children among the Plains People were being programed to absolutize reincarnation. How can he trust his feelings and convictions after this? Aren't all these beliefs, values, and customs just locally produced fictions that people mistakenly take to be true? Am I a believer in collective illusion? Is one idea or value system as good (or bad) as another?

Belief in cultural relativism thus subverts certainty in the truth and validity of one's own affirmations. Indeed, it can cultivate skepticism about the existence of ultimate truth and value. Because of this, sociology has contributed to a process of subjectivization in the Western world. We have lost a sense of truth and meaning being "out there," an objective truth that we can know. Now we must turn inward to our personal experiences, our subjective insights, our gut feelings, as a source of truth and meaning. What was once "This is true!" becomes "My people view this as true," which finally becomes "This is true for me." Needless to say, this is a fragile basis for truth and meaning.

Miguel's cross-cultural experiences have created in him a

sense of anomie—of homelessness. The cultural relativism pro-
moted by sociology produces the same rootlessness. Given what
sociology tells us, how can we claim to *know* something? I want to
know truth, but I fear that I am merely comforted by conventional
illusions. How can I make commitments, be confident enough in a
vision of right and wrong to invest myself in pursuit of values?
How can I take the risk of challenging and criticizing the given
social order? How can I be confident enough in my Christian faith
to step out into the risky unknown of discipleship?

Cultural relativism, when followed to its conclusions, is a
dead end.

A CHRISTIAN APPROACH TO CULTURE

Miguel Luis has returned home to his Lake People. His small
world has been expanded in sometimes painful ways through
months of living in a variety of cultures. He feels somewhat
rootless and unattached.

How should he now think about culture? Should he reinvest
himself in Lake People culture and readopt their customs, values,
and beliefs? Should he accept their assumption that Lake People
ways are the "one true way"? No, in that sense he can never go
home again. He has seen that all cultures view their ways as
naturally superior, but he recognizes the logical impossibility of all
of them being superior. He has seen that each culture has its
strengths and weaknesses, each has a logic, morality, and beauty
when viewed from within. Miguel knows that his people are
simply naive and ethnocentric when they claim the "one true
way."

Perhaps Miguel's experience of several different but equally
absolutist cultures has even convinced him that the whole culture
game is a sham. These customs, beliefs, and values are merely
human constructions posing as ultimate truths. But they cannot all
be ultimate—and in fact, none are. From this relativist stance,
Miguel would find none of these systems of "cultural fiction" to
be binding upon him. With no cultural commitments, he would be
floating free—free to do whatever he wanted or whatever he
could get away with. But he would be free, as well, from the
comfort and direction of a coherent vision of truth and justice,
beauty, and virtue. He would also be free from a community of
others who shared his vision. Life in such an anomic state of
"freedom" would be a journey through a desolate and pathless
terrain.

Now it seems to me that Miguel's dilemma may also be the
sociology student's dilemma. Both end up with broader cultural
horizons, both feel somewhat detached from their cultural traditions and people, and both may doubt that there are any ultimate

standards of truth, goodness, and beauty. The bottom line for both is the question of how to think about culture. Is my culture, or part of it, a reflection of God's truth—and thus a source of absolute standards and a foundation for commitments? Or is my culture simply a human product, jammed down my throat, but no more true than any other culture?

In response to these questions, I want to sketch the outlines of a Christian sociological approach to thinking about culture that may help you as you do more thinking and reading about these issues on your own. This approach will depart from the usual sociological way of thinking.

Sociology typically operates on naturalistic assumptions, taking as legitimate data only what is part of the material or "natural" world. Because this view ignores (or denies) "supernatural" forces or beings, it leads sociologists to conclude that there are no transcendent truths; truth, goodness, and beauty are merely human constructs that vary from culture to culture. My alternative approach begins with Christian assumptions about the human condition and uses these in conversation with sociological concepts (*see* Clark and Gaede, 1987).

Let me highlight three relevant Christian assumptions. First, God created humans as cultural beings and affirmed them as such. God made us creatures who need shared symbol systems, normative systems, and bodies of shared information in order to survive. We need culture to pool our learning and transmit our way of life to the next generation. He made us creatures who seek meaning, who desire to understand ourselves and our world, and who interpret and evaluate actions, persons, and events. He gave us the ability to appreciate and create beauty. Much of this is implied in God's command to subdue, populate, and cultivate the earth. In what is called the "culture mandate," humans are asked to work with the created order, to develop and maintain God's earth. He gave humans the responsibility to name the animals and create the institutions of work, government, marriage, and family. Clearly, God expects us to use the culture creating abilities he gave us. God also affirms culture in his use of human language, human images (father, mother, king, judge, shepherd), and human cultural forms (covenants, treaties) in relating to his people.

However, nothing reveals God's affirmation of human culture more than the Incarnation. In this act, the holy and righteous God (the creator and sustainer of the universe) became human. Jesus immersed himself in a particular human culture, taking its family roles, language, and work roles, sharing in its ceremonies, and telling stories in forms that could be understood by human audiences. The Incarnation is a clear declaration that culture is not inherently evil, but is our created, God-intended way of being in the world.

This creator God expected his human creatures to follow his direction in the use of their culture-building capacity. God is the source of all truth—truth that transcends mere human construction. He has intentions for our institutions, values, and norms. But there are constraints on our ability to know the truth and direction that God provides. This brings us to the second and third biblical assumptions.

We were created as *finite beings*. We are finite creations of an infinite God—not equal to the Creator in our capacities. We are not omniscient; we have finite brains, limited memories, and limited sensory and perceptual abilities. We are socially finite as well, in the sense that societies have limited and selective pools of experience, limited abilities to acquire, store, distribute, and apply cultural elements, and limitations in transmitting culture across generations. Each society then approaches its cultural task within the confines of its particular experiences, opportunities, resources, and concerns. Hence, God's infinite truth and meaning must be discovered, interpreted, communicated, and institutionalized by finite beings. Each culture's beliefs, norms, and values will thus necessarily be selective, incomplete, and particular.

Our final biblical assumption is that we are *fallen beings*. According to the biblical drama, God created humans with an ability to give him devotion and obedience—he did not force it. We were able to use our culture-building capacity in ways consonant with his intentions for us. But instead we used and distorted this capacity in our sinful rebellion against God and our fellows. We rejected the meaning, truth, and normative guidance that God provided. We declared ourselves to be the arbiters of truth, goodness, and beauty. Biblically, then, the Fall involves autonomous humans searching for and creating our own meaning systems, building institutions that serve the interests of the powerful, and constructing ideas and norms that justify our comfortable way of life (Walter, 1979). We fallen beings often do not want to know the truth, and we love "darkness rather than light" (John 3:19), when "light" would threaten our treasures or lifestyle. We are prone to cultural rationalizations, lies, and ideologies that legitimize evil systems. In effect, we use our truth-seeking and culture-building capacity not to honor God, but to promote our individual and collective interests.

We are cultural beings, finite beings, and fallen beings. What import do these biblical assumptions have for our thinking about culture? It seems to me that they suggest a stance toward culture that I call "critical commitment."

Relativists argue that each culture is its own standard—each has its own principles of truth, goodness, and beauty. Other relativists of more extreme nature go further, concluding that such standards are arbitrary human fictions and that the world is a meaningless canvas onto which we paint our puny illusions. Some Christians accept these relativist arguments. Some come to believe that culture must therefore be "worldly"—a mere human product. Therefore, to be a Christian means to resist human culture, to be elevated into a noncultural realm of spiritual truths and lifestyle.

But our Christian assumptions would suggest that these responses are unwarranted. The relativist denies that God created a meaningful world and human creatures who could apprehend that meaning—however imperfectly. The relativist denies God's authority over human culture, denies the existence of standards of truth and virtue that stand above and judge all cultures. And the Christian who recoils from relativism into an anticultural position is denying our God-created cultural nature.

As an alternative, Christians should be committed to culture. We should affirm, indeed celebrate, our cultural nature even as God did through the Creation and the Incarnation. Culture is flawed and infected by sin, but it remains an essential and worthy part of our created nature. Humans, in God's plan, are born as unfinished products. Culture and socialization are life-giving processes. Individually we need a language; we need to be surrounded by institutions and limited choices; we need to know who we are; we need to know how to do things; we need to know some norms and roles; we need some meaning; and we need focus, direction and vision.

In our life together as social beings, we need shared understandings and language; we need direction and focus; we need institutions and customs; we need socialization and social control. That is the God-created human way! Cultural institutions and customs, and the related processes of socialization and social control, can be vehicles of human well-being. They are the means through which we love and care for one another, promote justice, encourage peace, demonstrate mercy, resolve conflicts, and resist evil. They are also a means through which God loves us and works out his agenda for human history. God wants his human creatures to have an abundant life, and that is expressed through our nature as cultural beings.

An important implication of this is that it is rather silly to doubt your beliefs just because you were socialized into them by family, friends, and community. That does not mean that your beliefs are false or untrustworthy; it means only that you are human! How else but through social influences do humans get most of their beliefs and values? Indeed, the Holy Spirit may be acting through such processes. If you were brought to faith through social influences (as most of us were), be thankful! The key question is not how you obtained your beliefs; rather, the question is whether they are the most warranted beliefs (Clark and Gaede, 1987).

We cannot simply be committed to "culture in general"; for a starting place, we need commitment to a particular culture. For most of us, that will be the culture or subculture of our birth. When you commit yourself to a particular culture, you are making a choice of one culture over others. This choice carries the risk of being wrong. But all cultures carry this risk; there are no cultures that can legitimately offer guaranteed truth, the whole truth, and nothing but the truth. Not our culture, not their culture, and not the relativist's. We must all make risky choices and live with the consequences. But an important way to move toward the truth is to commit yourself to stand, in the absence of certainty, for what in your best judgment is true, good, and beautiful. By so investing yourself in a culture, pushing it, working with it, you may test its strengths and discover its weaknesses. Standing on the sidelines, uncommitted, is a risky option that will not help you move toward the truth.

But our commitment to culture must be a "critical commitment." Ethnocentrists are strongly committed to their culture; indeed they claim to have the one true way, tolerating no others. The problem is that their uncritical commitment to culture denies their finitude and fallenness. They identify the constructions of a people and their ancestors with the kingdom of God. That is nothing short of cultural idolatry. All cultures fall short. God stands above and judges all cultures as warped and incomplete representations of his will for us.

As an alternative to ethnocentrists' arrogance, Christians are called to humility by the awareness of our finitude and fallenness. We must become *limited* relativists (Mayers, 1987; Nida, 1954). That is, while we believe in God's ultimate truth and desire to live in it, we also recognize (as relativists) that our finitude limits, contextualizes, and diversifies our understandings of that truth. Furthermore, our fallenness leads us to resist, distort, and misuse the truth in self-serving ways. Our understandings of God's infinite truth, his Scriptures, and his creation are always flawed and incomplete—just as our efforts to translate understandings of his will into cultural customs and institutions will be imperfect. Though we disagree with relativists by believing that there are ultimate standards of judgment, we should appreciate the relativists' argument that any cultural element is shaped and conditioned by its cultural, social, and historical context.

Our commitment to culture thus needs to be self-critical. Our ultimate loyalty is to God, not a human culture. We can never embrace our culture as the last and only word. We are aware of the eternal gap between what is and what ought to be in our culture. We must be ever vigilant against the temptation to absolutize our institutions or nation—ever alert to the seductive pressures of conformity to the evil aspects of our culture. We must critically examine our culture in light of our best understandings of God's intentions for us. Our task, then, is to preserve the good in our culture and attempt to challenge and change what is corrupt, unjust, and false. Because we are committed to culture, but under loyalty to God, our goal is to join him in transforming human culture toward his creative intentions. It is a process of being "in but not of" this world—fully investing ourselves in this world while attempting to operate according to the values of another kingdom.

Finally, our Christian assumptions have implications for our thinking about other cultures. The first of these is a respect that flows from the recognition of our common humanity with all peoples as finite, fallen, cultural beings. The culture of another people represents their best efforts as cultural beings. We must allow others their cultural commitments and appreciate what they have accomplished. Until convinced otherwise, we should give other cultures the benefit of the doubt, respecting them as workable solutions to their problems and answers to their questions. All cultures, in varying degrees, are vehicles of human well-being. All cultures can be media of God's love and grace. The gospel can be communicated in any culture, and God can be known, worshiped, and obeyed in any culture—though more easily in some than in others (Hiebert, 1985). We can learn to appreciate the wide variety of particular ways in which God's general will for us can be expressed (Kraft, 1979).

Because we are critically committed to our culture, we should listen to others. As finite, fallen people, we may be wrong. We have much to learn from the rich diversity of human cultures. Each culture has opened up a part of the creation, solved certain problems, and learned from a history of experiences. By listening, we can also better understand their beliefs and customs from their point of view. We must also take seriously the views and criticisms of those with whom we differ, for they have much to teach us.

But the dialogue needs to flow both ways. Other people are also finite and fallen. They do not have the last word on culture, either. Because we are committed to our culture, we are convinced that others could benefit by listening to us. Moreover, our understanding of their ways does not require acceptance or even tolerance of those ways. We should encourage them to listen to the criticisms and challenges that grow out of our cultural commitments. Our integrity as Christians requires that we be witnesses against evil and injustice in our culture and theirs. If we are all to make progress toward truth and virtue, then, we must respectfully understand, listen to, and challenge one another as people critically committed to diverse cultures.

REFERENCES IN CHAPTER

Berger, Peter. 1969. *Rumor of Angels*. New York: Doubleday.
————. 1974. *Pyramids of Sacrifice*. New York: Doubleday.
Clark, Robert, and S. D. Gaede. 1987. "Knowing Together: Reflections on a Wholistic Sociology of Knowledge." In *The Reality of Christian Learning*, edited by Harold Heie and David Wolfe. Grand Rapids, Mich.: Eerdmans.
Hasker, William. 1980. "Cultural Relativity and Relativism." In *A Reader in Sociology: Christian Perspectives* edited by Charles DeSanto et al. Scottsdale, Pa: Herald Press.
Herskovits, Melville. 1972. *Cultural Relativism*. New York: Random House.
Hiebert, Paul. 1985. *Anthropological Insights for Missionaries*. Grand Rapids, Mich.: Baker Book House.
Kraft, Charles. 1979. *Christianity in Culture*. Maryknoll, N. Y.: Orbis.
Mayers, Marvin. 1987. *Christianity Confronts Culture*, Rev. and enl. ed. Grand Rapids, Mich.: Zondervan.
Moberg, David. 1962. "Cultural Relativity and Christian Faith." *Journal of the American Scientific Affiliation* 6:34–48.
Nida, Eugene. 1954. *Customs and Cultures*. Reprint. Pasadena, Calif.: Wm. Carey Library, 1975, 1982.
Walter, J. A. 1979. *Sacred Cows*. Grand Rapids, Mich.: Zondervan.

SOCIETY: THE SOCIAL CHARACTER OF HUMAN RELATIONSHIPS

S. D. Gaede

Society. A common term. We use it all the time. We talk about the society we live in, the friendship society we belong to, and the high society we wish we were a part of. Obviously, we feel comfortable with this concept. It's just a good, useful term.

Or so I thought. Until one day I was confronted with a most straightforward question: What does a society look like? At first blush, that didn't seem so difficult. A society is what I see when I attend a meeting of my fraternity or go to church or walk in a mall. A society is people doing things together. That's not so difficult.

But then I started thinking. When I walk into the church, are all the people I see members of my church or denomination? No, I had to admit, we sometimes have visitors. And if there is a meeting in our building, is it always a meeting of church members? No, sometimes we let other groups use our facilities. So then, can I conclude that what I see at a meeting in my church building is my church society? I guess not. You have to see a meeting of actual church members to really "see" that society.

But how do you know that? Can you actually see members of my church society? Do they look different from other people? Well, they are generally middle class. But when all is said and done, no, they don't look much different from anyone else. They are just people, after all. So how do you see a society member, anyway? How do you know for sure that you are visualizing a member of my church?

Unfortunately, you don't. At least not with your eyes you don't. It comes as a mild shock to most of us that we don't actually see societies at all. Nor do we see students, families, or parents. What we see are people, in a variety of different costumes and composures, acting as if they are students or parents or church members. And while you may guess that Heather is a student by the way she acts, you will not know this until you talk to her (or someone who knows her) and discover her status. In short, being a student or a professor or a society member is not a matter of seeing; it is a matter of *knowing*. Society is a product of the human mind.

By the way, none of this means that society isn't real. Try telling a father that being a parent is purely fiction, and he will laugh in your face. He knows the reality of parenthood, even though he can't see it. That is because it affects his life on a daily basis, from the time he hears his baby cry at five o'clock in the morning to the moment he puts his son to bed at night. For the same reason, we know that society is a rather profound reality as well. As Durkheim (1957) argued some years ago, we can measure its existence by determining its impact on our lives.

What it does mean, however, is that society is subject to a great deal of interpretation. If you and I were to sit down and look at a sea shell, for example, we would probably agree on a whole variety of things about the shell—from its color to its size to its original inhabitant. That is not because such things are obvious facts, as some might believe (*see* Wolterstorff, 1976), but because sea shells are a tangible, common part of our experience and we have learned to see and understand them in a certain way. Society, too, is a matter of experience and understanding, but it is neither tangible nor visual. As a result, the concept of society is a bit more slippery than that of the sea shell.

When something is slippery, either you get a firm hold on it, or you lose it. I hope that we will be able to get a good grip on the concept of society. In order to do that, however, we will have to ask some basic, but significant questions. The first is this: How do most contemporary sociologists conceive of the nature of society? That is important to know because sociologists are the ones who study society most directly. The second question is equally important: What kind of biblical wisdom can we bring to bear on the concept of society? This is an especially crucial question to me because I find the Scriptures to be incredibly relevant to the modern discipline of sociology. Finally, we will want to bring our answers to these two questions together and ask: What are the implications of a biblical understanding of society—for sociology, for the Christian, and for the Christian sociologist?

THE SOCIETY OF SOCIOLOGY

The slippery nature of society is evident the minute one opens up a text or two in sociology. After what may appear to be a straightforward definition of the concept, the reader may suddenly become confused in a wave of conflicting interpretations and observations. This is certainly the case if one peruses more than one textbook. But these days it is often true of any single text as well. Indeed, the standard book in introductory sociology is almost schizophrenic on the issue of society (*see* Eitzen, 1985; Taylor et. al., 1987).

On the one hand, a common observation is that society binds us to one another and enables us to meet one another's needs (Nisbet and Perrin, 1977). That tradition is best expressed by Durkheim (1937), who assumed that social solidarity is one of the human being's greatest needs. Instead of everyone going off and doing his own thing, society allows us to work together, protecting those who are weak and sharing the productivity of the strong and talented. If a parent doesn't feed and protect its offspring, the baby dies. If the farmer doesn't feed a nation, the nation dies. In short, social arrangements enable us to survive and to live productive lives.

But society's binding power does much more than just help us physically; it also gives emotional security to our lives. That is because it protects us from chaos (Berger, 1963:89). When you wake up in the morning, you do not have to ask: Who am I? What should I do? How should I do it? Normally, these questions are answered for you by your place in society. So, once you have pulled yourself out of bed and into the shower, you are able to say with some confidence, "I am Willy Wisdom, the son of Mr. and Mrs. Wisdom, currently a student at Wonderful College, and today I must read this sociology book or I'm going to flunk the test next Friday." In other words, your role as a student prevents chaos by providing you with direction.

Now this sounds pretty good, doesn't it? Three cheers for society and all of that. But just when you were starting to feel comfortable with this concept, you turn to the next chapter in your sociology text (or pick up another text), only to discover the emergence of a very different picture of society. Its most graphic scene shows society not as a cradle of peace and security, but as a prison holding people in intolerable conditions (e.g., Sherman and Wood, 1979). Society is not benevolent, according to this picture. It is an oppressor; and modern artists who paint such pictures often take their strokes from Karl Marx (1967).

The oppressive society, like the good society, is a highly nuanced sketching. It can be seen at both the physical and the emotional levels, and the level emphasized depends a great deal on the artist. Physically, for example, this view often shows society as the creator and sustainer of poverty (Ryan, 1977). Needing an abundant supply of cheap labor, society finds unemployment useful. Thus, it not only creates the economic forces that generate poverty but also provides the statuses and myths that legitimate poverty's existence. In this way, the poor are

trapped in the conditions of poverty and encouraged to think that
such conditions are either natural or divinely sanctioned. The
result is that the poor come to believe in their own impoverishment.

At the emotional level, society's oppression is variously
described. Some sociologists talk about the stress that comes from
living in degrading social conditions. They might point out that
poverty breeds feelings of despair, frustration, and alienation
(Liebow, 1967). For others, however, society's oppression goes
much deeper. That is because it applies not only to the poor but to
all humanity. We are all trapped in our social roles, according to
this view, constrained to play our parts—whether we like them or
not (Berger, 1963:93–121). Willy Wisdom did not choose to be
someone's son, and if he wants to be successful in our society, he
has little choice about being a student. Yet, these roles determine
his daily activities as well as his future. Willy Wisdom, like the rest
of us, is the product of his society.

THE ASSUMPTIONS OF SOCIETY

For the reader, the question immediately presenting itself is:
Whose view of society is correct? Good question. The problem is,
after a hundred years of debate and thousands of research studies,
sociologists do not agree on an answer. That is why the modern
introductory text is in such a dilemma over this issue. Some texts
try to solve this problem by siding with one perspective or the
other (e.g., Sherman and Wood, 1979). Others just present both
sides and let the reader decide (e.g., Eitzen, 1985). A few even
attempt to arrive at a creative synthesis (e.g., Lenski and Lenski,
1987). But all of them struggle.

The fact that all struggle with this problem should lead us to
an important realization: The debate about the nature of society is
not simply a dispute about social facts. It is also an argument
concerning social beliefs (Gaede, 1985). The debate has been going
on for many years now, and despite having generated lots of data,
the debate continues. This suggests that the problem is rooted in a
disagreement about what the facts are and about what they mean.
In other words, this debate results from a conflict of *assumptions*,
not just data.

The significance of assumptions in this debate ought to drive
each of us back to the question: What do I assume to be true about
the nature of society? Unfortunately, that important question has
not always been asked by sociologists themselves. As a result,
there has been far too much confusion in the sociological
community about this issue—a matter about which we will have
more to say shortly. But, for now, it is important simply to note

that the facts do not stand alone. They must be perceived, interpreted, and reinterpreted.

That process—called understanding—is greatly influenced by what we believe. To understand society (and the sociological debate about its nature), we must know the facts and also have a clear picture of the perspective from which we see the facts. We must begin with the following question: *What do we believe about society?*

The minute we ask this question, however, we may be thrown for a loop. Why? Well, for one thing, many of us have never thought of it before. Some of us haven't asked the question because we thought it had already been answered; we assumed that society is an obvious fact. Still, there are others who have asked the question, but haven't had the foggiest notion of how to go about finding an answer. This can be a troubling question indeed, especially for those with no clear understanding of their own world view.

Theoretically, the Christian should not have trouble with this. The Christian ought to have a biblically rooted world view from which a myriad of insights about the nature of society should be forthcoming (*see* Storkey, 1979; Walter, 1979). Generally, however, this has not been the case. Instead, most of us have assumed that being a Christian is a private matter only, having personal consequences certainly, but having little to do with the way we think about society. Such an assumption is understandable—*since that is precisely what our world wants us to believe*—but it is grossly unbiblical (Guinness, 1983:71–90). The Scripture is unequivocal about one thing: Our God is the Creator and Lord of all things. Nothing exists outside of his interest or authority. Individuals who ignore his wisdom and guidance do so at great cost and great peril.

THE SOCIETY OF SCRIPTURE

For thinking Christians, then, the question is: What biblical insights can we gain about the nature of society? Well, it turns out that the Bible addresses this issue with a multitude of teachings, proverbs, parables, and laws relating to society (Mott, 1982). Indeed, Scripture itself was given in the context of a particular society and it constantly critiques and assumes aspects of its own context (Clark and Gaede, 1987). Unfortunately, we don't have the space to delve too deeply into this subject. We can, however, look specifically at the issue concerning the nature of society, which was raised in our discussion about sociology textbooks.

When we do that, a rather surprising thing happens; the Bible seems to present the same dichotomy found in the introductory text! Scripture clearly teaches that human beings need one another and that human relationships exist for our own good. One of the more amazing biblical statements comes after the creation of Adam. Prior to this point, as God has been creating the world, Genesis ends each day with the statement: "And God saw it was good." That is God's conclusion about the man he created as well. But then, in direct contrast to all this goodness, God says, "It is not good for the man to be alone" (Genesis 2:18 NIV). This doesn't mean that God goofed, of course. It means that God had yet to finish his work, that the creation of Eve was necessary to truly complete the human being. The crucial issue for our discussion is that the Creator himself declares that human isolation (loneliness) is not good and that human fellowship (togetherness) is good. In other words, God created us to be together. We need one another because we were created with such a need.

The rest of the Bible backs up this creational fact. Time and time again, God shows himself to be concerned about human relationships—their quality (Leviticus 19:18), durability (Ruth 1:16–17), and strength (Matthew 19:6). He implores husband and wife to be faithful to each other (Ephesians 5:21–33), children to honor their parents (Deuteronomy 5:16), kings to protect the weak and oppressed (Psalm 72:1–4), citizens to submit to the rule of legitimate authority (Romans 13:1–4), Christians to fellowship regularly with one another (Hebrews 10:24–25), neighbors to love one another (Matthew 19:19), wealthy to give to the poor (Deuteronomy 15:7–11), the strong to aid the weak (Luke 10:25–37), and on it goes. One simply cannot read Holy Scripture and conclude that God is unconcerned about social relationships. On the contrary, God is deeply aware of the relational need he put within the human heart, and He has given us laws and teachings to enable us to hold the fabric of society together.

But that is not all the Bible has to say about society. If we stopped our discussion here, we would have a very one-sided view of human relationships. For just as the Bible shows that relationships exist for our good, just as surely we discover that human relationships are highly problematic. It starts in the Garden when Adam blames Eve for his sinful behavior (Genesis 3:12). It continues when Cain, in a rage of anger and spite, kills Abel (Genesis 4:8). And from there things go downhill. Marriage relationships are perverted (Genesis 6:1–3), kings oppress the weak (Isaiah 1:23), the rich take advantage of the poor (Amos 4:1), and neighbor exploits neighbor (Genesis 19:4–9). Even God's most loyal servants pervert relationships through incest (Lot), murder (David), false pretense (Jacob), and denial (Peter). In short, relationships are not only a difficulty for some people, they are a horrendous problem for all people.

Now we need to stop at this point and ask, What's the problem here? How can relationships be absolutely good on the one hand, but so positively awful on the other? For the Christian, there is no great mystery here nor any need to beat around the bush. The problem, quite simply, is sin. That is why the problem begins in the Garden after the fall of Adam and Eve and expands geometrically from that point on. That, too, is why its influence is so pervasive, affecting even the relationships of those who seek to be God's faithful followers. Sin, as most of us have discovered, is no respecter of persons or societies.

Although the problem of sin is obvious, it is an easy one to ignore. The reasons are many, but it boils down to the fact that sin is most effective when its presence is unrecognized. When sin is exposed, its tactics must be defensive. When sin is thought to be inconsequential, however, it can mount a full-scale invasion, and no one will even notice or care. (Note the advice given to Wormwood in *Screwtape Letters* [Lewis, 1950].) That is extremely important to remember when we go back to the concept of society as it is found in the introductory sociology text. On the one hand, it helps explain why the problem of sin is unlikely to be part of the text's discussion of society. Following a naturalistic methodology (*see* Gaede, 1985), most social scientists believe sin is not a legitimate scientific subject—a belief that must inspire songs of jubilation in the nether world. On the other hand, it is precisely because the text is unable to acknowledge the problem of sin that it is caught in a quagmire with respect to the nature of society. Indeed, I would assert that most sociologists struggle with the contradictions in modern society because they are unwilling to confront its core problem.

SOCIETY WITHOUT SIN

Let's look at an example. Some sociologists assume that social relationships are essentially functional. What exactly that means is hotly debated, even among those who call themselves functionalists. But on the whole, a functional relationship is one that contributes positively to the growth and stability of society (Perdue, 1986:69–90). Once this assumption is made, however, the sociologist is in the predicament of explaining the existence of relationships that don't seem to promote a healthy society. Like the economic relationships that maintain poverty, for example. Or the sexual relationships that promote prostitution. How do poverty and prostitution square with a functional assumption about relationships?

To deal with this problem, two different types of explanations have been given. First, there are those who would argue that these relationships are indeed functional and that our moral blinders prevent us from seeing that fact (*see* Gans, 1972). Prostitution, for example, may be disgusting to us, but it also provides a sexual outlet for individuals who are unable to find satisfaction through conventional means. Moreover, prostitution is a major source of employment, an obvious need in every society. Poverty, too, can be seen as functional if one does not concentrate on the human misery that it entails. For one thing, poverty reminds us of the consequence of unemployment—thus motivating wage earners to be industrious workers. It also serves as a source of cheap labor for many undesirable jobs. Who would pick grapes if it weren't for the poor? In short, prostitution and poverty fill a need in society. Their existence testifies to their essentially functional character.

Thanks be to God, many sociologists remain unconvinced of the merits of this interpretation. Most sociologists, like most other people, cannot look into the eyes of the impoverished, or contemplate the future of the prostitute, and declare nonchalantly, "This is functional, or this is good." Thus, a large number of functionalists have sought to distance themselves from this interpretation by asking, "Functional for whom?" and by embracing the concept of "dysfunction" (Merton, 1968). Armed with these tools, they would suggest that though poverty may be functional for certain employers, it is not functional for the poor themselves. Moreover, they would assert that poverty is generally dysfunctional (read, "is not healthy") for society as a whole. In this way they admit to the existence of different perspectives on functionality as well as the presence of many social relationships that are not, on the whole, functional.

But if functionality is relative to the perceiver, and if many human relationships are not functional, in what sense is the original assumption—that human relationships are functional— helpful? Or even true? What one ends up with, I'm afraid, is an assumption so fraught with qualifications and countertendencies that it is not much of an explanation at all. Now, don't misunderstand me on this point. I certainly prefer the qualified functionalist's viewpoint to that of the consistent functionalist. Without doubt, it lines up more closely to my own view of human relationships. Nevertheless, a theory that says relationships are functional. . .maybe. . .sometimes . . .but not always is simply not a very robust theory. And it tends to lead us into a quagmire concerning the exact nature of society.

This view of society is not the only one in the sociology literature, of course. As I mentioned earlier, some sociologists see social relationships as essentially imprisoning or destructive (e.g., Habermas, 1975). I shall not take the time to explain such views. But it is important to note that those sociologists have the same problem as the ones who view relationships in a positive light. They must explain the existence of exceptions. Once again, they do that either by denying that there are benevolent relationships (it is only our "false consciousness" that makes us think they exist) or by arguing that they are not the most significant or salient relationships in our society. The first option enables them to put forward a consistent theory, but it also means they must impugn everyone else's intelligence or motives to make their case. It also seems patently wrong to me. The second option, while closer to the truth, assumes agreement on what is a "significant relationship." Not only is that unlikely, but it also puts us right back into the quagmire of saying that relationships are (this time) malevolent. . .maybe. . .sometimes. . .but not always.

SOCIETY WITHOUT BLINDERS

What all of this suggests is that by ignoring sin, the modern social scientist is not only ignoring a crucial element of society but also stripping sociology of an important explanatory tool. One cannot attain a full appreciation of human relationships without understanding that they are, at once, good gifts of God and the ever-present loci of sin. Thus, one ought not talk about human relationships as if they are wholly good or wholly bad—they are both. Nor would one suggest that relationships are either functional or dysfunctional—they are both. In short, from a Christian perspective, the effort to characterize human relationships as naturally benevolent or malevolent is a totally fruitless one. It will result neither in truth nor in good sociology.

The acknowledgment that sin is at the core of the problem does not suddenly make sociology easy, of course. Far from it. Sin is ingenious, and its ability to subvert human relationships is certainly equal to the Christian sociologist's ability to understand. When Christians say that "such and such social problem exists because of sin" and then stop speaking, they have demonstrated that they have a second-grade grasp of biblical truth but little else. Knowing the basis of a social problem is only the beginning of understanding—not the end. No Christian motivated by the love of Christ can stop there. For the sociologist, the primary benefit of taking sin into account is not for ease but for accuracy. If society is infected by sin, ignoring it will lead to quagmires and to a distorted picture of human relationships. First and foremost, then, it is for the sake of truth that the sociologist needs to take sin seriously.

That brings up another question: If the contemporary social scientist's analysis of society omits the effects of sin, does that mean that the insights are without merit or wisdom? No, it does not. I think some of the most perceptive analyses we have of human relationships come from the pens of modern sociologists. The problem with these analyses is not that they are wholly wrong, but that they are without wholeness. They are incomplete.

They show us, in great depth at times, how relationships can be oppressive or liberating, but they rarely note that they are both at the same time. More problematically, they have no basis upon which to explain such contradictions even when they are recognized, precisely because they appear to be contradictions rather than God's good creation groaning under the weight of sin.

However, such knowledge should be of great benefit to Christians. For one thing, it ought to prevent us from buying into some of the currently fashionable notions of society. I am forever amazed at how easy it is for Christians to accept simplistic descriptions of social relationships, especially those outside their immediate experience. For example, when Christians talk about family relations (of which they are quite aware), their insights are generally biblically informed. As a result, they understand the tug of war between good and evil that haunts family relationships, and they would never think of denying the presence of either sin or goodness in those relationships. But if you ask them about social relations in politics or economics, something entirely different takes place. Instead of assuming that same tug of war, they immediately discuss them in either-or, black-and-white terms.

Why is that? Well, a full answer is complicated, but a simple answer is that we have not allowed biblical wisdom to penetrate our notion of society. In the absence of such wisdom, we are inclined to adopt the views of those around us and, not incidentally, the views that are easiest for us to believe. Thus, the successful Christian in business is likely to view economic relationships in positive, functional terms, but the Christian social worker may tend to see these same relationships in quite negative terms. If you ask them why they have such views, they will tell you their views derive from their experiences—the person in business has seen the good while the social worker has witnessed the bad in economic relations.

Although there is some truth in these claims, it ought to be offset by two things. First, both will have been involved in economic relationships that do not support their one-sided interpretations of society. Second, even if their experiences in the economic realm have been skewed, their understanding should be balanced by a biblical perspective on human relationships. The fact that it is not suggests that their views of society are primarily informed neither by the Bible nor by their experiences, but by their self-interest. By seeing economic relations as either good or bad, they are promoting their own jobs. That is not only sad, it is tragic. But it is a preventable tragedy for those with a genuine thirst for a biblical understanding of society.

Finally, social perspective rooted firmly in Scripture ought to give us direction as we seek to faithfully confront the problems of our society. Two tendencies have marked the efforts of those who have attempted to deal with modern social problems: (1) a hopeless utopianism and (2) a utopian hopelessness. In the first, all things are possible for those willing to change the structure of society. In the second, nothing is possible before the advent of a new age. The first offers promises that cannot be kept; the second promises nothing but an escape by a god who seems forever in slumber. Both are wrong.

The fact that human relationships are good creations marred by sin ought to prevent us from being either overly optimistic or overly pessimistic about the possibility of social change. On the one hand, the presence of sin means that no matter what changes take place in the design of relationships, problems will persist. I do not believe that all social forms are of equal value; I prefer democracy over dictatorships, monogamy over polygamy, and so on. Nevertheless, democracy and monogamy are still highly problematic social forms because they remain tainted by sin. For me to assume, therefore, that a change from one to the other will bring about heaven on earth is completely contradicted by a biblical understanding of evil. It may improve life, but it will not end social problems. To believe otherwise is naive and dangerous.

On the other hand, those who deny the possibility of social improvement deny as well God's redemptive activity in the world. Sin, remember, is a usurper—it doesn't belong. And in God's own good time, it will be completely overcome. In the meantime, the strategic battle has already been fought and won. Jesus Christ has already gained the decisive victory over sin at the cross. Those of us who claim to be Christ-followers are on the winning side. Thus, we have no business acting like sore losers, waiting for some future escape from our perennial defeats. Rather, we are God's agents of change now, bringing the words and deeds of redemption to all people, in all kinds of social relationships. Sins can be forgiven. Broken relationships can be restored. And the love of Christ can bring real healing—not only to individual hearts but also to families, neighborhoods, economies, and any other social arrangements devised by the human imagination.

In the end, then, recognizing the influence of sin in society is not merely a matter of sociological accuracy. Nor is it simply a way of avoiding the pitfalls of much modern social theory. It is all of that, to be sure, but it is much, much more. In the final analysis, it is the realistic hope we have for a better society. For just as only the contrite heart can know redemption, so only the society that knows its own sin can be saved from it.

REFERENCES IN CHAPTER

Berger, Peter L. 1963. *Invitation to Sociology*. Garden City, N.J.: Double-day/Anchor Books.

Clark, Robert, and S. D. Gaede. 1987. "Knowing Together: Reflections on a Wholistic Sociology of Knowledge." In *The Reality of Christian Learning*, edited by Harold Heie and David L. Wolfe. Grand Rapids, Mich.: Eerdmans.

Durkheim, Emile. 1933. *The Division of Labor*. Translated by George Simpson. New York: Macmillan.

_____. 1951. *Suicide*. New York: Free Press.

Eitzen, D. Stanley. 1985. *In Order and Conflict*. 5th ed. Boston: Allyn & Bacon.

Gaede, S. D. 1985. *Where Gods May Dwell*. Grand Rapids, Mich.: Zondervan.

Gans, Herbert. 1972. "The Positive Functions of Poverty." *American Journal of Sociology* 78:275–89.

Guinness, Os. 1983. *The Gravedigger File*. Downers Grove, Ill.: Inter-Varsity.

Habermas, Juergen. 1975. *Legitimation Crisis*. Boston: Beacon Press.

Lenski, Gerhard, and Jean Lenski. 1987. *Human Societies*. 5th ed. New York: McGraw-Hill.

Lewis, C. S. 1950. *Screwtape Letters*. New York: Macmillan.

Liebow, Elliot. 1967. *Tally's Corner*. Boston: Little, Brown & Co.

Marx, Karl. 1967. *Capital: A Critique of Political Economy*. 3 vols. New York: International.

Merton, Robert K. 1968. *Social Theory and Social Structure*. New York: Free Press.

Mott, Stephen Charles. 1982. *Biblical Ethics and Social Change*. New York: Oxford University Press.

Nisbet, Robert, and Robert G. Perrin. 1977. *The Social Bond*. New York: Alfred A. Knopf.

Perdue, William D. 1986. *Sociological Theory*. Palo Alto: Mayfield.

Ryan, William. 1977. *Blaming the Victim*. Revised ed. New York: Random House, Vintage Books.

Sherman, Howard J., and James L. Wood. 1979. *Sociology*. New York: Harper & Row.

Storkey, Allan. 1979. *A Christian Social Perspective*. Leicester, England: Inter-Varsity Press.

Taylor, Maurice C., Laura H. Rhyne, Steven J. Rosenthal, and Korsi Dogbe. 1987. *Introduction to Sociology*. New York: Macmillan.

Walter, J. A. 1979. *Sacred Cows*. Grand Rapids, Mich.: Zondervan.

Wolterstorff, Nicholas. 1976. *Reason Within the Bounds of Religion*. Grand Rapids, Mich.: Eerdmans.

ARE GROUPS REAL?

Brendan F. J. Furnish

When my son was growing up, one of our neighbor's kids was his best friend. This boy was the son of a university psychologist, who always seemed overly concerned with his son's future. My boy was somewhat less than perfect, and according to my neighbor, his son was better behaved than mine. Regardless of their respective manners, both boys were (as individuals) fairly well-behaved. However, whenever these boys got together for even the shortest length of time, they would invariably get into some sort of mischief. Jointly, their creativity in concocting stressful situations for adults was just short of phenomenal.

As I think back about this, two alternatives come to mind that might explain this strange behavioral transformation. Was it possible that my neighbor and I jointly overestimated the goodness of our kids? Or was something else going on that meant that when the two boys formed a group together, their individual behaviors were significantly altered? Is behavior in a group different from what we would expect by knowing how the individuals in the group act independently?

To put this in a larger context, were the Germans in Nazi Germany cruel and inhumane as individuals or only when they were acting in their Nazi party group roles? How could officers in the Nazi death camps behave in an absolutely ruthless manner toward camp inmates but act with gentleness and compassion as husbands and fathers?

To put it succinctly, are groups real? Is there something about putting clusters of people together in long-lasting interactional situations that changes the nature of relating? Does a group of individuals constitute a reality that transcends its individual members? This has been an important issue within the field of sociology—one that differentiates a sociological perspective from a psychological orientation. This is also an important issue for the biblically minded Christian.

Because we live in a culture that strongly fosters a radical type of individualism, it is sometimes rather tricky to clearly understand the nature of this issue. The topic is important because it enables us to determine whether the individual or the group is the proper unit for sociological analysis. Moreover, it is important for biblical understanding, since by imposing the incorrect cultural interpretation on Scripture, we may grossly misunderstand the biblical message as it applies to our contemporary life.

In sociology, the issue of the individual versus the group has been termed the "unit of analysis debate" and centers on what sociologists consider the basic sociological unit—the group. Just what a group encompasses is the focus of this discussion. In sociology, the issue boils down to a couple of fairly straightforward positions.

Nominalism stresses the centrality of the individuals who make up the group. This position holds that groups per se are not "real" units, but are merely collections of individuals. Proponents of this position claim that if we view the group as containing anything other than an assembly of individuals, we are in danger of committing the fallacy of reification—that is, it is possible to turn an idea into a concrete entity, which it may not be. After all, how can we assume that the group can be explained in any other way than by looking at the behavior of individuals?

Because people who subscribe to the nominalist viewpoint tend to see the individual as the sole form of reality, they believe that in considering group actions, the only thing that can be explained is the collective behavior of the individuals who make up the group. That is, a group (or by extension, a society) can develop a sense of identity that is based strictly on the collective actions of the individuals who comprise the group. In this type of orientation, the focus is on the personalities of the people in the group and not on the group or the social system itself. The notion that the individual is the only sure form of existence has also been termed "ontological reality." This position has been favored by behaviorist psychologists such as B. F. Skinner and a great many past and present American sociologists.

Realism is an opposing view. It was originally posed by the French sociologist Emile Durkheim, who held that groups (and societies) are in fact more than the sum of interacting individuals. When you put people together in long-term, meaningful interaction (for example, a nuclear family), the behavior of the group is more than the sum of the actions of the individuals in the group. In other words, something rather mystical develops when people interact for long periods of time. Durkheim extended this idea to society and referred to it in almost metaphysical terms. Thus, he said that the "collective consciousness" is "a unity of consciousness of the society over and above that of the individuals comprised within it" (Bogardus, 1968:459). Societies (and groups) become involved in a type of synthesis that "surpasses the individual as the whole surpasses the part." In doing so, the group does not depend on the nature of the individual personality; rather, it becomes a new thing: *sui generis*—a unique class by itself (Simpson, 1965:17ff.). Durkheim would hold that "irrespective of the actors, society is."

There are a variety of middle-of-the-road positions between the poles of nominalism and realism. The most familiar and significant of these in sociology is *interactionism*. This approach attempts to bridge the gap between the nominalist and realist poles by stressing that, in fact, the two are inseparable. One of the major founders of the symbolic interactionist approach, Charles H. Cooley (1922:33), observed that

> A separate individual is an abstraction unknown to experience, and so likewise is society when regarded as something apart from individuals. The real thing is Human Life, which may be considered either in an individual aspect or in a social, that is to say a general aspect; but it is always, as a matter of fact, both individual and general. In other words, "society" and "individuals" do not denote separable phenomena but are simply collective and distributive aspects of the same thing.

That is, you cannot have individuals without the group and vice versa. Furthermore, understanding groups can come only by analyzing the complex patterns of interaction that take place in particular group situations (Warriner, 1956:549–550; and Smith, 1967).

The interactionist position does provide us with the opportunity to acknowledge the reality and importance of the group and to recognize that without interacting individuals there would be no groups. Furthermore, the interactionist position has provided sociology and social psychology with the best and most useful theoretical insights regarding the process of socialization. Indeed, through the process of interaction, children are changed from near animal, unsocialized creatures into functioning human beings. Regrettably, a fuller treatment of this position is outside the scope of this chapter.

Unfortunately, although the interactionist position holds much promise for mediating a position between the extremes of nominalism and realism, it fails to resolve the problem—not because of its orientation, but because most of its followers tend to favor the nominalist orientation. The major criticism of interactionism and other similar approaches—by those who favor a realist position—is that all the other orientations inevitably subject sociology to "reductionism." By this we mean that rather than focus our attention on the group and its relations to other groups and social structures, we reduce our inquiry to psychological investigations of the individual personalities of those who comprise the groups being studied.

The problem this poses for sociology is that it makes our discipline synonymous with psychology, and it may also prevent us from being able to explain the real reasons for many kinds of social phenomena. By way of illustration, consider the problem of suicide. For centuries most people believed suicide was a desperate act of people who were simply crazy. Many people still believe that all suicidal behavior is the consequence of mental illness. This individualistic, psychological explanation was challenged by Emile Durkheim, who discovered that societal forces accounted for much of the suicide that occurs (see Durkheim, 1951).

Durkheim initially set out to develop an explanation of social integration; he wanted to find out why societies and groups stayed together. As he pursued this investigation, he discovered that different factors affected the integration, or cohesion, of groups and societies. He began to realize that whenever factors of malintegration existed in particular segments of society, these portions of society would experience an increase in suicide directly proportional to the amount of malintegration.

Durkheim found three significant, general types of malintegration. The first type, *egoism*, was a condition that occurred whenever individualism became excessive in society or its groupings. When this condition developed, the individual attachment to community was weakened, and the individual no longer felt bonded to any societal grouping. This resulted in a feeling of detachment and led people to be more willing to kill themselves than they would have been if they had been more strongly related to others. For example, Durkheim found that single people would be much more prone to commit suicide than would married people with families.

On the other hand, Durkheim observed that one could become excessively attached to the community, to the point of willingly dying in order to attempt to save one's primary group or community. This is what motivated the Japanese Kamikaze pilots to intentionally crash their aircraft into Allied warships during World War II; their sacrifice was because of their overattachment to Japanese society. Most Americans feel that such behavior was bizarre, to say the least. Yet American soldiers who attempted to save the lives of their friends by throwing themselves on live hand grenades were lauded as unselfish heroes who gave their lives out of pure altruism. In both cases, the individuals involved were committing *altruistic* suicide because they had excessively high rates of group cohesion. In this regard, heroism or insanity is a matter of social definition; however, the causes of the suicidal acts are the same.

A final variety of societal malintegration proposed by Durkheim had to do with *anomie* (a concept to be discussed further in chapter 8). This has to do with the sudden breakdown of the usual rules and ways of conducting oneself. In this type of situation the ordinary ways of doing things no longer seem to work. The commonplace illustration of this concerns the wealthy man who loses all in a financial crash. However, in terms of self-destruction, a more dangerous situation is, in fact, the poor person who becomes suddenly wealthy and has no idea of what is expected of him by the new circumstances and groups of which he now finds himself a part. (Examples of this type of suicide would include such entertainers as Freddie Prinze and possibly John Belushi.) Likewise, the person who is suddenly divorced or whose spouse unexpectedly dies is in a situation where the former sets of group rules and expectations no longer seem relevant. Such a person is no longer integrated into a primary group and may be in jeopardy of self-destruction.

The point of this lengthy example concerning Durkheim's theory of suicide is to demonstrate that this unfortunate act may not be psychological at all. Rather, suicide occurs because of predictable social causes involving the individuals' integration into groups and society. Despite this rather elegant theory (which, incidentally, had strong empirical support), Durkheim's ideas about suicide and social integration were not initially well received in the United States, even among sociologists. In fact, to this day, group realism is not a popular position among American sociologists. To see why this is so, we need to look briefly at the issue of the individual versus the collectivity in American culture. As we do this, we will want to pay special attention to the role of the church regarding this issue, mainly because the Protestant church played a significant role in shaping these particular aspects of our culture.

One of the major characteristics of American culture is its strong and historic commitment to individualism. The Puritans of New England were committed to an ethic of self-sufficiency and brought a highly nominalistic Protestant faith to the New World. These two aspects of their lives had a profound influence on subsequent cultural developments in the United States (although it should be observed that the Puritans themselves could not be classified as believing in radical individualism—actually quite the opposite was true in their case).

After the Revolutionary War, the forces of "utilitarian" individualism became dominant. From the time of the post-Revolutionary period, it was a crucial cultural viewpoint that what was best for society was individual self-improvement. Because this orientation was congenial to a Protestant world view, it was widely accepted in America—despite the fact that it was not a particularly Christian teaching. As Max Weber pointed out in *The Protestant Ethic and the Spirit of Capitalism*, the theological underpinnings of the Protestant work ethic in the United States had begun to give way to a much more materialistic world view. This metamorphosis brought about an even greater emphasis on individualism, since it slowly but gradually removed the notion of Providence and tradition from human activity and substituted individual acquisition as the basis for our cultural value orientation. The process of secularization (i.e., eliminating both God and the supernatural realm from the ideas that explain and define reality) of both the work ethic and culture continued at an even more accelerated pace from this point. Likewise, our culture continued to choose individualism with the same velocity that it desired materialism and secularization. A more detailed discussion concerning the causes and consequences of these cultural shifts is beyond the scope of this chapter (if you are interested in pursuing the topic, see Bellah et al., 1985 or Lasch, 1978).

The theme of individualism as a societal problem has been prevalent in the sociological literature for many decades. Tocqueville, Marx, Durkheim, Weber, Simmel, and others have cautioned that increased individualization and materialism, combined with the proliferation of structures needed to control mass society, would lead to grave societal consequences—not the least of which would be the depersonalization of humanity. This phenomenon has now been epitomized in contemporary American culture. Durkheim saw a paradox in all this, since the culture that allowed the phenomenon of hyper-individualism to develop would in time be destroyed by the radical individuals it created, because they were no longer interested in the collective maintenance of the culture.

Although the spiritual residuals of both the Protestant work ethic and Protestantism in general still haunt our cultural ethos, most Americans have no real understanding of how or why these cultural orientations came about. Thus, we feel guilty about "wasting" time or money, but do not usually attach this to the formerly widely held belief that time and money were gifts from God—to be cherished and used with care. Likewise, we fail to see how the Protestant emphasis on the individual in general, and the individual's salvation in particular (while scripturally correct in many ways), has also introduced some significant distortions to both modern culture and our understanding of what God is calling us to.

Clearly, Protestantism was one of the major forces that led to our present widespread desire for individualism and self-sufficiency; it also provided fertile ground for the strong aspirations for self-improvement. Naturally, many of these elements were good in themselves; however, without Christian underpinnings, they had the potential to become sources for idolatry, which is often the case in our contemporary culture (*see* Walter, 1979).

The Evangelical wing of Christianity generally adapted and accepted this cultural package and enthusiastically joined the movement toward individualism, secularism, and generalized "modernity" with about the same rate of velocity as the rest of society. Perhaps it might be useful to look at some specific factors of Protestant nominalism manifest in the contemporary Evangelical church.

First, nominalism in general is not a biblical teaching. This is true from the very early parts of the Bible where we find God calling out a *people* to himself. This teaching extends into the New Testament where again we hear God calling out a people for his name's sake (1 Peter 2:9–10). To be sure, there may be a spokesman for the people, but the spokesman can be understood only as a part of the special body of God's people. If we examine the Scripture carefully in this regard, we will see that there is no substantive disjunction in the biblical view of humanity between the "I" and the "We." Likewise, in the Old Testament, there is no distinction made between the self and the nation of Israel. Many other Scriptures point to the importance of the corporate in both Old and New Testaments.

Evangelicals have neglected the sense of biblical community and corporate realism that is so evident in the Bible. In fact, there is a tendency to reject communal forms of any kind since they have "Socialist" implications. In doing so, we slight the implications of the radical identification that Christ makes between himself and the church. We also ignore, at great cost, the strong interdependencies that the mystical corporate church must foster with and for individual Christians.

Second, instead of emphasizing the corporate realism of the faith in all its varied elements, the contemporary Evangelical church seems to emphasize and promote "self-improvement" psychology, as any quick inspection of most "Christian" bookstores will reveal. Psychology as a discipline is individualistic by nature and tends to stress nominalism. Furthermore, our need for "pop" psychology is harmful to us, since most of our problems come from lack of belonging to a meaningful community within the church and not because of some sort of psychological maladjustment. This infatuation with psychology is also harmful to the church's mission to the larger society since the psychological approach urges us to adjust to the culture. In doing so, it tends to stifle the prophetic voice of the church, which, rather than adjusting, should be crying out against injustice and ungodliness created by a culture that is separated from and at enmity with God.

Third, with its emphasis on the sermon, Protestant worship usually discourages the spirit of community and encourages radical individualism. The worship format used in most Evangelical churches is indicative of this. On Sunday morning we invariably discover a nonparticipatory audience watching a performance orchestrated by a strong, authoritarian leader. Little wonder why so many people who have bought into a secular cultural ethos opt out of the local churches and now sit in their homes and watch the electronic church! After all, if the corporate is not stressed as necessary, why not watch a far more professional production on television?

Additionally, we cannot help wondering if some of the excesses of the contemporary charismatic/pentecostal movement are not merely further manifestations of radical individualism among Christians. In many of the circles where such teaching occurs, the emphasis is on "spiritual gifts" for the *individual* believer and not for the corporate body. It is important to recall that the charismatic gifts of the New Testament initially fell on a group of 120 believers who were in joint prayer in the Upper Room (Acts 2). Likewise, this same nominalistic tendency can be seen in the teachings of the so-called health-and-wealth movement. Here the emphasis is invariably on material gifts to the individual and not to the corporate body of Christ.

Fourth, professionalism—which is a logical product of modern culture—has co-opted the church in the same way it has had an impact on rest of modern culture. Pastoral duties have shifted from reliance on qualified lay church officers and leaders to "professional" staffs who are certified to do psychological counseling and who may have specialty skills in such areas as fund raising and "church growth." Within this environment, the biblical gifts and offices (formerly distributed by the Holy Spirit) are now superseded by professionally trained experts. Here, Martin Luther's teaching about the priesthood of all believers becomes a ghostly relic of an antique time.

Finally, and most importantly, because of its heavily nominalistic outlook, the Evangelical church has failed to act as a crucial primary group. It is obvious, as one reads the New Testament, that the early church had many more functions than to meet for an hour in formal worship. The early church frequently met around meals, provided welfare for needy members, and gave emotional support and friendship to all members of the body. In general, it fostered a sense of community and acted as a primary group. Very few contemporary Evangelical churches develop primary group functions. As a consequence, the socio-emotional function of the church has been passed on to the only other major primary group remaining in our society—the nuclear family. Small wonder that the family becomes emotionally overloaded and often cannot supply the emotional support its members need in this complex, individualized, and alienated culture. The result has been an increasing deterioration of the family unit—a deterioration that continues in spite of professional courses in "parenting" and psychological counseling by church staffs.

From all this, I suggest that Protestantism had much to do with the development of nominalism in contemporary culture. Furthermore, I also imply that instead of recognizing this as a problem, the contemporary Evangelical church assists the larger culture on the path of nominalism—a path that may well lead to the ultimate destruction of American culture as we know it.

Having said all of this, perhaps we should conclude by returning to the unit of analysis debate. Which position is the most correct interpretation of reality: nominalism, realism, or interactionism? I suppose that for the purposes of sociological research, all three perspectives are useful in explaining social behavior under various conditions and circumstances. This, however, is obviously not a very courageous answer—nor is it very satisfying relative to our faith concerns. Therefore, allow me to venture out on somewhat more speculative ground concerning the issue of group realism.

If we examine the New Testament church, it is obvious that something superorganic makes the whole (the church) more than the sum of the parts (see 1 Corinthians 12). However, we should note that not only does the Holy Spirit empower the church, but the Spirit's agents are people. The church can function as a collectivity (in the realist sense) only when the members are willing to serve the Lord *and* one another in a consistent and dedicated way. This realism can also extend to other primary groups, but only to the extent that it is allowed by the group's participants. Therefore, the issue of group realism is existential and volitional—groups can be real if the group members *will* them to be so. In other words, to the degree that we willingly commit ourselves to our primary groups, these groups do take on a reality that exceeds the inputs of the individual actors.

By way of illustration, let us consider the marriage relationship. The dyad consists of two individuals and is the simplest of all social groups. As a result of the process of physically and spiritually uniting and cleaving to each other, the Bible says that the two shall become one (see Genesis 2:24; Mark 10:6–9, and Ephesians 5:31). This same metaphor is used to describe our relationship with Jesus Christ (2 Corinthians 11:2). So in the biblical sense, true group realism can be experienced in marriage. But both partners can exercise their will and can, at least to some extent, choose the degree of realism to be manifested in their marital group. Both can become intensely involved in each other's lives, or they can become what Marriage Encounter participants call "married singles"—sharing their lives in only the most tangential ways. They can will to deeply love each other, or they can will to break their vows and commitment and destroy the group.

Thus to a large extent, group realism may be built on a paradox. Group reality is a product of the willingness of the individual members to be committed and dedicated to the group. This principle applies to entire societies as well as to dyadic relationships. In this regard, we might say that God is giving us a glance of his kingdom by allowing us to become co-creators of group reality. One can hope that we may learn to apply this creative power in our own lives, before our groups and society fall into the anarchy that will come from the further evolution of a hypernominalistic orientation.

It is my hope that the reader will not dismiss this chapter lightly, but will realize that with the understanding gained from this and other chapters of this book comes responsibility to use sociological insights for the kingdom of God. The biblical mandate is to live one's faith, to be involved in "praxis"—as Rich Perkins points out in the last chapter of this book. To be an acting (as well as believing) Christian surely implies opposing much of the culture of which we are a part. In this case, it means becoming aware of what biblical group realism is all about and then creating groups and communities to live out this reality (as Perkins has done). It must be emphasized that simply opposing cultural individualism—or any other cultural manifestation—is not sufficient. God is calling us to demonstrate, in tangible ways, what his kingdom is all about. The signs of cultural disaster increasingly abound among us—the effects of radical individualism are simply manifestations of a pending calamity. Surely the Lord will call us to account if we continue to remain comfortable with the existing state of affairs.

REFERENCES IN CHAPTER

Bellah, Robert, Richard Madsen, William Sullivan, Ann Swidler, and Steven Tipton. 1985. *Habits of the Heart*. Berkeley and Los Angeles, Calif.: University of California Press.

Bogardus, Emory S. 1968. *The Development of Social Thought*. New York: David McKay.

Cooley, Charles H. 1922. *Human Nature and the Social Order*. New York: Charles Scribner's Sons.

Durkheim, Emile. 1951. *Suicide*. New York: Free Press.

Lasch, Christopher. 1978. *The Culture of Narcissism*. New York: W. W. Norton.

Simpson, George. 1965. *Emile Durkheim*. New York: Thomas Y. Crowell & Co.

Smith, David Horton. 1967. "A Parsimonious Definition of a Group: Toward Conceptual Clarity and Scientific Utility." *Sociological Inquiry* (Spring): 141–167.

Walter, J. A. 1979. *Sacred Cows*. Grand Rapids, Mich.: Zondervan.

Warriner, Charles K. 1956. "Groups Are Real: A Reaffirmation." *American Sociological Review* (October): 549–54.

SYSTEMS OF INEQUALITY

Zondra G. Lindblade

Social stratification: the systematic, unequal distribution in society of valued objects, opportunities, and life chances. This system is like a layer cake—the top layer gets the frosting, and the bottom layer bears the weight. For many, the "American Dream" means getting a greater individual share of the frosting. Personal "success" is defined by achieving higher position and symbolized by material goods and elite services—cars, fine houses, cruises to the Bahamas, and season tickets to the symphony. Social esteem is also associated with success. Admired persons (we know they are admired because these are the ones we select to be the elders in our churches, the presidents of community organizations, and the chapel speakers in our colleges) are those who have fulfilled the obligation of striving for high status and who have won over the competition. Upward social mobility is seen as a goal of a college education—the satisfaction of parents' hopes and a sign of God's blessing.

But the "Dream" is a zero-sum game—only a few win the frosting, many bear the weight, and some scramble for the leftover crumbs. Whether we are looking at experiences of the elderly, women, the poor, and/or ethnic minorities, we find the situation of the bottom layers repeated—demeaning environments, often inhuman and unloving treatment from the "frosting" group, and subtle injury to human dignity and self-respect. *Do we care as long as we are moving toward the frosting?*

But it is also possible that the winners are really losers. The ones who get the frosting come to think of themselves more highly than they ought to think. Their activity often is focused on the symbols of accomplishment—prestige, recognition, money—rather than the substance of achievement itself (Abrahamson et al., 1976). As Christians run toward the frosting, our momentary rejection of servanthood and even integrity may become permanent. The culture has "squeezed us into its mold," and we center most of our activities on protecting favored positions in society or on getting closer to the frosting.

Most sociologists refer to this system of frosting, cake, crumbs, and resulting alienation by using technical-sounding phrases such as "social class system," "system of inequality," or "stratification system." These conceptualizations hide the stark, ugly realities of injustice that are generic to any kind of status hierarchy. Christians, along with others, use complex rationalizations to support social inequality. "Blaming the victim" is a favorite—unequal treatment is deserved because the group has gotten old, has an unacceptable skin color, is defined as lazy, and/or was created to be helper, not leader. Or we dislike the inequality, but shrug and recognize that "this is a sinful world" and will remain so until Christ returns. Eschatology helps to take care of any momentary sense of responsibility for the losers. Some of us even rationalize that injustice can be used by God to bring the group to faith in him, that social position will change when the group is reconciled to God, or that God will help persons adjust to their degrading social positions.

We need to examine the sociological descriptions of systematic inequality and its destructive effects. We also need to expose our carefully packaged rationalizations and see them for what they are. They are not truth; they are lies.

THE QUESTIONS

Is stratification a "law" of human behavior? We do find inequality in every society and during every era of history. Is the unequal distribution of valued things an inevitable result of individual differences? We know persons have varied abilities, but must the differences be ranked with some judged worthy and others ignoble? Are systems of inequality necessary to attract qualified persons for difficult tasks in society?

These questions are not new. Throughout human history, poets, writers, philosophers, and social leaders have pondered the persistence and purpose of social stratification. These questions are important because God challenges us to have mercy and do justice (Micah 6:8), and to be the salt of the earth (Matthew 5:13) and the light of the world (Matthew 5:14). Where and how do we begin to understand what "justice" involves, and where do we start trying to be "salt" and "light"?

Perhaps a chapter on stratification in a sociology text begins the process; but many have read these chapters in the past, and others will do so in the future. The continual and growing presence of systematic inequality suggests that studying *about* inequality has not done the job; we do not yet understand the injustice, nor do we act. Looking at three contemporary examples of social inequality may deepen our understanding and move us to action.

Example #1: Poverty—"Loose Morality"

Recent media attention has focused on the "underclass" in the United States. This group is made up of those living in poverty from one generation to the next. They are quasipermanent recipients of social welfare who live out the attitudes of the "culture of poverty"—lack of goal striving, apathy, hopelessness, and perception of external barriers to getting ahead (Lewis, 1966). Sometimes a loose sexual morality is associated with the welfare dependence of this group. Let's examine the evidence related to loose morality and investigate how the social inequities of American society may contribute to the situation.

It is true that pregnancies among unmarried teenagers have increased to epidemic proportions in the underclass (NCHS, 1984). Health care indicators show a cycle of related physical miseries—malnourished teen-age mothers producing low birth-weight and/or physically handicapped infants who have diminished life chances, diets with insufficient protein for the child's healthy brain development, deprivation in parenting skills, and lack of positive coping mechanisms for mothers raising children alone. These miseries seem to be the result of individual and immoral choices. However, in what ways could the inequities of the system shape these choices?

As we look more closely, we find young women with little education, no opportunities, and few career goals trying to gain self-esteem and identity by bearing children. Traditionally, women have found this role to be one of deep meaning; even as a choice of last resort, being a mother is being someone. Children also provide hope for the future. Read what one welfare mother says about the meaning of children in her life:

> To me, having a baby inside me is the only time I'm really alive. I know I can make something, do something, no matter what color my skin is, and what names people call me. When the baby gets born I see him, and he's full of life, or she is, and I think to myself that it doesn't make any difference what happens later, at least now we've got a chance, or the baby does. You can see the little one grow and get larger and start doing things, and you feel there must be some hope, some chance that things will get better; because there it is, right before you, a real, live, growing baby. . .at least he's *some* sign.

If we didn't have that, what would be the difference from death? (Coles, 1964)

But why no marriage? One of the effects of social inequality is to diminish the number of underclass males who fit the "suitable mate" pattern—most are unemployable with little hope of access to formal education. Since a postindustrial society uses education as an avenue by which jobs are filled, schooling could provide a way out of the underclass. But if men and women are functionally illiterate (cannot read or write at a fourth grade level), little possibility exists for anything other than repeating the generational cycle of welfare.

Why hasn't public education taught the necessary skills to members of the underclass? Housing patterns provide one answer; schools are supported by property taxes, and the underclass is concentrated in low-income areas. Neither the local government nor the state has incentives to upgrade the quality of education for those who can least afford it, and who are not likely to become politically influential. Neither has the middle class (not even those who are religiously motivated) generally been willing to sacrifice time, money, or effort to address the difficult task of education for the poor. After all, we might have to live in their communities in order to teach effectively. We might have to sacrifice expenditures for our children in order to pay for upgrading education in the slums. We might slow down our social mobility if we try to increase theirs.

In the underclass, then, lack of functional literacy is a characteristic of potential marriage partners; such men are not very good risks as husbands, fathers, and providers. The actual supply of "good" marriage partners is also limited. Some underclass males are already in prison, some are drug or alcohol addicts, some have committed suicide, and some are dead as a result of street violence.

Perhaps sexual immorality explains less about teen-age unmarried pregnancies in the underclass than does the social stratification system and its many inequities.

Example #2: World Systems—Dependency/War

We live in a shrinking world. Geographically distant events affect the United States and our personal hopes and dreams. Americans and others are taken hostage in Lebanon, and we consider creating detention centers for Lebanese nationals (who might be terrorists) working or attending school in America. Japan increases/decreases the number of automobile imports coming into this country, and we wonder what will happen in Detroit. Isolation is no longer a viable choice. Even those nations that have attempted closed borders—the Soviet Union, China, Nepal—discover their survival requires economic, political, and social interaction with other countries. Unfortunately, that interaction is structured by a global stratification system. Wallerstein (1979), Chirot (1986), and others have written extensively about a three-tiered world system. The "core" societies have industrialized, with resulting economic and political advantage. The USSR, Japan, West Germany, and the United States would be examples of this powerful group, sometimes referred to as "MDC" (more developed countries). The "peripheral" or Third World societies are the underdeveloped nations or ones with few natural resources. Mexico, El Salvador, Afghanistan, and the Philippines are some examples. These are labeled "LDC" (less developed countries). Between these two are the "semi-peripheral" countries with developing industry, but still dependent for their economic health on the activities of the core nations. Italy, Spain, and Austria are examples.

Tension and conflict are characteristic of this global stratification system. Both world wars and the continuing military-guerrilla outbreaks represent extreme measures that the core, peripheral, and semiperipheral nations take to protect and/or better their economic and political positions. Twentieth-century nations do not seem to recognize that characteristics of national moral fortitude, generosity, concern about global human rights, and a high quality of social and spiritual life also could bring respect, power, and authority. Mahatma Gandhi suggested these were the qualities India needed for achieving independence from England and for developing into a strong, influential nation (*see* Erikson, 1969). Perhaps the nations believe moral values will be automatically nourished when economic and political positions are strong.

In trying to explain global inequality, some would again "blame the victim." A nation is backward and traditional—still kinship-based with little interest in high-level technology or efficient organizational structures. The people are lazy, event-oriented, nonambitious, or illiterate. If only the LDCs would become more like the developed world, the global inequities would diminish. But the core nations are so far ahead in their control of the world market and in applications of sophisticated technology, that it seems unrealistic to hope the Third World will ever taste the frosting.

Exploitation may be one reason for the core nations being far ahead of the others. Many of today's less developed countries were colonies of Europe (and especially of England) in the last century. The colony provided raw materials for the successful industrializing of Europe, but little capital was returned for the colony's own development. Although some historians suggest there were benefits for the colony in this arrangement, it seems clear that the system exaggerated the gap between the rich and the poor by rewarding the land-owning elite at the expense of the general population and the economic development of the colony.

Today many of these countries, now independent, are experiencing "neocolonialism"—the domination of their economies by multinational corporations and outside investors. Multinationals often discourage indigenous manufacturing, choosing instead to sell to the LDC the manufactured products of the core (Barnet and Muller, 1977). The LDC attempts to export crops such as coffee, sugar, and tea, hoping that these will bring in capital to fund industrialization. Instead, the small group of land-owning elite again benefit, and all others remain poor. At the same time, communication networks beam by satellite the TV panoramas of "Dallas," "Dynasty," and other extravagances of the core. The Third World desire for material goods adds to the internal restlessness and destabilizes those countries barely surviving on the crumbs.

What does it mean for Christians from the United States to recognize the stratification system of the world's winners and losers? We shrink from the enormity of the problem, especially when we understand its self-perpetuating nature. We remind ourselves that we really cannot do much. We forget that God is more powerful than the global system and that he is the one calling us to do justice.

Example #3: Gender—Biology/Creation Order

Societies differ in the type and amount of social inequality that exists. The simplest and most common systems are based on age and sex. All human societies—present and past—are stratified on at least these two characteristics. Let's examine some of the inequalities based on the sex of the person.

Although some would suggest that women in prehistory were the dominant leaders (E. Davis, 1972; Stone, 1978), most evidence indicates that patriarchies have been the cultural norm (Rosaldo and Lamphere, 1974). Patriarchy is a system in which males have the primary decision-making power. Control over other members and over dispersal of valued objects in the society belongs to the males. Opportunities for valued life chances come first to them.

Anthropological explanations for patriarchy focus on biology and environment (Harris, 1977; Chodorow, 1978). Female reproductive cycles of menstruation, pregnancy, childbearing, and the nursing of infants require a "close to home" lifestyle for women. Because of the emotional and physical bonding of the mother and infant, women are "instinctive" mothers. Males, however, are not "natural" fathers. Society must carefully teach, reinforce, and reward fathering behaviors (Mead, 1975). Part of the male reward is higher status, power, and more frosting. Male duties include protection, providing for the family, and controlling whatever surplus he has gathered. The surplus is an important feature of one analysis of gender inequality, since it encouraged individual ownership of property (Engels, 1942). If the property can be increased and protected it can be used for barter and for power to control others. Females usually do not control the property or have access to the power it creates. High status and dominance, therefore, belong to males.

This explanation is not adequate. Why would private property become the source of higher status? Since both property *and* children are vital to the survival of any group, why would both not be equally valued and equally rewarded? Similar questions are asked today: Why are the "masculine" characteristics of logic, assertiveness, and dominance valued and rewarded while the "feminine" qualities of intuition, long-suffering, and submission are not praised but taken for granted? Why is the male point of view regarded as the human point of view (Gilligan, 1982)?

Some writers use the biblical record to explain male dominance (Elliot, 1976; Clark, 1980; Bloesch, 1982). They suggest that God assigned both function and position for women and men. He planned gender roles to be complementary and hierarchic. Males are strong, decisive, dominant, and external in their activities because God made them that way. Females are a weaker creation: nurturant, subordinate, and meant to function inside the home.

However, viewing gender as complementary is not a distinctive drawn from the biblical record. Dualism has been prominent in human philosophy. For example, an all-encompassing dualistic world view expressed as "yin" and "yang" structured activities and human relationships in traditional China.

When the "creation order" is used to validate male dominance—Adam was formed first, and then woman—the chronology described in Genesis 2 presents difficulties. What do we do with the animals when we accept patriarchy based on this order of creation? Most of us do not think that males get the top frosting, animals the frosting in the middle, and women bear the weight. The chronological perspective also suggests that Adam bears God's image and the woman bears Adam's image. She would be subordinate to the man, who is subordinate to God. First Corinthians (11:3, 8–9) often is used to support this idea: "But I want you to understand that Christ is the head of every man, and the man is the head of a woman, and God is the head of Christ. . . .For man does not originate from woman, but woman from man; for indeed man was not created for the woman's sake, but woman for the man's sake" (NASB). Reading on in the passage, however, we find the Bible careful to complete the picture of who comes from whom, and "all things originate from God" (1 Corinthians 11:11–12). God has made the "hierarchy" into a circle.

The creation account in Genesis 1 raises different questions. The order here is one of ascending complexity and achievement. If chronology is a necessary and sufficient explanation, then woman is the crowning achievement and should be given the highest status (Bilezikian, 1985). Using the creation order as a basis for gender inequality raises more questions than it answers.

THE QUESTIONS REVISITED

Poverty, global stratification, and gender hierarchy exist everywhere and are stubborn in their persistence—advantageous for some and devastating for others. Why do these systems of inequality exist? And what might be appropriate Christian responses to the answers given to that question?

Answer #1: Individual Differences

Stratification persists because it is a result of basic individual differences. Achievement is determined by genetic abilities (Wilson, 1978). Every person has a natural difference in talent that no amount of social manipulation can change. Rewards for these differing abilities gradually develop lopsided social systems of inequality. Aristotle says: " It is thus clear that there are by nature free men and slaves, and that servitude is agreeable and just for the latter. . . .Equally, the relation of the male to the female is by nature such that one is superior and the other is dominated." (in Kerbo, 1983).

Because he is the creator, giver of individual abilities, and ruler over all things, God ordains some to have the frosting and others to bear the weight or get the crumbs. This argument indicates that the appropriate response to structured inequality is acceptance.

A Christian Response

Who can argue against the reality of individual differences? And who would dispute the need to divide up jobs to be done, matching ability to job? A Christian response accepts both of these to be real, but sees the ranking of them in any kind of hierarchy to be a social construction. Arbitrary measures of worth are assigned, usually by those in power and along lines of their own self-interest. The ranking of human abilities suggests that God created some characteristics noble and others disreputable. Scripture warns about such thinking: "The eye cannot say to the hand, 'I have no need of you'; or again the head to the feet, 'I have no need of you.' On the contrary, it is much truer that the members of the body which seem to be weaker are necessary. . .on these we bestow more abundant honor." (1 Corinthians 12:21–23 NASB).

Individual differences do not presume or require ranking. Accepting stratification because it reflects individual differences is rejected.

Answer #2: The Requirements of Social Order

Systems of inequality are necessary for the smooth, efficient functioning of society. Many jobs in society are not pleasant, and some require rigorous and long preparation. Qualified persons are difficult to find. The stratification system offers the incentives of prestige, power, and money to attract competent persons and leaders (Davis and Moore, 1945).

This perspective also recognizes that people at the top may exploit their positions, further exaggerating the inequalities that natural talent conceived. Exploitation is unfortunate, but does not disprove the fact that a stratification system remains the most efficient way to attract and reward gifted persons for taking on the priority tasks of the group. It is built on our understanding of human nature, varied abilities, and factors of motivation.

This second perspective suggests that the appropriate response to social stratification is appreciative acceptance, with restraint put on excessive exploitation.

A Christian Response

The necessity argument is based on society's growing demand for leadership and the assumption of a dwindling supply. Perhaps much more is occurring. First, an "efficient" society is seen here as an end—a value in itself—rather than as a means toward human goals. Second, it is not clear that the importance level of a task is intrinsic to its ranking. Some people have unpleasant, dirty but important jobs and do not receive high status. Garbage collectors are one example. Also, some tasks require extensive training, but receive only moderate prestige and money. Pharmacy might be an example. Third, if the importance of the task is not intrinsic, then who decides which jobs are essential? Fourth, the supply has not dwindled; rather, qualified persons are denied leadership opportunities because of race, sex, or religion.

The stratification system also tends to crystallize the top roles and then draw only from this pool. Consider the medical doctor. This person may be selected for a church leadership position because "physician" is a prestigious and highly regarded profession rather than because the person is wholeheartedly following God and willing to be his servant. Others in the church who are not doctors or lawyers or successful business persons may possess valuable and needed spiritual gifts but are not chosen.

For the Christian, leadership is servanthood. Jesus put it this way: "Whoever wishes to be great among you shall be your servant" (Matthew 20:26 NASB). Servanthood fits best in a system where leadership is flexible rather than hierarchic. The "needs" of the social order cannot be used to justify stratification.

Answer #3: Power and Domination

Stratification is a result of power and the domination of the many by the few. Such a system does not reflect individual differences, nor is it necessary for society to function. In fact, stratification limits the discovery and use of human abilities present in a group. Many never have opportunity to contribute, even though they may have great gifts. Qualified persons are scarce, not because no one wants the job, but because those in power keep others out. Favored positions are protected by restricting recruitment, training, and access to opportunity. This represents the exercise of power, not nature or necessity (Dahrendorf, 1968).

A rationale supporting social inequality as natural, morally right, and good for all is created and communicated by those at the top. These persons also control the institutions of the social system—education, politics, economics, the law, and family life. Since both the rationale and the system are embedded in each person's world view, any challenge must be directed first against the deceptive rationale and then against the system itself. Because the powerful will not easily give up their advantages, the appropriate response to stratification is revolution.

A Christian Response

Both Old and New Testaments warn us about the deceptions of powerful people and express God's special care for the oppressed. We recognize that power can corrupt. Marx suggests revolution as the appropriate response—smash the offending systems and something beautiful will grow out of the ashes. But revolution doesn't work that way; it merely recycles the oppressed and the oppressor. The oppressed-turned-ruler will "lord it over" others when the opportunity comes. The Christian should reject revolution as an appropriate response to structured inequality.

Answer #4: Rebellion/Sin

Structured inequality is present everywhere and persistent not because it is built on individual differences created by God, nor because it is functional and necessary for social order, nor merely because some are powerful and exploit others. Hierarchy exists because the woman and Adam rebelled against God. Stratification was not part of his original plan. The mandate containing instructions to "be fruitful and multiply," to "fill the earth and subdue it," to "have dominion. . .over every living thing" was given by God equally to both created persons (Genesis 1:28).

But the woman and the man disobeyed God. The first and most destructive effect of their sin was separation from him, and then from each other. What happened next is instructive for our discussion of hierarchy and injustice. The sweeping mandate given to the woman and Adam changed; their roles radically diminished in scope and function. The woman's activities now focus on *childbearing*. She receives the "be fruitful and multiply" aspect of God's original commandment. Adam names the woman "Eve" because she is the mother of all the living (Genesis 3:20). Adam's activities diminish to those of worker. He receives the "subdue the earth" part of the mandate. Thorns and thistles plague him; sweat and toil are his constant companions. Not only have their activities narrowed, but their relationship with each other now is asymmetrical. Adam will "lord it over" Eve— dominance and hierarchy are now part of their experience, as they are of ours today.

Since Adam and Eve, every one of us has sinned and is separated from God and from one another. Why, then, should we be surprised to discover hierarchy and dichotomized roles present everywhere and persistent? But they are not natural; they are not necessary. They are the results of evil. And they are so culturally familiar that we must be reminded that they are sin.

The appropriate response to social stratification is not acceptance or control or revolution, but repentance and reconciliation.

OUR RESPONSE

Let's assume this fourth answer is correct. Stratification is not a "law" of human behavior; it is the result of evil. Can it be changed on earth? Many groups—the Marxists, Jim Jones's group, the Oneida Community—have tried to abolish stratification. None succeeded. Oppression was recycled, or leaders turned tyrants, or ends were used to justify immoral means.

Erich Fromm (in Kerbo, 1983) and others have noted that social change cannot occur unless people have undergone *moral change*. Christians know that believing in Jesus Christ begins such moral change. We start to see ourselves and others with new eyes. But the moral change isn't automatic or instantaneous. We can choose to open our eyes wide or to stay blind, to work for the kingdom or to be squeezed into the culture's mold.

Suppose Christians caught a glimpse of human partnership as it was before sin. Suppose Christ's work on the Cross was understood to reconcile the twisted horizontal relationship among humans as well as the broken vertical relationship between us and God? Suppose working for the kingdom of God meant social action against all expressions of hierarchy in the human group? Where would you begin?

Start where the problem first began. Restore mutuality between the woman and the man. Allow the reconciling love of God to make a difference. Judge the hierarchy for what it is; refuse to make it sacred or absolute. No contemporary issue is more volatile than gender inequality. Maybe there is good reason. The serpent wants us to continue to "enjoy" the fruits of rebellion, and will work hard to frustrate any attempts at reconciliation. As we read the human story in Genesis, we find the "lording it over" activities begin with the male and female, quickly are adopted by Cain, and then generalized to nations. Israel eventually fell to the lowest level of global stratification, becoming a slave nation. The fundamental gender hierarchy provided the model for other patterns of domination.

But do redemption and reconciliation in Christ really speak to these issues? Does God intend male dominance to diminish as a result of belief in Christ? If he does, the New Testament should indicate changes in the relative position and activities of women and men. Five pieces of evidence from the New Testament may whet your appetite for further biblical study.

1. *Education for women.* Contrary to the expectations and in spite of the disapproval of his disciples, Jesus taught women in ways that violated cultural norms. He assumed intelligence, ability to understand spiritual truth, and wanted them to have personal experience with the Son of God (John 4). In the disagreement between Mary and Martha, Jesus took Mary's side. The culture did not encourage education for women; Jesus affirmed that spiritual study was for both women and men (Luke 10:38–42).

2. *Baptism.* The Old Testament sign of Israel's covenant relationship with Jehovah was male circumcision. In the New Testament, the sign of belief is baptism. Wonderfully, the Acts 8:12 account of baptism specifically mentions that women joined men in publicly proclaiming their relationship with God.

3. *Priesthood of all believers.* In the Old Testament, priests who handled the sacred things and mediated between the people and God had to be males from the tribe of Levi. The change in the New Testament is startling. Old Testament rituals required to approach God are no longer necessary; immediate access into his presence is possible for every believer. No longer are women required to go through a male to approach God or to know his will for their lives. The Book of Hebrews describes the new priesthood of all

believers. Men and women are priests—both can intercede for others, both can know his will directly, and both are called to be his ministers.

4. *Spiritual gifts.* Now the work of God is to be carried out by those assigned spiritual gifts rather than those with religious roles assigned by birth and sex. The Bible does not divide the gifts by sex—with men being given those of administration, preaching, and teaching and women given hospitality and helps. Rather, the Holy Spirit gives the gifts to whomever he wills (Romans 12; 1 Corinthians 12), and each of us is responsible to nurture and use our gift as loving service for him.

5. *In Christ, no hierarchy.* Galatians 3:23–28 focuses on three hierarchic relationships of New Testament culture: Jew-Gentile, slave-free, and male-female. The context of these verses initiates the end of social hierarchies for those "in Christ."

For Christians, then, structured inequality—whether "vindicated" by individual differences, supposed societal need, power, or even scriptural proof-texts—cannot be justified. Christ's redemptive work reconciles us not only to God, but also to one another. Gender mutuality, not hierarchy, powerfully models his kingdom. Mutual respect, responsibility, and opportunities for leadership for both women and men need to be developed at all levels in the church, at the workplace, in the family, and in governing structures. We need to socially construct our social worlds so they are characterized by *structured equality* rather than structured inequality.

Perhaps you would choose, instead, to first diminish stratification among the poor or between the races. But do not overlook the fact that the initial result of rebellion against God was *gender* inequality. Modeling mutuality in this relationship includes all our life experiences—it is daily, and deeply personal. As the style of life together in the kingdom of God, male-female mutuality has potential to affect the inequities in all other relationships: race, poverty, occupation, and among the nations of the world. Without the modeling of gender mutuality, stratification will persist, along with inadequate justifications sustaining it.

REFERENCES IN CHAPTER

Abrahamson, Mark, Ephraim H. Mizruchi, and Carlton A. Hornung. 1976. *Stratification and Mobility*. New York: Macmillan.

Barnet, Richard J., and R. E. Muller. 1977. *Global Reach: The Power of the Multinational Corporation*. New York: Simon & Schuster.

Bilezikian, Gilbert. 1985. *Beyond Sex Roles*. Grand Rapids, Mich.: Baker Book House.

Bloesch, Donald. 1982. *Is the Bible Sexist?* New York: Cornerstone.

Chirot, Daniel, and Robert E. Merton. 1986. *Social Change in the Modern Era*. New York: Harcourt, Brace, Jovanovich.

Chodorow, Nancy. 1978. *The Reproduction of Mothering*. Berkeley, Calif.: University of California Press.

Clark, Stephen B. 1980. *Man and Woman in Christ*. Ann Arbor, Mich.: Servant.

Coles, Robert. 1964. *Children of Crisis*. Boston: Little, Brown & Co.

Dahrendorf, Ralf. 1968. *Essays on the Theory of Society*. Palo Alto, Calif.: Stanford University Press.

Davis, Elizabeth Gould. 1972. *The First Sex*. New York: Penguin.

Davis, Kingsley, and Wilbert E. Moore. 1945. "Some Principles of Stratification." *American Sociological Review* 10:242–49.

Elliot, Elisabeth. 1976. *Let Me Be a Woman*. Wheaton, Ill.: Tyndale House.

Engels, Friedrich. 1942. *The Origin of the Family, Private Property, and the State*. New York: International.

Erikson, Erik. 1969. *Gandhi's Truth: On the Origins of Militant Non-Violence*. New York: W. W. Norton.

Gilligan, Carol. 1982. *In a Different Voice*. Cambridge, Mass.: Harvard University Press.

Harris, Marvin. 1977. "Why Men Dominate Women." *New York Times Magazine*, November 13.

Kerbo, Harold R. 1983. *Social Stratification and Inequality*. New York: McGraw-Hill.

Lewis, Oscar. 1966. "The Culture of Poverty." *Scientific American* 215:19–25.

Mead, Margaret. 1975. *Male and Female: A Study of the Sexes in a Changing World*. New York: Morrow.

National Center for Health Statistics (NCHS). 1984. *Advance Report of Final Natality Statistics*. Washington, D.C.: National Center for Health Statistics.

Rosaldo, Michelle Zimbalist, and Louise Lamphere, eds. 1974. *Women, Culture, and Society*. Stanford, Calif.: Stanford University Press.

Stone, Merlin. 1978. *When God Was A Woman*. New York: Harcourt Brace.

Wallerstein, Immanuel. 1979. *The Capitalist World Economy*. Cambridge: Cambridge University Press.

Wilson, Edward O. 1978. *On Human Nature*. Cambridge, Mass.: Harvard University Press.

ALIENATION AND FREEDOM

Brendan F. J. Furnish

Although an often discussed topic among contemporary scholars, alienation as a concept represents the timeless and universal angst of the human condition. In the last few decades, concern over this notion has intensified, and there has been a fairly concerted effort to favor a definition of humanity that avows our condition as detached and meaningless. The vanguard of this concern was originally made up of writers and playwrights, perhaps typified by Camus, Sartre, Genet, Albee, and Salinger. Later, especially in the United States, the term became a key word in the vocabulary of the intellectuals.

Although the concept is clearly present in many sociological writings, the term itself is frequently not used. Despite some considerable effort to satisfy the more scientifically oriented by attempting to define the expression in more objective terms, the meaning of the concept of alienation remains somewhat vague and elusive. Consequently, we find the expression used to refer to human alienation from nature, as was the case in the writings of D. H. Lawrence and the romantic novelists; or perhaps the more recent existential use of the term in which we find that we have become alienated from ourselves; or perhaps the type of alienation that represents estrangement from God. Nevertheless, while the struggle to refine the concept continues, there seems agreement that humanity is becoming successively alienated in an increasingly complex world. All too frequently, this alienation is a matter of our own creation.

About twenty-five years ago, Kenneth Keniston (1965:3) prophetically described this ongoing cultural current when he observed, "The drift of our time is away from connection, relation, communion and dialogue, and our intellectual concerns reflect this conviction. Alienation, once seen as imposed on men by an unjust economic system, is increasingly chosen by men as their basic stance toward society."

BIBLICAL ESTRANGEMENT

No sociological explanation is totally sufficient in explaining the deep-seated anxiety and despair inherent in the human condition. Only by examining the biblical causes of alienation can we begin to grasp the root causes of our universal estrangement— all social manifestations are but a reflection of the spiritual realities present in our natures.

The focus for the biblical treatment of alienation is found in the third chapter of Genesis. In this chapter, humanity is led astray by Satan who, in his own rebellion against God, successfully incites God's human creations to disobey his norms, infringe on his sovereign rights, and attempt "to be like God." The consequences for these actions were banishment from Eden, the introduction of death in the world, and a general disarray of the entire natural order. Moreover, the Fall had other, direct consequences for the human psyche. The disobedience, questioning, and, doubting of God led to a set of character defects that are still manifest in humanity. We fear that we will lose something by being obedient to God. We also lack confidence in fully trusting in him, and we become intensely anxious about our lives. As a consequence, the "natural human" tends to believe that association with God will not satisfy the hunger in his or her life.

Thus, our sin is not simple rebellion. Brunner (1939:132) put it well when he said that "sin is composed of the mingled elements of distrust, doubt, and defiant desire for freedom." The outcome of this is that the unregenerated members of the human race (and unfortunately most Christians, also) suffer from an underlying condition of anxiety and at the same time believe (in an unconscious manner) that they can become God.

It is against this biblical background that we must now compare sociological theories of alienation. To do this, we shall look at the concepts of alienation found in the writings of some important early sociologists, and we shall pay particular attention to seeing how well these theoretical ideas "fit" our Christian world view.

POWERLESSNESS AND THE RESTRAINT OF FREEDOM

One of the more commonplace discussions of alienation in contemporary introductory textbooks concerns Karl Marx's use of the term to describe the plight of the industrial worker in modern society (*see* Robertson, 1987: 459–60). In the Marxian analysis, the workers (the proletariat) are exploited by the owners of the means of production (the bourgeoisie). This exploitation is not only economic; more important, the exploitation is existential. That is, the creative powers of the workers are taken away from them and in exchange for wages paid. The workers also exchange their creativity for highly specialized production activities. Accordingly, because of the lack of creative input by the workers, much of what passes for work in modern society is meaningless and intensely boring. The condition of the workers' lives is further impoverished by the fact that the laborers are not free to determine the outcomes of their lives, but find themselves having to obey the dictates of those who manage their productivity. As a result, they experience the sensation of powerlessness (see Seeman, 1959:784).

Many of Marx's ideas came out of theology, and in some sense it may be said that Marx developed a peculiar type of Christian heresy. That is, Marx was very greatly influenced by the German philosopher Hegel. For Hegel, the history of humanity since the Genesis fall was a history of alienation. Although Hegel's use of the term was a sort of general intuition (rather than a specific concept), it nevertheless provided Marx with useful ideas. Hegel felt that humanity had come into a world that was no longer theirs, a world that seemed to oppose the gratification of basic human needs—"a strange world governed by inexorable laws; a 'dead' world in which human life is frustrated" (Marcuse, 1960:246–47).

Further, Hegel felt that the world's social institutions had distorted even the most personal and private relations between people. These social institutions have come about during the process of alienation, and they especially manifest themselves in the form of goods and private property. To Hegel, human activity is continually consumed by the objects that humans create. People alienate themselves by abstracting the things they create and making these things the products of the human consciousness. When they do so, they reduce their understanding of themselves to merely a set of "things." The products of human labor become transferred into an objective transcendent power that gets out of control and eventually blocks inner expectations. Humans change from self-determined creators into other-determined creatures (see Lefebure, 1968: 9ff).

Marx accepted Hegel's basic ideas, but felt they lacked any practical substance. Marx did not view the distortion of humanity as the outcome of the biblical event of the Fall, which to Marx, the atheist, was a "pseudoevent." Rather, he asserted that "the essence of Man's alienation is private property—man's alienation from himself occurs in capitalist work" (Nisbet, 1966:281). Thus Marx sought a secular cause for human alienation and found it in the dehumanizing forces of the nineteenth-century industrial order.

Marx concluded that capitalism is the causal mechanism whereby the laborer becomes a commodity—an object to be used by wealthier people. Because the worker is turned into an object, he or she is no longer able to achieve human fulfillment and becomes a "dehumanized being." Workers are condemned to live in societies where they are denied satisfaction of their activities by a few greedy capitalist owners.

One should not lightly dismiss Marx's ideas. Class-capitalism does present many problems that require rectification, particularly for Christians who, because of the nature of the gospel, are required to seriously assist the exploited among us. This Christian social action should include restoring dignity and autonomy to workers at all levels of work. Likewise, the emotional and real economic costs incurred on our society by alienated workers caught in meaningless and repetitious jobs are increasingly difficult to sustain. Indeed, this may be one of the main reasons why production in the United States is falling behind that of other countries. After all, how would you feel if upon leaving college you could only look forward to a clerical job filling out endless and repetitious forms for the firm of Dullum, Dullum, Dullum & Bore? In the last several years, sources within the various fields of industrial relations have made proposals to alleviate this type of alienation. One would hope that Christians would be at the forefront of the attempts to restore meaning to much of our human activity.

Furthermore, although we may not be willing to admit it, the problem of the contemporary homeless is, in large part, a consequence of our particular form of capitalism. After all, it was not too many years ago that American industries willingly employed large numbers of basically illiterate and unskilled manual workers. Now, with changes in technology, many of these same workers have been rather casually cast aside as superfluous. This is usually done by corporations that perceive no moral or social reason to either retain or retrain such people for other types of occupations. Additionally, we have, as a nation, tolerated and often envied the "takeover" machinations of a few Wall Street barons. These opportunists have frequently enriched themselves and at the same time destroyed the livelihoods of tens of thousands of blue-collar workers. This is very much in line with what Marx had in mind when he discussed how capitalism inevitably led to the increasing impoverishment and misery of the proletariat.

Although we may disagree with the Marxian analysis of alienated society, Christians simply cannot escape Christ's concept of who our "neighbor" is—this includes the unemployed and the homeless. In a democratic society, Christians need to examine and reform the structural factors contributing to the impoverishment and further alienation of our neighbors.

There is much food for thought in Marx's theory of alienation, but some crucial problems must be understood in order to put it into proper perspective. To begin with, the nineteenth-century capitalism that Marx encountered in Great Britain is no longer in existence in the Western democracies, especially in the United States. It appears foolish to attempt to suggest that this theory, which was bound to a particular time period (admittedly an appalling time for industrial workers), is applicable to our contemporary situation—a reality that the Chinese Communist leaders have recently acknowledged. The simple fact is that Marx just did not understand the flexibility of capitalist democracies. Likewise, he did not anticipate the powerful effect that the trade-union movement would have on reforming the workplace. Finally, we must question Marx's utopian vision in light of historical experience. Despite over seventy years of the application of "communism" in the Soviet Union and other countries, we have yet to see either the elimination of worker alienation or the development of a true "classless society." The reason for this is that while Marx correctly identified one form of alienation, he misunderstood the true causal factor—that of the development of modern forms of organization. We shall deal with this issue when we examine the ideas of Max Weber.

More to the point of this chapter are the problems that the Christian encounters in a close reading of Marx. These problems largely center on the *assumptions* that Marx made about the nature of humanity. Marx picked up the dominant ideas of the European culture of his day and incorporated them into his theorizing (in this regard *all* social and behavioral science theories are influenced by the historical and cultural epochs in which they are framed).

The most important assumptions Marx drew from his culture were those of *innateness* and *perfectionism*. Marx believed that humanity was innately good. To him, sin and evil were not spiritual problems (remember, in his way of thinking, such things were religious, and therefore were pseudoevents), but were products of the corrupting influences of class-societies. Coupled to innateness was the idea of perfectionism. Intellectuals of his time believed that given the right social circumstances, humanity could be made perfect. To Marx, this meant that when the corrupting influences of capitalism were removed, the human race would be capable of perfection. Indeed, the premise was that humanity had the potential of becoming Godlike. These beliefs are still widely held.

This, of course, brings us back to the third chapter of Genesis (v. 5) and also causes us to pose a final question regarding Marx's notions: Can work ever be made completely satisfying and nonalienating? What are the implications of Adam's curse (Genesis 3:17–19) on contemporary society and the nature of modern work? Rather than attempt to answer this for you, we think it best to let you spend the next few decades of your life working out your own response.

MAX WEBER AND THE OVERORGANIZED SOCIETY

Max Weber was certainly no great supporter of Karl Marx. He was, however, someone who had read most of Marx's writings, and was very familiar with the works of the Socialists and Communists being studied during the first few decades of this century. Weber disliked the premises of the far left because he felt that the systems they proposed did not free humanity from the effects of alienation, but intensified the very forces that led to the mental and physical enslavement of humanity. To Weber, it seemed that as long as the fundamental forces unleashed by industrialization were allowed to continue and grow, people would be increasingly alienated, regardless of who owned the means of production (*see* Zeitlin, 1968:120f.). Socialism, with its inevitable emphasis on centralized planning and large bureaucratic control organizations, tended to enhance the depersonalization of modern life.

In most introductory sociology textbooks, Weber's name is associated with the study of bureaucracy and formal organizations—a field of study that he pioneered (e.g., Schaefer, 1986:137f.). Unfortunately, most introductory discussions of Weber and his organizational theories fail to communicate the depth of his pessimism toward the increasing alienation of contemporary society. Weber never used the term *alienation*; rather, he used the term *rationalization* . By this, he meant that modern society was rapidly abandoning traditional values in order to develop the necessary rational-bureaucratic organizational structures needed to govern modern society. However, in doing so, all forms of *enchantment* had to be eliminated; rational and quantitative processes became the sole bases of modern society. Thus, everything that could not be objectively accounted for was eliminated for consideration in the new forms of governance. This made for highly efficient organizational structures, but it also led to what Weber claimed was "the disenchantment of the world" and the dooming of modern society to the "iron cage" of rationalism (Weber, 1958:180–83).

To us, this means that our culture has taught us (although we may want to deny this) that there are no mysterious and unknown powers in our lives. This course is best seen in the scientific approach to life. The presumption that what cannot be observed is not real has infiltrated deeply into our culture. As a consequence, the objective approach to life has penetrated into the innermost parts of our psyche. We now demand a rational explanation for all that occurs in life.

Consequently, many of us find it increasingly difficult to understand, let alone accept, a concept such as "love" in any of its biblical variations. To be sure, we may discuss *agape* in an intellectual manner, but our actual understanding of this term may be quite different from that of our ancestors several centuries removed. Perhaps even more telling is our changed understanding of *eros* love. To a person steeped in secular modernity, the idea of romantic love increasingly appears ludicrous. In contemporary society, eros has come to simply mean some sort of sexual activity. Accordingly, the romantic activities of the medieval troubadours (pursuing courtly love with women they could not possibly have sex with) seems truly bizarre to most of us. Less weird and rather startling is the documented fact that courtship not involving sexual intercourse was more or less normative only two decades ago—a reality almost incomprehensible to today's younger people.

Weber feared that without some reliance on tradition and the unexplainable but significant elements of life, humanity would become a great regimented, mechanized mass in which all sense of reason had been destroyed in order to allow secular bureaucracy to become preeminent. Weber noted that already in his day (1920s) people were becoming used to being dealt with in an increasingly custodial manner—allowing their affairs to be regulated in ever smaller ways (*see* Nisbet, 1966:294).

Today the situation may be even worse. Lacking the understanding of nonempirical notions such as freedom, we willingly relinquish control of our lives to professional managers. One does not have to look very far to discover examples of bureaucratic intrusion that is increasingly welcomed into our lives. Not too long ago, raising children was far more of a private family matter than it is now. These days the family is besieged by an army of professional "experts" who impose their views on the proper means of "parenting" at various points in the life cycle of the family (a provocative discussion of this appears in chapter 7 of Christopher Lasch's *The Culture of Narcissism* [1978]), and many of these "experts" are single people who have not had children of their own. Personal experience (once highly valued in traditional society) is no longer valued in today's rational-objective society.

This process of rationalization has other ramifications for contemporary society. It is a force that penetrates all aspects of culture and leads to the questioning of everything, particularly cultural value systems. Hence, in the last few decades Western civilization has witnessed a sharp decline in support for traditional

Judeo-Christian values. In the short term, such changes appear to grant freedom, but as experience proves, such freedom is illusory and transient (*see* Ellul, 1976).

As the system of values becomes weakened, the societal rules of conduct give way—since norms not supported by values simply will not be obeyed. As the usual means of regulating behavior disappears, we may be faced with the prospect of either anarchy or an unknown form of culture. In time, the facade of civilization will begin to crumble.

An intriguing aspect of the denial of the unexplainable—and obviously by extension the denial of the supernatural—is the spiritually oriented cultural reaction to rationalization. The explosion of interest in occultism and the very rapid growth of Eastern religions and other metaphysical concerns are clear indications that individuals possess a need to deal with the unknowable.

All this poses a vital challenge to Christians. By understanding the cultural forces that have brought about this state of affairs, we can (with the guidance of the Holy Spirit) develop strategies for bringing light to a darkening situation. Specifically, we must oppose the excessive rationalism of our culture. We should also strongly reidentify ourselves with Christian supernaturalism and begin to deal with the transcendent nature of humanity.

We should cease being ashamed of providing Christian moral and normative guidelines for ourselves and for our culture. We have too long let the church's voice be muted in the interest of not being offensive to our pluralistic society. Increasingly, the body of Christ has been afraid to counter the spurious morality and destitute values offered by the "professional" opinion setters of our culture. In doing so, we had better be sure that such guidelines are firmly grounded in biblical principles rather than in the subcultural notions of Christianity or, worse yet, in the transient theories of the social and behavioral sciences.

GEORG SIMMEL AND THE URBAN PERSONALITY

Simmel was a sociologist who was a contemporary and acquaintance of Max Weber. Simmel is especially significant because many of his ideas were brought into American sociology early in the development of the discipline in this country, although he was unfortunately never given credit for many of these concepts (*see* Levine et al., 1976a and 1976b). Simmel's ideas about alienation were carried into American sociology by Louis Wirth, who wrote a now famous essay concerning the "urban personality" entitled "Urbanism as a Way Of Life" (1938).

With Weber, Simmel shared many of the apprehensions concerning the negative drift toward increased alienation in Western culture. However, with regard to the speed and intensity of the process of alienation, Simmel was far more pessimistic than Weber. Like so many other social theorists, Simmel did not use the term *alienation* directly, rather he talked about *objectification*— an idea that is somewhat similar to Weber's term *rationalization*. Like Weber, Simmel was also concerned with modern forms of organization, but his focus was rather specifically on the modern metropolis—where he saw the forces of alienation truly running amuck.

Simmel was concerned with the separation of the individual from the group—the loss of community. This particular estrangement from the group is the result of progressive cultural forces, which seem to shape the nature of humanity. Simmel suggested that modern industrialized people must develop a culture to sustain them and also allow them to develop their potential as individuals. However, paradoxically, this same cultural elaboration has within it the capacity to eventually destroy them as individuals. Thus, Simmel proposed a series of pessimistic contradictions, or dualisms, which (unlike the Hegelian-Marxian dialectic) humanity has no ability to resolve.

These forces of cultural estrangement come to fruition in the culmination of human cultural development—the metropolis. According to Simmel, human interaction and interdependence achieve their full potential in the modern city. It is also within this urban culture that harmful changes occur to the individual. In the metropolis we become less than human as we become routinized, regimented, and calculating creatures due to our ever increasing alienation.

In his various works, Simmel presented these ideas at two different levels—the "micro" and the "macro." At the micro, or social-psychological level, he observed that cities are places where the circle of one's acquaintances is wide and relatively unrestricted. Although this discourages the strength of communal bonds, it encourages individual achievement and specialization. These factors would be stifled in the smaller primary group since excessive specialization and accomplishment are destructive to the similarity necessary to maintain primary group bonds (*see* Wolff, 1950:416). This feeling comes out strongly in Simmel's discussion of the stranger, a person who is not merely a transient visitor, but a permanent resident who is quite unbounded by group ties. The stranger is the urban archetype. He or she is an innovative but marginal individual who is not restricted by confining group norms. This person can be objective and yet remain a member of the urban society.

Such freedom is nevertheless costly since it removes protections for the individual found in more close-knit societal arrangements. Because human interaction in urban situations is unrestrained by the type of norms and values found in the more primary relations of small communities, a fear of exploitation develops (often for good reason). After all, urban dwellers frequently do not know (in a wholistic manner) the person with whom they are interacting; rather, they know one another by status categories in highly specific situations. In such circumstances, they get to see only selected pieces of people and then usually as actors on some type of stage, a condition frequently described by the modern social theorist Erving Goffman.

The consequence of this situation, for most city dwellers, is to develop what Simmel termed a "reserve"—a sort of mental attitude that manifests itself in "devaluating the whole objective world—a devaluation which in the end unavoidably drags one's own personality down into a feeling of the same worthlessness" (Wolff, 1950:415). Thus, urban people tend to interact with some degree of caution and try to be highly rational and sophisticated (objective) in their relations with others.

At the macro, or institutional level, we find a complementary set of alienating structures. At this level we are concerned with the normative and value patternings of the culture. Simmel pointed out that in the metropolis we find formal patterns of relationships, particularly those emphasizing social control and placing heavy reliance on formalized sanction patterns. Such structures allow individuals maximum freedom since they are not subjugated to the close personal control found in the small community (community in this sense meaning a place of individual identity and "wholeness" instead of merely a location). On the other hand, they also allow considerable deviation from the laws since formalized social controls are relatively remote from the urban individuals. Consequently, this can lead to fairly unrestrained activities, generating the fears of exploitation in the minds of many urban dwellers.

This same urban milieu produces a culture that emphasizes personal achievement and encourages increasingly high degrees of specialization. Intangible elements, such as morality and integrity, are put aside for the more tangible evidence of success and achievement. Thus, "competency" and symbolic demonstrations of "ability" supplant the moral virtues that held the older traditional community together in mutual bonds of trust.

Simmel proposed that the most compelling cultural characteristic of the urban society is *rationality* in our dealing with others. This is manifested in our preoccupation with legal contracts, money, and a host of other material factors. Mostly though, it is epitomized by the economy of modern urban society. Simmel pointed out that money reduces all human values down to a common denominator, and replaces personal preferences as the basis of human association: "Money is concerned only with what is common to all. It asks for exchange value and reduces all quality and individuality to the question: 'How much?' " (Wolff, 1950:411; see also Spykman, 1925:221ff.). Within this arena, issues such as "comparable pay" and "comparable worth" make sense to many people.

Simmel grappled with the problem of how one can develop and maintain individuality and freedom in modern society and at the same time avoid the trap of objectification of life (his particular term for alienation). Unfortunately, he had no solution. Indeed, the reader is left with a deep sense of pessimism since all Simmel foresaw was the "crashing of society."

Much in Simmel's works speaks to the human condition, especially the condition that results by allowing human cultural systems to place Christians in bondage. It is true that the idea of being a "stranger" is an important biblical trait—referring to the believer's marginality in a culture that is almost always at enmity with Christ and the Christian faith. However, in contradiction to biblical teaching, Christians have allowed themselves to become strangers to one another. As we saw in chapter 6, biblical teaching does not support a church of radical individuals. However, moving from being the individualistic "stranger" to Christian community involves a loss of human freedom that many of us refuse to give up, even if the result is severe alienation. Yet, Christ calls us into community with others—a community where estrangement can be finally vanquished.

Christians need to carefully examine and, when necessary, reject social systems that require participants to become uncaring to other individuals. This once again means becoming involved with our "neighbor" in the biblical sense. Such involvement implies a cost, not the least of which may involve interacting with people we would ordinarily prefer to avoid.

Likewise, Christians need to reject the bondage that comes from viewing people in a purely "objective" manner. Measures of wealth, power, and prestige that we feel are indicative of human worth actually enslave us by not allowing us or others to penetrate to the authentic men and women hidden behind the symbols of status. This illusionary world is antithetical to the teaching of Scripture. It needs to be exposed and renounced wherever possible.

EMILE DURKHEIM AND THE DISINTEGRATION OF SOCIETY

Durkheim shared with Weber the notion that in destroying tradition, people destroy something in themselves. However, he differed from Weber in claiming that alienation is not caused primarily by overorganization; rather, Durkheim claimed that modern organizational life has become *meaningless* (contemporary writers would say *absurd*).

Differing from the Marxian alienation concept involving estrangement from work and self, Durkheim was concerned with the human situation where the rules of the group—or, by extension, society—no longer limit human impulses. Durkheim saw alienation coming about as a result of human isolation from traditional society and values. He posited a situation in which the regulating bonds of society (mainly the societal norms) are loosened to the point that the individuals are without adequate regulation for their lives. *Anomie*—a situation of "rulelessness" is the intolerable condition where social relationships are unpredictable (*see* Durkheim, 1964).

In most social situations, norms not only regulate behavior but they also impose predictability and orderliness in the lives of the participants. For example, when you interact with one of your professors, you expect that the individual will conduct appropriate academic business with you. It would be an intolerable state of affairs if, on the other hand, you found yourself in the position of never knowing if the professor would stick to business or would instead sexually assault you. Durkheim claimed such uncertainty in society can lead people to commit *anomic suicide*—to destroy themselves because of their inability to adequately comprehend the course of their lives. Because of the disruption of societal regulation, life became meaningless and absurd to such victims (*see* Durkheim, 1951).

It must be emphasized that Durkheim's concern with the meaning of anomie has to do mainly with society and not necessarily with the individual. As we saw in chapter 6, Durkheim believed that the collectivity, and not the individual, was the most important component of society. Nevertheless, the *individual* is affected when the bonds holding community together are weakened.

In effect, Durkheim said that modern society has created a built-in paradox. Modern culture encourages ever-increasing individualism (a situation that is especially acute in the contemporary United States). However, in becoming purely individualistic, we devitalize the sense of community that enabled our individuality in the first place. Loneliness, despair, and the eventual collapse of society are the products of the process of individualism.

THE CHRISTIAN IN AN ALIENATED WORLD

Having presented this admittedly pessimistic overview of the varieties of sociological treatment of alienation that characterizes contemporary American society, we need to examine how these ideas affect our lives and formulate a Christian response. While, on the one hand, it is true that modern people are living in situations that contribute to increasing alienation, we do not, on the other hand, need to accept the conditions that lead us into being alienated. We can pursue several courses of action in an attempt to remove the despair of alienation.

The first step is to try to understand the things that bring about our alienation. The study of sociology can be helpful in this regard, since we can acquire insights into the nature of our culture and society. An understanding of sociology can help us interpret our social conditions—making it less likely that we will become ignorant victims of our social circumstances. A sociological imagination can allow us to comprehend the implications of powerlessness in our lives as well as to come to grips with our feelings of abandonment brought about by the isolation in modern society.

A second possible step in dealing with alienation is to develop a strong understanding of what Christian freedom is all about. This involves the realization that alienation is more than a sociological or an economic phenomenon. Rather, it is essentially a moral and spiritual phenomenon.

We are alienated largely because we choose to accept many elements of life as necessities rather than options. Furthermore, we mistake certain liberties as freedom, when in fact these are false licenses that enslave us and put us in additional alienating bondage. Our contemporary culture's fascination with eroticism and "liberated sexuality" is a case in point. In our haste to pursue these new liberties, we may have placed ourselves in a new form of alienating estrangement and at the same time, have allowed our true freedom to be taken away from us in a perverse exchange process (see Ellul, 1976:23–50).

A third likely step in reducing alienation is to learn to examine and criticize the materialism of our culture. We tend to pursue consumerism with the idea that "one more acquisition is going to make it all better." This way of thinking, of course, is false; the purchase of anything cannot reduce our angst, but may increase it. While we spend our passions in consumption, our will to change the structural evil of our culture is drained away. In this sense, consumerism is demonic; it fails to produce the peace that it promises and also prevents us from carrying out biblical mandates regarding the redemption and restoration of society.

One suspects this also supports a quasi-Marxist interpretation; since the members of the proletariat have become so preoccupied with the consumerist goals of acquisition, they fail to discern the depths of their exploitation by the ruling classes. Jules Henry's writings regarding the "American Dream" are helpful in understanding how the process of consumerism leads us into further alienation and to great personal self-contempt (Henry,

1963). Likewise, Richard Foster's *Freedom of Simplicity* (1981) is well-suited in assisting Christians in coming to grips with some of the alienating burdens that we have defined as necessary.

The fourth step in eliminating alienation is to establish a balance between community and individualism. We have discussed the idea of community in chapter 6 of this book. Additionally, we must continuously uncover and examine the mechanisms promoting hyperindividualism in our culture. One of the most potent of these, and one that has penetrated almost all elements of the American church, is our ever increasing fascination with "pop" psychology. This fascination is a reflection of the narcissistic selfism running rampant in contemporary culture. There is, however, a more troublesome aspect to it if our obsession with becoming "adjusted" obscures from us the fact that our culture is becoming increasingly hostile and alien. Much of the thrust of the new pseudopsychology accepted by the bulk of the church asks us to make peace with and adjust to the alienating forces of our culture. Instead, we must realize that we, as Christians, are here to change culture. Jacques Ellul (1970) points out that human culture is naturally at enmity with God, and Christians have a mandate to work at restoring the fallen creation until Christ returns.

A fifth step in retarding the forces of alienation is to reclaim the Reformation concept of "calling". Our commitment to materialism has caused us to forget that God wants to call us to our vocations. One of the reasons why our work alienates us is because we view our employment primarily as a means to some type of material or power-related ends. One suspects that our attitudes about our jobs would be significantly altered if we earnestly sought God's will in our career choices. Likewise, Christian employers and managers should strive to make dignified and meaningful work available to people in their employment.

Finally, one of the most compelling steps we should take is to restore meaning and purpose to our lives. Most people in contemporary society have no idea why they are here. If they do believe in some kind of supreme being (and most Americans do), they feel he, she, or it has deserted them and left them to face a world that is basically absurd. The church's virtual silence in the face of a crisis of meaning has intensified the experience of alienation in contemporary society. As members of the body of Christ, we must cease being ashamed of evangelization and Christian supernaturalism. If we really believe that Christ is the answer to our dying world, then we should start telling our neighbors about him.

CONCLUSION

One of the major themes of the New Testament is the call to freedom (John 8:36; Galatians 5). This call is not exclusively for freedom from the bondage of sin; it concerns freedom from all bondage—including alienation. It is sometimes difficult to see the effects of Christ's victory on the cross against the forces of evil and alienation. An analogy from recent human history might be useful to illustrate the magnitude of his victory.

On June 4, 1942, less than six months after the Pearl Harbor attack, United States naval forces scored an important victory over the Imperial Japanese Navy in the Battle of Midway Island. At the time, no one on either side of the conflict fully realized just how decisive that battle was. Although the war persisted for another three years, as a result of that one major battle, the Japanese were forced to move from an aggressively offensive position to one of desperate defense. This battle was the turning point of the war (*see* Prange, 1982).

We do not mean to trivialize the sacrifice of Christ by comparing the Atonement with a human battle; nevertheless, we hope you can see the moral in the illustration—the forces of death and alienation were defeated on the cross at Calvary. Although the fight goes on, the victory is assured. Our job is to continue the struggle against evil and alienation until he returns.

REFERENCES IN CHAPTER

Brunner, Emile. 1939. *Man in Revolt*. Philadelphia: Westminster.
Durkheim, Emile. 1951. *Suicide*. New York: Free Press.
_____. 1964. *The Division of Labor in Society*. New York: Free Press.
Ellul, Jacques. 1967. *The Technological Society*. New York: Vintage Books.
_____. 1970. *The Meaning of the City*. Grand Rapids: Eerdmans.
_____. 1976. *The Ethics of Freedom*. Grand Rapids: Eerdmans.
Foster, Richard J. 1981. *Freedom of Simplicity*. San Francisco: Harper & Row.
Goffman, Erving. 1959. *The Presentation of Self in Everyday Life*. Garden City, N.Y.: Doubleday.
Henry, Jules. 1963. *Culture Against Man*. New York: Random House.
Keniston, Kenneth. 1965. *The Uncommitted*. New York: Harcourt Brace.
Lasch, Christopher. 1978. *The Culture of Narcissism*. New York: W. W. Norton.
Lefebure, Henri. 1968. *The Sociology of Karl Marx*. New York: Pantheon.
Levine, Donald N., et al. 1976a. "Simmel's Influence on American Sociology." *American Journal of Sociology* 81 (no. 4): 813–45.
_____. 1976b. "Simmel's Influence on American Sociology II." *American Journal of Sociology* 81 (no. 5): 1113–32.
Marcuse, Herbert. 1960. *Reason and Revolution*. Boston: Beacon.
Nisbet, Robert A. 1966. *The Sociological Tradition*. New York: Basic Books.
Prange, Gordon, et al. 1982. *Miracle at Midway*. New York: McGraw-Hill.

Robertson, Ian. 1987. *Sociology*. 3d ed. New York: Worth Publishers.

Schaefer, Richard T. 1986. *Sociology*. 2d ed. New York: McGraw-Hill.

Seeman, Melvin. 1959. "On the Meaning of Alienation." *American Sociological Review* 24 (no. 6): 783–91.

Spykman, Nicholas J. 1925. *The Social Theory of Georg Simmel*. Chicago: University of Chicago Press.

Weber, Max. 1958. *The Protestant Ethic and The Spirit of Capitalism*. New York: Charles Scribner's Sons.

Wirth, Louis. 1938. "Urbanism as a Way of Life." *American Journal of Sociology* 44 (July): 1–24.

Wolff, Kurt H. 1950. *The Sociology of Georg Simmel*. New York: Free Press.

Zeitlin, Irving M. 1968. *Ideology and the Development of Sociological Theory*. Englewood Cliffs, N.J.: Prentice Hall.

THE FAMILY: HEAVEN OR HAVEN?

Jack Balswick and Judith Balswick

Sociologically, the family is the basic unit of society, for it is the social unit into which children are born and socialized. It is also the primary source of economic status and social identity for most people. The theological centrality of the family can be seen in the biblical use of familial imagery: God as the *father* of his children, Christ as the *bridegroom* , and his church as the *bride* . In addition, the family is the primary metaphor used for the church in the New Testament; its members are described as being *adopted* into the household of God, after which they become *brothers* and *sisters* in Christ.

Although it can be argued that the family is the basic unit in society, it is also true that the family does not exist in a vacuum, but is instead an integral part of the wider web of societal relationships and structures. It is common to hear the claim that the contemporary American family is in trouble since approximately half of all couples who begin marriage by saying "'til death do us part," actually become divorced or separated long before death. Moreover, the effect of such partings goes well beyond the marriage partners themselves; nearly 50 percent of all children in the United States will *not* live out their growing years under the care of the same two parents. There is trouble with our fragile and fragmented nuclear family system, and much of the disruption is a reflection of changes that have taken place in the wider society.

When we consider societal change from a long-term perspective, it can be seen that family structures are related to societal types. Thus, in societies that subsist on such activities as hunting and gathering, families are very small because their economic base cannot support more than a few people. However, in agricultural societies, the extended family is the norm since domesticated animals and harvested crops create a sturdier economic base. And with the emergence of the industrial revolution in the Western world people started to move from rural to urban areas, thereby creating still another type of family system.

Any useful analysis of the contemporary American family must take into account how it has been affected by the tremendous rate of social change that has occurred in the United States during recent years. Economically, the family is no longer the basic unit of production, but has instead been reduced to the basic unit of consumption. In addition, the structure of our modern-day economy demands that family members work outside the home, and its system of training and advancement also necessitates the periodic uprooting of families. This, in turn, contributes to a sense of widespread societal instability. Furthermore, as a variety of extrafamilial social agencies and institutions have taken over many of the traditional family functions, the very meaning of family life is being reevaluated.

Societal responses to the current crisis in family life often take one of two predictable extremes. One is the reactionary stance adopted by many conservative Christians who seek to return the family to an idealized image of the past. This solution is based less on an attempt to discern what a proper biblical perspective on the family should be in modern society than on a nostalgic defense of the "good old days." Indeed, it is a common mistake for Christians to assume that the particular family form that has existed in their past is, in fact, God's ideal! With the confusion and fear created by modernity and rapid social change, many Christians are holding up a nineteenth century patriarchal model of the American family as being the biblical family.

The opposite extreme is an adaptive or "progressive" response, which is often based on naturalistic and relativistic assumptions about the family. In avoiding the pitfall of idealizing a particular cultural or temporal form of family life, proponents of this approach claim that there are no lasting normative structures or functions for the family. In what we will describe as the "modern, open response," the family is re-created into any form that might appear to be best suited to the personal demands of individual self-fulfillment and the insatiable demands of other societal institutions. Such a response not only ignores scriptural mandates pertaining to the family but also promotes the narcissistic needs of individuals and social institutions that can, in turn, be destructive to Christian family values.

A THEOLOGICAL BASIS FOR FAMILY RELATIONSHIPS

One reason for the contradictory versions of the ideal biblical family has to do with the diverse ways in which Christians use

Scripture. One common method of interpretation is for each person or group to pick and arrange a bouquet of Bible verses into the configuration that supports a particular point of view. Such a method, when devoid of exegetical analysis, results in an abuse of scriptural data. In this chapter, an attempt will be made to base a family model on broad scriptural themes that will serve as a foundation for developing a theology of family relationships.

We propose that a sound theology of family relationships may be constructed on four logically sequential but nonlinear elements of relationship—these being *covenant, grace, empowering,* and *intimacy.* These particular elements are derived from an examination of certain biblical writings that speak of God entering into and sustaining a relationship with the people of God (Balswick and Balswick, 1987).

Covenant: To Love and Be Loved

The relationship between God and the chosen people, Israel, began with the establishment of a covenant with Abram (Genesis 15, 17). Although God initiated the covenant by making an unconditional, unilateral commitment, God's desire was for people to bring this covenant to bilateral maturity by continually responding positively to this unconditional love. Although the Lord called these people to be obedient, such obedience was not a necessary precondition for the establishment of the initial covenant. Thus, Israel's disobedience did not annul the covenant since God's covenant is more than a bilateral and conditional contract.

God's covenant with the church is also properly understood in terms of unconditional love. Such love is spoken of in 1 John 4:19, "We love, because he first loved us," and in 1 John 4:10, "In this is love, not that we loved God but that he loved us." This unconditional love is offered to those who believe in Christ (John 3:16). Covenantal love provides the foundational commitment upon which a biblical view of marriage is to be based. When children are born into a family, covenantal love is the commitment required by the parents and other family members.

Grace: To Forgive and Be Forgiven

By its very nature, covenant is grace. From a human perspective, the unconditional love of God makes no sense except as an offer or covenant of grace. *Grace,* which is a relational word, can be understood in its biblical context in terms of God calling us into a gracious relationship of unmerited favor.

Family life was designed by God to be lived out in an atmosphere of grace and not law. Family life based on a contract leads to an atmosphere of law; family life based on covenant leads to an atmosphere of grace and forgiveness. A family grounded in legalism is a discredit to Christianity since our faith is based on grace. At both the individual and the family levels, law leads to legalism while grace provides freedom from legalism and a motive to act responsibly. Moreover, grace provides the security and structure within which family relationships may be nurtured.

Empowering: To Serve and Be Served

Out of an atmosphere of grace can come empowering—this being the action needed for mature family relationships. In an atmosphere of law, power is often used in a negative way to influence or control others. We believe, however, that the biblical mode for the proper use of power is empowering or the quality of upbuilding and developing another's God-given potential. Empowering is not merely yielding to the wishes of another person or giving up one's own power. Rather, it is the active, intentional process of developing power within others. Thus, the person who gains power does so because of the empowering behavior of the other.

Jesus' central message was that he came to empower: "I came that they may have life, and have it abundantly" (John 10:10). The apostle John put it this way, "But to all who received him, who believed in his name, he gave power to become children of God; who were born, not of blood nor of the will of the flesh nor of the will of man, but of God" (John 1:12–13). From passages such as these, it is clear that power is given by God apart from either physical or conventional means.

Jesus' teaching about power was so central to his mission that its use became to him the basis for all human relationships. Therefore, in response to the request of his disciples James and John that they be permitted to sit on his right hand and left hand in glory, Jesus replied, "Whoever would to be great among you must be your servant, and whoever would be first among you must be slave of all. For the Son of man also came not to be served but to serve, and to give his life as a ransom for many" (Mark 10:43–45). Jesus redefined the understanding of power by his teaching and life; according to the Master, power is not to be used to control others but to serve, to lift up the fallen, to forgive, to encourage responsibility and maturity, and to give power to the powerless.

Jesus' relationship with his disciples demonstrates the empowering theme. When preparing his disciples for his leaving, Jesus replied to their question, "Lord, will you at this time restore the kingdom to Israel?" (Acts 1:6) by saying to them, "You shall receive power when the Holy Spirit has come upon you" (Acts 1:8). As a consequence of this Pentecost empowering, the first

Christians formed a tightly knit community. Thus, Acts 2:44–45 states, "All the believers were together and had everything in common. Selling their possessions and goods, they gave to anyone as they had need" NIV). The result of these disciples taking Jesus seriously was to give up those very resources upon which conventional power is usually based. In Jesus, we see power defined as strength for serving, something that all family members should seek to embody with regard to one another.

Intimacy: To Know and Be Known

Human beings are unique among living creatures in our ability to communicate elaborately with one another through language, a capacity that makes it possible for us to *intimately know* one another. This is supremely modeled by God's relationship with the children of Israel. Our God is distinct from the "gods" of Eastern religions insofar as God wants to be *personally* related to us. Indeed, one of the major themes stretching throughout the entire Bible is that God wants to know us and wants to be known. We are encouraged in Scripture to share our deepest thoughts and feelings through prayer. We are told that the Holy Spirit dwells within us and, knowing our innermost thoughts, "groans" on our behalf (Romans 8:26–27 NIV).

While in their perfect state, Adam and Eve stood before God vulnerable, transparent, and without guilt and fear. It was only after they had sinned that they tried to hide from God out of a feeling of nakedness and shame. Likewise, prior to the Fall these two individuals stood naked before each other without shame (Genesis 2:25). Intimacy was possible when they were free to be themselves before each other and had no need to play deceptive games.

Shame is a product of feeling that one should hide oneself. When shame is present, family members put on masks and begin to play deceptive roles before one another as if they were an audience rather than fellow human beings. However, when the Book of Genesis describes the nature of human relationships prior to the Fall, the emphasis is on intimacy—on knowing and being known.

In a family based on covenant, there can be an atmosphere of grace in which family members engage in mutual empowering, which in turn fosters true intimacy. It is a way of knowing, understanding, caring, and serving one another. This is a biblical model of family relationships we will use in exploring family issues in contemporary society.

HOW MODERN SHOULD THE FAMILY BE?

Our strategy for dealing with family issues in contemporary society will be to consider three generalized family styles. The first, the *traditional-patriarchal* type, represents the style of family life as it has existed in the past. The second, the *modern-open* type, presents the family according to the current secular humanistic perspective. And the third, the *biblical-ideal* type, embodies the themes of covenant, grace, empowering, and intimacy.

We realize that claiming knowledge of the "biblical ideal" for anything inevitably results in being charged with encouraging cultural encapsulation. Nevertheless, we believe that although God desires certain characteristics—such as unconditional love— to be found in all family systems in all societies, there can be a variety of culturally alternative ways in which God's purpose for family life may be carried out (e.g., nuclear versus extended family systems). Our task is to suggest a model of what a biblical-ideal type of family might be, given the nature of contemporary society.

Family life is an integral part of a wider social and cultural structure. Thus, any attempt to construct a model of the biblical-ideal family, which supposedly transcends cultural and temporal boundaries, is difficult. Therefore, our discussion of *family commitment* will be based on the biblical theme of *covenant*, our consideration of *family roles and adaptability* will center on the theme of *grace*, our consideration of *family authority* will be grounded on the biblical view of *empowering*, and our discussion of *family communication* will focus on the theme of *intimacy*.

Table 1 summarizes what we believe are the major characteristics of the traditional-patriarchal, the biblical-ideal, and the modern-open types of families. These three systems are compared in terms of the four broad categories of family commitment, family roles and adaptability, family authority, and family communication.

Family Commitment

Under the traditional-patriarchal family system, divorce was rare because built within the system was a commitment to marriage as an institution. Most of our grandparents and great-grandparents stayed married because it was unthinkable to violate the strongly held belief that divorce was morally wrong. At that time, it was also true that there were fewer alternatives for people who were divorced. The economic pressures of raising a large family and little work opportunity for women contributed to the stability of this system.

Largely as a result of the countercultural movement of the 1960s, this view came to be regarded as an invalid reason to

TABLE 1. TYPES OF FAMILY RELATIONSHIPS

Traditional—Patriarchal	*Biblical—Ideal*	*Modern—Open*
FAMILY COMMITMENT		
To the family as an institution	Covenant between family members	Contract for Self-fulfillment
Dutiful sex (male pleasure)	Affectionate sex (mutual pleasure)	Self-centered sex (personal pleasure)
External coercion	Internal cohesion	Disengaged
Bondage	Bonded	Unbonded
FAMILY ROLES AND ADAPTABILITY		
Law	Grace	Anarchy
Role segregation	Role differentiation (interchangeable)	Undifferentiated roles
Mothering	Coparenting	Minimum parenting
Rigid/stilted	Adaptable/flexible	Chaotic
Predetermined	Creative and Regenerative	Undetermined
FAMILY AUTHORITY		
Ascribed power Possessive power	Empowering	
Authoritarian	Suffering servant	No authority
Male headship, wife submissive	Headship, mutual submissiveness	Neither submissive
Male centered	Person and relationship centered	Self-centered
Authoritarian parenting	Authoritative parenting	Permissive and neglectful parenting
FAMILY COMMUNICATION		
Distant	Intimacy	Pseudoinstant intimacy
Pronouncement	Discussion	Declaration
Legislate	Negotiate	Stalemate
Nonassertive (withdrawal)	Assertive	Aggressive

remain in a marriage. It was argued that too many people were more committed to institutional norms than to self-fulfillment. As this intense focus on the self continued throughout the 1970s—in the form of such a phenomenon as the encounter-group movement—an attitude of narcissism became firmly implanted within American culture. It became more important to seek personal happiness and new growth experiences than to nurture marital and family relationships.

In the early 1970s, a dramatic rise in the divorce rate began to occur, and it continued for nearly ten years. Social scientists now believe that one of the major reasons for this was that persons who were unhappy in their marriages increasingly turned to divorce as a means of escape. They believed they had a choice and a right to happiness, and this value took precedence over a commitment to the sanctity of marriage as an institution.

These values of self-fulfillment and individual happiness constitute the core commitment in the modern-open form of marriage. Indeed, a main criterion that sociologists of the family now use to measure marital success is marital happiness. In the biblical-ideal marriage, however, both individuals are as committed to nurturing each other as they are to maximizing their own happiness and potential. In family relationships there is a mutuality of commitment which expresses itself in cohesion and bondedness between family members.

Still another difference among the three family types concerns the issue of sexuality. In the traditional-patriarchal marriage, sex is viewed as a right to pleasure for the male and as a duty to be endured by the female. In the modern-open marriage, the emphasis is placed on each partner's right to personal pleasure. Thus, there has been a literal deluge of sex manuals focusing on bodily techniques that purportedly can bring the greatest sexual pleasure. We would argue that while sexual fulfillment between marriage partners is certainly very important, the fuller meaning of sexuality is lost when such fulfillment becomes the sole focus of attention.

The biblical-ideal type, however, emphasizes affectionate sex or the expression of affection. From this perspective, the relationship is the focus, and mutual pleasure is derived for mutual benefit (1 Corinthians 7:3–5). The decision made by both persons is to give and receive love from each other.

Any covenantal relationship is based on an unconditional commitment. God's ideal for family relationships is a *mature covenant*—*a bilateral, unconditional commitment*. However, relationships may be either unilateral or bilateral. For example, the birth of a child necessarily begins as an *initial covenant (a unilateral, unconditional commitment)* since the infant is unable to make a commitment or reciprocate the covenantal commitment at this stage. Reciprocity occurs as children and parents develop socially, emotionally, spiritually, and physically throughout the life span, contributing to one another in a bilateral commitment of love and action. Later, as parents grow older and may become more dependent on their adult children, this unconditional commitment has come full cycle. The bilateral covenant commitment provides a sense of security and assurance that stabilizes relationships. Whereas at every age reciprocity is possible since even the smallest child is able to contribute to and elicit an emotional response in the adult, it is the more mature, bilateral reciprocity that leads to the intended level of covenant commitment.

Put very simply, God's ideal for parent-child relationships is for initial unilateral covenants to develop into mature, bilateral relationships. Although young children are dependent on their parents for many things, as teen-agers they gain independence and the accompanying responsibilities of that stage. A part of maturity is not only gaining independence and freedom but also assuming responsibility in family relationships. Relational maturity depends on personal maturity, and it is a rewarding time of life when both parents and adult children become supportive friends and establish such natural commitments.

Family Roles and Adaptability

Shakespeare wrote that all the world is a stage and each of us has his or her exits and entrances. This is no less true of the family, which is the "stage" where much of private life is played out. The key question we are dealing with here is the amount of rigidity or flexibility that family members should have in acting out their respective roles.

The primary characteristic of family life based on covenant is that of *grace* . Family life based on contract leads to law. However, such life was designed by God to be lived out in an atmosphere of grace. Just as the meaning and joy of being a Christian are largely nullified if we perceive of our relationship with God primarily in terms of law instead of grace, so is it true of the family. At both the individual and the family levels, legalism is opposed to grace. Grace fosters freedom and the ability to forego personal rights for the sake of the family's good and growth.

In the traditional-patriarchal family, marital roles are segregated. Thus, the husband usually assumes the role working outside the home, and the wife is the homemaker and caretaker of the children. However, most persons who argue for this separation in marital roles are not aware that this phenomenon is actually a quite recent occurrence. Until the time of the industrial revolution, 90 percent of all American families lived on farms. All family members worked together to accomplish the tasks that needed to be done. Both mother and father, and even a grandparent or two, took responsibility for parenting the children. It was more a cooperative effort rather than a duty assumed by the mother only.

Marital role segregation largely originated with the emergence of the urban family. Therefore, it became quite common for the male to work outside the home and very uncommon for the female to do so. It can thus be seen that on the basis of both social history and biblical evidence, it is difficult to argue that a woman's "natural" place is in the home while a man's place is outside the home.

Largely as a reaction to this type of role segregation in the traditional-patriarchal system, the modern-open marriage has come to be characterized by anarchy and undifferentiated roles. That is to say, there are no clearly agreed-upon arrangements designating which family member or spouse will perform a given role or responsibility. What often happens is that no one takes responsibility! Not only is there no arrangement for designating who does what in the home, but everyone has individual interests at heart and does not want to be bothered by others. For example, simple chores like taking out the garbage, doing dishes, or mowing the lawn are not routinely handled. Although everyone experiences the disorganization, no one takes the responsibility.

Social exchange theory can help us here in understanding how things are accomplished in a modern-open marriage. This theory suggests that persons try to get at least as much as they give in relationships. It's a "tit for tat" or "this for that" arrangement. Let's imagine that a couple is trying to decide who will cook the evening dinner. The conversation may begin with the husband suggesting that his wife cook because he has had a hard day at the office and also because he cooked last night. The wife may respond that she has had an equally hard day at work and that she has cooked three of the last four evening meals. The husband may then suggest that he will cook if she will clean up, wash the dishes, and take out the garbage. (At this point, you may be thinking that this couple should eat out or else they are headed for a stalemate!) Needless to say, unless family members possess good bargaining and negotiating skills, lack of role differentiation may be disastrous to family relationships.

Roles in a biblical-ideal family will be differentiated, but not segregated. In other words, in role segregation, certain tasks are designated for females and others for males, with very little overlap occurring. But role differentiation involves the exchanging of duties among family members depending on the given situation. With respect to their particular interests, skills, and time available, members choose how to divide their family responsibilities instead of being bound to a rigid societal model developed in the past. For example, the wife may find that it is more convenient for her to take the car in to get the tires rotated, whereas the husband can be home earlier and cook the evening meal.

In the traditional-patriarchal family that has emerged in our urban and technologically oriented society, most parenting has been done by mothers. The typical father commutes to work and is not present physically or emotionally with his family. The mother is expected to take the primary responsibility of caring for and nurturing the children. As a result, mothers are often as over-involved with the children as fathers are underinvolved. Because the weakest aspect of parenting today centers on the role of fathering, there is a great need for the church to address the importance of coparenting.

In modern-open families, proper parenting is often neglected due to the inordinate stress placed on maximizing one's personal happiness and self-fulfillment. While the contemporary day-care movement partially reflects a response to the unique needs of working parents—especially single parents—still another reason for the growth of these facilities is the desire of some modern parents to avoid the difficult role of parenting.

A biblical-ideal family stresses the necessity of both mother and father being actively involved in the parenting process. Moreover, if such parenting is to be based on the model presented in Scripture, fathering would certainly appear to be as important as mothering. In fact, a recent accumulation of research demonstrates the significant impact that strong father bonding has on family relationships.

In the traditional-patriarchal family, roles are often rigidly defined. However, in the modern-open family, role expectations are undetermined and so loosely defined that family life can become chaotic. Where family life is lived out in a spirit of grace, roles will be structured yet flexible and adaptable.

The family dinner hour illustrates these different family types. In the rigid family, every supper is routinely served at exactly 6:00 P.M. with little or no tolerance for tardiness or variation. The chaotic family, at the other extreme, has no specified time for the supper hour or any plan for who is in charge of cooking the meal. Family members are left to fend for themselves, hoping that someone has taken the responsibility to buy groceries for the week. The biblical-ideal family will be characterized by a structured, yet flexible, style that can serve the unique needs of all family members. In regard to the example of dinner hour, parents will set clear guidelines, but will be willing to be flexible about the time for supper. Such grace, which is regenerative, permits family roles to be creatively lived out without simultaneously denying individual differences and needs.

Family Authority

One of the strongest criticisms being leveled against the contemporary family concerns the subject of a "crisis in authority." Many societal problems (such as discipline in public schools, crime, and divorce) may be traced to a crisis in familial authority— the essence of such authority is the phenomenon of power.

Power is the ability to influence someone else, and this use of power most dramatically distinguishes the traditional-patriarchal from the modern-open family. In the patriarchal family, power is given to a person—based not on individual qualities, but on status. Thus, power is reserved for the husband-father because it is believed the man should have ultimate power in the family. It is therefore wrong for a wife to exercise power independently of her husband, because doing so is perceived as reducing his power.

One contemporary defense of the traditional-patriarchal type of family often put forth by Christians is that family members are, by nature, in a chain of command whereby power passes from God to the father, who has authority over the mother. Together, they exercise power over their children.

In contrast, power in the secular humanistic-based, modern-open family is something to be achieved via personal resources. Thus, the more resources a family member has that are valued by other family members, the greater that person's power. In a modern-open marriage, for example, power is based on each spouse's ability to provide such things as a good income and nurturance.

Although the sources of power differ in the traditional-patriarchal and modern-open types of families, the concept of power as a *commodity in limited supply* is similar. Neither of these views is consistent with a biblical view of power, which is that authority is designed for the *purpose of serving others*. In the biblical-ideal family, power will be used to empower rather than control family members. Empowering is the active and intentional process of developing power within another person.

Empowering others in no way diminishes one's own power; rather, it breaks free from the notion of a limited supply or finite quantity view of power. For example, when children have a sense that they are valued and disciplined consistently and fairly by parents, they begin to be empowered to take responsibility and contribute in cooperative and productive ways. While parents definitely remain in the *position* of power, all members benefit and feel powerful in the process. When parents demand obedience, they may feel powerful. When parents fail to give guidelines, children may feel powerful. But in both situations, power is actually diminished to a commodity in which everyone loses personal power. Both parents and children can feel powerful and simultaneously children will come to *want* to do what is responsible and helpful.

Although the question of who should possess power within a marriage is currently a controversial issue among Christians, it need not be. Traditionally, both Christians and non-Christians have adhered to the idea that the husband is the authority. In fact, until just a few years ago, it would have been difficult to locate a Christian article or sermon exhorting husbands to love, serve, and submit to their wives as seen in the example of Christ. Instead, authority in marriage was interpreted as the husband's right to rule over his wife.

The scriptural passage that most directly addresses the question of authority in marriage is the fifth chapter of Ephesians. Many, in fact, cite Ephesians 5:22–23 as the origin of Paul's teaching on marital authority. It is here stated, "Wives, be subject to your husbands, as to the Lord. For the husband is the head of the wife, as Christ is the head of the church." A consistent exegesis of this passage, however, requires that these verses be interpreted in light of the previous verse (Ephesians 5:21), which says, "Be subject to one another out of reverence for Christ." And in verse 25, husbands are told to "love your wives, as Christ loved the church and gave himself up for her." Thus, just as Christ served his church, so must a husband serve his wife. It is quite evident that the male authoritarian model of marriage finds little support here. In Christ's example we see a compassionate servant who gave his life for his bride, the church.

Partly as a reaction to the excesses in the traditional-patriarchal marriage and partly as a result of hyperindividualism within modern society, there has been a reaction against virtually any notion of authority or hierarchy in marriage. Therefore, modern-open marriages stress democracy, freedom, and the right to self-fulfillment.

Authority or decision-making power will go to the one with the most resources, which are likely to be such things as money, sex, nurturance, protection, and security. Accordingly, research has brought forword some evidence to suggest that wives who work outside their homes have greater power in their marriage relationships than wives who do not. Since the money that is earned can be converted to power, this strengthens the authority of these women. In a biblical-ideal marriage, husbands and wives will seek to empower one another rather than to accumulate resources that can be used to control the other. Each partner will want the other to reach full potential and full power. The specific gifts, talents, and characteristics that God has given each family member will be honored and valued. Each will encourage the others to become proficient and competent rather than dependent.

Much of the present-day fury pertaining to the issue of

familial authority centers around the parent-child relationship. In the past, there was little doubt about who was in control of the home since parenting within the traditional-patriarchal family was clearly *authoritarian*. The saying that "children are to be seen and not heard" was not too far from reality, especially when it came to questions of authority. In contrast, the parenting style of the modern-open family is much more *permissive*. Parents allow their children to make more of their own decisions at increasingly younger ages. In addition, they often fail to assist, support, and model decision making for their offspring.

Social science research demonstrates that the most effective parenting style combines the two qualities of social *support* and social *control* (Maccoby, 1980; Rollins and Thomas, 1979). This combination corresponds quite closely to the biblical parenting model; God exhibits both discipline (high control) and love (high emotional support) toward his children (Chartier, 1978). This parenting style is properly termed *authoritative*. The empowering of children can occur most effectively within just such a context of authoritative parenting.

Just as God provided specific guidelines for the children of Israel, he also gave them freedom to respond. God's covenant love supported them through difficult times, which were often generated by their own mistakes and rejection of God's way. As an applied example, when parents seek to empower their teen-agers to drive a car, they offer controls in the form of guidelines, instruction, and good modeling. The support comes when they show confidence in their teen-ager's ability to make good judgments, and in reaffirming such confidence when inevitable mistakes are made. Rather than viewing beginning mistakes as total failures in competence, empowering parents offer a supportive and caring attitude that will encourage a child to succeed in doing better. Parental empowering consists of a building up, rather than a tearing down, in response to a child's mistakes and shortcomings.

At the community level, Christians are called to live according to exceptionally high social expectations. Though we are sinners, we are nevertheless empowered by God to live an extraordinary family life by following Christ's example. As we seek to understand what a biblical ideal is in family life, we must be realistic with regard to our own sinfulness and brokenness. Yet we should be optimistic because God's grace and power enable us to live according to the intended purposes of the Creator.

Family Communication

Verbal communication is often quite limited in the traditional-patriarchal family. In this setting, communication may be accomplished through a series of pronouncements made by the patriarch. The husband-father tends to legislate and often talks "at" his family members rather than "with" them. In addition, he may make decisions without consulting his wife, such as bringing guests home for dinner unannounced. Conflicts and delicate issues are often sidestepped at the husband's prerogative. He assumes that his wife is there to serve him and does not take time to consider her feelings. She does not mention her disappointments, and as a result, unspoken resentments are often held. Within this system, marriage is primarily an institutional arrangement designed to provide individuals with a certain amount of financial security and social status. It is not necessarily expected that the socioemotional and companionship needs of individuals will be met within the marital relationship.

Alternatively, communication in the modern-open marriage can be characterized as a series of freely expressed declarations and demands that each family member makes toward the others. The wife may declare that she intends for them to spend their upcoming vacation at the beach. The husband states that he is looking forward to going to the mountains. She lets him know in no uncertain terms that he'll be spending it there alone. The kids interject that they want to go to Disneyland. The independence tends to discourage mutually agreed-upon decisions because individual freedom and self-fulfillment are more highly valued than are joint decisions or the family relationships. Confrontation, which is avoided in the traditional-patriarchal family, is rarely stifled in the modern-open family. Although such openness may be refreshing when compared with the lack of communication in the traditional-patriarchal pattern, the combative posture that is often adopted can prevent each family member from sensitively caring for the needs of the others. It may also promote an atmosphere of aggressiveness or even hostility. The result is that no one's needs and concerns are met in a satisfactory manner, and demands and counterdemands lead ultimately to a stalemate.

In the biblical-ideal family, members will communicate and express themselves in a caring and concerned manner toward one another. Thus, when one talks, the others will listen attentively, and differences will be dealt with by placing the other's needs and desires before one's own. In the vacation scenario, all family members will express their desires, but will also listen to the expressed desires of the others. They will work together to find a mutually satisfying solution as they desire to understand the other's needs, and they are willing to consider alternative plans. They may choose a place where various needs can be satisfied or satisfy needs on alternative years.

The most important communication ingredient is listening and making choices beneficial to the relationships. The adoption of this servant attitude enables one to be submissive and loving. This in turn fosters joyous and fulfilling familial relationships. To develop interdependence in relationships, it is sometimes necessary to give up some of one's own needs and desires. When family members have this kind of attitude and perspective, there can be a common ground for communication, and the relationships benefit.

The capacity for family members to freely communicate their feelings with one another is contingent upon not being afraid of one another. John gives us an important insight at this point when he says, "God is love. . . .There is no fear in love, but perfect love casts out fear" (1 John 4:16, 18). God expresses unconditional love because he is perfect. Such unconditional love allows family members to freely communicate with each other without fearing rejection. When parents initiate and communicate unconditional love to their children, the children will be confident and free to reciprocate this love toward others.

In the person of Jesus, we have a model of the type of communicative intimacy that family members should strive to develop. During his last days on earth, Jesus questioned Peter three separate times, "Do you love me?" Why three times? It may be more than coincidental that Peter had denied Jesus three times. Perhaps Jesus was giving his disciple the opportunity to assert what he had previously denied. Peter certainly had a need to express his loyalty after it had been denied through his actions, therefore restoring his relationship with Jesus. So, too, family relationships become strained as we disappoint, fail, and even betray those whom we love the most. However, God desires that we verbally communicate our feelings of love, forgiveness, and affection toward one another and therefore fulfill the intended covenant nature of family relationships.

How modern should the family be? No more than it was meant to be in the Garden of Eden. By examining biblical themes that have a bearing on the nature of family relationships, we have concluded that

— Family commitment is to be based on the concept of covenant, and marriage is to be grounded in a mature covenant—an unconditional, bilateral commitment. Moreover, although parents' devotion to their children begins as unilateral commitment, God intends for it to mature into an unconditional, bilateral commitment.

— The establishment and maintenance of family roles are to be done in an atmosphere of grace.

— Regardless of who holds power in the family, or how such power was obtained, family authority must be used to empower and not coerce.

— Intimacy is the goal of family communication. Based on

covenant commitment and fostered in an atmosphere of grace, family members will share intimacy as they mutually empower one another.

DO WE WORSHIP THE FAMILY?

Few Christians would disagree with the assertion that the contemporary family is in trouble. In the above section, we discussed certain solutions to this problem—some of which we hold to be untenable. Many Christians today envision the family in terms of an idealized image from the past. This false hope is based on at least two fallacies: (1) that the golden age of family life is best represented by the nineteenth-century patriarchal family and (2) that the traditionally dominant patriarchal families represent the biblical ideal for contemporary society. This approach generally ignores the complexity of the pertinent issues involved in family life today.

A second false hope, the modern-open marriage, is adaptive or progress oriented. In addition, it is often based on naturalistic and relativistic assumptions about the family. In attempting to avoid the pitfall of idealizing a particular cultural or temporal form of the family, proponents of this approach fail to recognize any normative familial structures or functions.

Our suggestions as to what the biblical-ideal family should embody could prove to be equally sterile if we ignore certain sociostructural changes that are currently needed with respect to the family. Certainly one such change centers on the nuclear family, which is an isolated, self-contained unit that is thought to be able to meet all of the social and emotional needs of its members. This has been expressed by the authors of *Habits of the Heart* (Bellah et al., 1985:111-12). What would probably perplex and disturb Tocqueville (whose writings were the subject of *Habits of the Heart*) is that the family is no longer an integral part of a larger moral ecology—tying the individual to community, church, and nation. The family is the core of the private sphere. Its aim is not to link individuals to the public world, but to avoid it as much as possible.

The family, as a self-contained unit, is an unrealistic ideal doomed to fail in modern society. Setting up this form of family as the idol to be worshiped is inconsistent with the biblical injunction that the family ought to be inclusive and not exclusive.

While we do believe that the emphasis in Genesis on *leaving* father and mother and *cleaving* to one's spouse establishes marriage as the basis of family life, we question the notion that God intended the family to be an isolated unit. The typical family in the United States is a partial community at best. On one side, it is affected by the demands and intrusion of mass society; on the other, it has become increasingly narcissistic—reflecting the American emphasis on hyperindividualism. The isolated family has become increasingly unable to adequately provide for the nurturance, care, and identity of its members. The result has been the rapid growth of such extra-familial social structures as day-care centers for children, retirement centers for the elderly, and institutions designed to care for the handicapped.

What we need most is to recapture a biblical understanding of family life. The family needs to be a *koinonia* community characterized by covenant love, an atmosphere of grace, and relationships that are empowering and intimate.

In addition, the family must become inclusive instead of remaining exclusive because the Bible forbids family members from becoming content with any form of amoral familialism. This refers to a social ethic that recognizes social obligations to family members, but none to the poor and needy of the world. Much in the teaching of Jesus suggests that one's loyalty is too limited if it resides only in the nuclear family. Accordingly, Jesus described discipleship in terms of "leaving," "dividing," "disuniting," and even "hating" the family or family members (Luke 12:52–53). Coupled with the fact that Jesus chose to remain single, one might plausibly argue that he undermined the ideology of familialism. Taken as a whole, though, the Master's teaching endorses strong family life.

Contemporary Christians need to realize that loyalties must extend beyond the family to the larger Christian community and to the larger secular populace. Jesus made this point evident in his reply, "Who is my mother? Who are my brothers?" As he looked around at those who were sitting in the circle about him, Jesus said, "Here are my mother and my brothers! Whoever does God's will is my brother and my sister and my mother" (Mark 3:33–35 NIV). The common membership we have in the body of Christ binds all believers to one another as a family of God. This Christian community is drawn together in a covenant love and a commitment to minister to the hurting world.

THE MEANING AND HOPE OF FAMILY LIFE

Hope for sound family life is to be found in recapturing the biblical meaning of the family. We believe that such meaning is bound up in the relational experience made possible by covenant love. We also believe that hope for all human life in the larger society is to be found in covenant love. In this regard, it has been suggested that the family is the cornerstone for the moral order of society. Therefore, if we are currently experiencing a crisis in the moral order of society, it may well be at least partially because of the crisis presently occurring with respect to family life.

Our society desperately needs to recapture the biblical meaning of family that entails the practice of covenant love and the manifestation of that love through grace, empowering, and intimacy. Although God intends for covenant love to be supremely experienced and exemplified in the context of the family, God also intends for it to be the basis for moral authority in the church and secular society. However, persons who are deprived of the nurturing found in covenant love have often not experienced the bondedness that enables them to love others.

The lack of hope and moral authority in contemporary American society is a mere reflection of the lack of moral bondedness on the individual level. In this regard, the psychiatrist Eric Fromm has defined socialization as getting a child to want to do what it has to do. Sociologically, moral authority is considered effective to the extent that a society operates on an internal rather than an external means of social control. However, our society has, of necessity, come to depend increasingly on punitive and coercive means of social control. Bellah et al., (1985:111) have correctly observed that "the family is no longer an integral part of a larger moral ecology which ties the individual to community, church, and nation." The truth of this statement is to be seen in the declining effectiveness of our society's moral authority; social relationships are governed more by contract than covenant, law than grace, coercion than empowering, and alienation than intimacy.

It is hardly an overstatement to argue that the hope of society must begin with a recapturing of the meaning of family life. Covenant love, which is the biblical basis of family life, is necessary for the proper ordering of a society because it encourages the committing of sacrificial acts for the sake of others. Jesus taught that we must be prepared to extend this covenant love to socially different persons, who just might be placed in positions in which we are called to be their neighbor (Luke 10:25–37).

A poignant incident in the life of our Lord is recorded in John 19:26–27. According to this passage, "Jesus saw his mother, with the disciple whom he loved standing beside her. He said to her, 'Mother, there is your son,' and to the disciple, 'There is your mother'; and from that moment the disciple took her into his home" (NEB). The meaning and hope of family life is that our relationships are conducted in such a manner that Jesus would want to send his own mother to be a part of our families (Anderson, 1985:23).

REFERENCES IN CHAPTER

Anderson, Ray. 1985. "The Gospel of the Family." Fuller Theological Seminary. Unpublished paper.

Balswick, Jack, and Judy Balswick. 1987. "A Theological Basis For Family Relationships." *Journal of Psychology and Christianity* 5/3 (Summer): 37–49.

Bellah, Robert, Richard Madsen, William Sullivan, Ann Swidler, and Steven Tipton. 1985. *Habits of the Heart*. Berkeley and Los Angeles, Calif.: University of California Press.

Chartier, Myron. 1978. "Parenting: A Theological Model." *Journal of Psychology and Theology* 6:54–61.

Maccoby, Eleanor. 1980. *Social Development: Psychological Growth and The Parent-Child Relationship*. New York: Harcourt, Brace, Jovanovich.

Rollins, Boyd, and Darwin Thomas. 1979. "Parental Support, Power, and Control Techniques in the Socialization of Children." *Contemporary Theories About The Family*, vol.1, edited by Wesley Burr, Reuben Hill, F. Ivan Nye, and Ira Reiss. New York: Free Press.

IS FAITH A SOCIAL CONSTRUCTION?

Michael R. Leming

As I enter church this bright and beautiful Spring morning, I am greeted by the sounds of the choir singing "Oh Lord, our Lord, how majestic is Your name in all the earth." At the conclusion of this song, the worship leader opens the service by speaking these words: "When two or more of you gather in my name, I am with you." In the invocation for the service, my pastor prays these words:

> Thank you, God, for these people who have come to worship you. May our worship unite us in this hour, and as a result of being here, may we sense our membership in your church—the body of Christ. Furthermore, may we realize that in being members of Your body we are to be a servant church—ministering to the needs of a world that needs your touch. For we pray these words in the name of Jesus, who is our example, leader, and guide. Amen.

For me spiritually, everything is just right! I feel the presence of God, and I feel a sense of unity with my family and the persons (some of whom are my closest friends) who are sitting all around me. I know intellectually *and* emotionally that God is in his heaven, that he cares about me personally, and that all will be right with the world.

As I pause to reflect on my feelings, some other words come to me from my readings of the past week: "The worship of God is the disguised worship of society. For God is the projection of the group's norms, values, and goals." They are from Emile Durkheim, a French sociologist, who was interested in the role of religion in creating societal cohesiveness. But wait, what does Durkheim know of my Christian faith? His parents were Jewish, and some of the members of his extended family were rabbis. He was expected to become a rabbi until he became an agnostic (Parsons, 1968:311). As an outsider and a "value-free" sociologist, he could not possibly understand the complex mysteries of my faith and religious experience. If Durkheim were a visitor in my church, he would gain a new and more enlightened view of religion. But would he? How might Emile Durkheim interpret the worship service of which I was a participant? Would he discover the transcendent God of the Bible, or would he discover a transcendent group or society that had been projected into inherent meanings of the universe?

If you observed this service from Durkheim's perspective, you might feel that the empirical evidence you gathered from your visit to Emmaus Baptist Church provides support for your contention that the worship of God is the disguised worship of the group. Furthermore, the activity of worshiping creates a sense of group cohesiveness among the participants. As I look around my church, I encounter more sociological data that explains the intensity of the fellowship found in this social group. All of the participants come from rather homogeneous neighborhoods. They have similar educational and social class backgrounds. In their Sunday school programs, they divide into age-stratified groups and rarely discuss issues that would divide them or destroy their feeling of group consensus.

The sociological perspective on religion is unsettling. Is there other empirical evidence available to support Durkheim's claim? I look around my church with a "different set of eyes" and observe the following facts:

— There is an American flag in the church sanctuary.
— In the hymnal I find the following songs: "America," "America the Beautiful," and "The Battle Hymn of the Republic."
— In the morning prayer the pastor prays for the president and the members of Congress.
— The church is used as a polling place for federal, state, and local elections.

All of this evidence raises doubts in my mind regarding my taken-for-granted understanding of religion. What is religion? What is its function in and for society? Is what I understand to be God's activity merely a part of the natural process? Is there a difference between faith and religion? Is it possible to be a committed Christian and a serious student of sociology? In this chapter we will explore these questions.

WHAT IS RELIGION?

Sociologists employ two strategies in defining religion. One type of definition—*substantive definition*—tries to establish what religion *is*. These types of definitions attempt to distinguish religious activities from nonreligious behaviors by providing necessary criteria for inclusion as religious phenomena. The substantive definition used most frequently by sociologists of religion is the one formulated by Emile Durkheim in his *Elementary Forms of Religious Life* first published in 1915: "A religion is a unified system of beliefs and practices relative to sacred things, that is to say, things set apart and forbidden—beliefs and practices which unite into one single moral community called a Church, all those who adhere to them." In this definition, Durkheim designates four essential ingredients of religion—a system of beliefs, a set of religious practices or rituals, the sacred or supernatural as the object of worship, and a community or social base. Most substantive definitions of religion employed by contemporary sociologists will incorporate these four key elements. However, some sociologists have argued that to be inclusive of phenomena most people consider religious, it might be proper to exclude the necessity of having a sacred point of reference. Buddhism, for example, does not have a supernatural being to which beliefs and rituals are oriented.

The second strategy by which sociologists define religion is the *functional definition*. Functional definitions define religion in terms of what religion does for the individual and society. This definitional strategy focuses on the consequences of religion rather than on the content of religious belief and practice (McGuire, 1987:8).

Attempting to provide a functional definition of religion, Thomas O'Dea (1983:14–15) designates the following six tasks as the primary functions of religion:

1. Aids the individual in providing support, consolation, and reconciliation.

2. Provides a transcendental relationship with the sacred.

3. Makes sacred the norms and values of established society.

4. Calls society's norms and values into question.

5. Provides a sense of individual identity and helps with the self-concept formation.

6. Aids in the growth and maturation of the individual and his passage through the various age gradings.

O'Dea (1983:16) brings together these basic functions of religion for society and the individual with the following definition:

Religion identifies the individual with his group, supports him
in uncertainty, consoles him in disappointment, attaches him to
society's goals, enhances his morale, and provides him with
elements of identity. It acts to reinforce the unity and stability of
society by supporting social control enhancing established
values and goals, and providing the means for overcoming guilt
and alienation. It may also perform a prophetic role and prove
itself an unsettling or even subversive influence in any particular society. The contributions of religion to society may be either
positive or negative—religion may support society's continued
existence, or religion may play a part in undermining society.

The substantive and functional definitions of religion give us
a sociological understanding of religion and its role in contemporary society. This may be somewhat less than satisfying for a
committed Christian because although it occasionally attempts to
take into account participants' point of view, the sociological
perspective is primarily concerned with an objective and external
analysis of religious phenomena. This more limited view of
religion is primarily concerned with *extrinsic issues*—what are the
consequences of a particular religion that can be empirically
measured, how can individuals benefit from religious experiences,
and how does religion promote societal maintenance? Such
questions tend not to be the concerns of individual believers who
are preoccupied with *intrinsic issues* related to ultimate truth and
personal meaning.

If it is possible for the value-committed individual to realize
that the sociological perspective is only one perspective contributing insight regarding religious phenomena, there are many
personal benefits to be gleaned from studying the church as a
social institution and religion as a social construction.

RELIGION AS A SOCIAL CONSTRUCTION

In my opinion, Peter Berger's *Sacred Canopy: Elements of a
Sociological Theory of Religion* (1969) is the most important sociological analysis of religion ever written. In his book Berger synthesizes
the theoretical writings of Emile Durkheim, Karl Marx, and Max
Weber—historically considered to be the most significant sociologists. Berger accomplishes this integration using a "sociology of
knowledge" perspective.

According to Clark and Gaede (1981:4), the sociology of
knowledge is "an effort to understand the interrelationships of
socially shared knowledge and the social conditions of existence in
which people produce and accept such knowledge." A sociological understanding of knowledge explores the content, social
context, and the method of transmission of a group's beliefs. This
perspective on knowledge does not account for, or take into

consideration, revelation—which is assumed to be true, regardless of how people define it.

Berger applies this perspective to religion, arguing that society is a human product. The material and nonmaterial aspects of culture are produced by human beings with the purpose of providing order for their existence. Furthermore, Berger contends that while society is nothing but a human product, it continuously acts back upon its producers. It is within the society, and as a result of social processes, that the individual becomes a person, that he or she attains and holds onto an identity and carries out the various projects that constitute his or her life.

Berger's statement reflects the essential dialectical character of social living—human beings are both the creators of society and the products of society. According to Berger (1969:3), this dialectical relationship consists of three processes: externalization, objectivation, and internalization. *Externalization* is the process whereby human beings construct their social world. This process includes the construction of symbols (meaning systems), values, beliefs, social structures, and all forms of social institutions. In the process of *objectivation* the socially constructed world takes on a self-generating reality of its own (*sui generis*)—independent of its creators.

A personal example might help to illustrate the externalization-objectivation process. When my wife and I were first married, we established norms, family traditions, and a division of household chores (externalization). Some of these behavioral patterns had been established in the families in which we had been raised, but others were of our own creation. Today, I find that we continue to act in accordance with this "family script" that we had "written" in 1970. Certainly we are free to change, but we both feel comfortable with this taken-for-granted social order.

According to Berger, *internalization* is the process of reappropriation by human beings of the reality that has been externalized and objectified. Internalization transforms the objective structure of the social world into the structure of the individual's subjective consciousness. Berger cites two examples of internalization: language and roles. Humans invent or create a language only to discover that their thoughts and speaking are dominated by its grammar. The roles we play also reflect the internalization process. When an individual performs the role of father, he also *becomes* a father, in terms of whatever "being a father" implies for the society in question. Berger (1969:13–14) summarizes the relationship between the objective social world and the subjective understanding of personal identity with the following words: "The individual's own biography is objectively real only insofar as it may be comprehended within the significant structures of the social world. . . .Society assigns to the individual not only a set of roles but a designated identity."

As we can see from this discussion of the "chicken-egg" relationship between human beings and the social order, the process of creating a social world is, above all, an ordering of experience for individuals and groups of individuals. Maintaining this ordered world requires social control, socialization of society's members, and social legitimation. These social processes explain to the members of society the "why" of the social order and enable them to locate their lives in a meaningful context.

However, the socially constructed order is always inherently precarious because it is a human product. As a consequence, the social order can be reduced to chaos by any of the following social processes: social change, social revolution, and cultural assimilation. On an individual level, people may experience anomie (lack of purpose or meaning) whenever their personal order is challenged by crisis events such as unemployment, disease, divorce, or death. For these reasons, individuals and societies need a protection against anomie and social chaos. Therefore, the social order takes on a sense of ultimacy causing the taken-for-granted meanings of society to be projected into the meanings of the universe. It is in this context that religion becomes the chief legitimator in society because it explains the "why" of the social world by placing it within an ultimate, sacred, and meaningful cosmos.

On the personal level, religion serves a basic function of protecting the individual from anomie—discovering that his or her life is meaningless. However, the price that the individual pays for escaping anomie is alienation—he or she must deny any role in creating and sustaining the "revealed" social order. Through alienation, the cosmos is viewed as being ultimately real rather than created by human beings. However in reality, although humans deny it, the relationship between human beings and society remains dialectic. Thus, from the perspective of the sociology of knowledge, religion is part of the sociocultural reality (created by humans) that serves to legitimate the social order by producing alienated believers.

SOCIAL GROUPS AS PLAUSIBILITY STRUCTURES

At this point we return to the importance of the group in maintaining the meaningful cosmos posited by religion. In the words of Berger (1969:45):

> Worlds are socially constructed and socially maintained. Their continuing reality, both objective and subjective, depends upon specific social processes, namely those processes that ongoingly

reconstruct and maintain the particular worlds in question. Conversely, the interruption of these social processes threatens the reality of the worlds in question. Thus each world requires a social "base" for its continuing existence as a world that is real to actual human beings. This "base" may be called its plausibility structure.

Consider the following verses from the Bible emphasizing the importance of the group as a plausibility structure:

> For where two or three are gathered in my name, there am I in the midst of them (Matthew 18:20).

> Let us hold fast the confession of our hope without wavering, for he who promised is faithful; and let us consider how to stir up one another to love and good works, not neglecting to meet together, as is the habit of some, but encouraging one another, and all the more as you see the Day drawing near (Hebrews 10:23–25).

The church is the plausibility structure of the Christian faith. Intellectually, we know that our faith does not depend on the people around us, but our experience convinces us of our need of other people who provide a plausibility structure for our faith. As a social institution, the church preaches the message of the Christian gospel, makes disciples of all nations, teaches the commandments of God, and proclaims the presence of God— Father, Son, and Holy Spirit (Matthew 28:19–20). The strength of our faith diminishes and our religious doubts increase as a result of not attending church and/or not meeting with our Christian friends.

Does this mean that our faith is only a figment of our collective imaginations? Again the thoughts of Durkheim come back to haunt us.

> God is the hypostatization of society, the group made into a personalized living entity. Religion is the sacralization of the traditions, embodying society's requirements for human behavior, upon which society ultimately rests. Society is greater than the individual; it gives him strength and support, and it is the source of the ideas and values which render his life meaningful. It makes him a social being. The worship of God is the disguised worship of society, the great entity upon which the individual depends. (Durkheim, cited by O'Dea, 1983:12)

It might be easy to come to Durkheim's conclusion if one were concerned only with functions that religion performs for society. The problem with Durkheim's argument is that he reduces religion to the empirical consequences, benefits, and/or outcomes of religious experience. Reductionism of this type gives us a distorted view of the totality of religious phenomena.

Let me provide an example that demonstrates my point. I love my wife, and I find in her a supportive friend, a primary confidante, and an intimate partner. In our marriage relationship, we created a division of labor where we each perform tasks within our home ensuring the maintenance of our family. As a result, we are keenly aware of our mutual dependence on each other. One might view this relationship from a functional perspective and say, "Leming, you don't love your wife! You are just using her to fulfill your needs. You think that your life is more meaningfully ordered and structured by your marriage. But, you are using love as a legitimation for your need to exploit your wife for personal gain. Your love is only the disguised projection of your own inadequacy and dependence on another person with similar needs."

Is this true? I think not! Functional arguments of this type attempt to explain things away by reducing complex phenomenon with "nothing but" statements. If the truth be known, I love my wife *and* I need her. In fact, my dependence on her may be caused by my love—and not the reverse. However, from the objective perspective of an observer (one who is not involved in the relationship), it is impossible to determine whether or not my love is authentic. Just because my relationship provides me with happiness and need fulfillment does not preclude its authenticity. The same is true of one's relationship with fellow believers in the context of worship. We need not reject the existence of God because our awareness of him is heightened when we come together for worship. In these types of issues (the authenticity of love and the existence of God) science cannot resolve our ontological questions. The empirical method is applicable only to phenomena that lend themselves to sensory investigation. Hence, sociologists of religion concern themselves with the consequences of religious behaviors and experiences and not the objects of worship. It is illegitimate to conclude that the empirical realities are the only components of religious phenomena.

THE SOCIOLOGY OF RELIGION
AND SOCIAL RELATIVISM

If we have protected ourselves from social reductionism— religion is only a social construction—we are still vulnerable to the problem of social relativism. Sociologists of religion who employ a sociology of knowledge approach would contend that knowledge always has a social context. Furthermore, as we have demonstrated, the truth of the knowledge is not as important as the consequence of knowing. Sociologists of religion would affirm the following conclusion of W. I. Thomas: "If something is defined as real, it will be real in its consequences." For example, if I believe that I love my wife and that she loves me, my behavior will be affected by this belief. If I believe that "in everything God works for good with those who love him, who are called according to his purpose" (Romans 8:28), then in my daily experience I will find evidence of God's touch on my life. From this perspective, the reality defined by the plausibility structure will be affirmed in the experiences of members of the group and in the group as a whole.

Since American society is so pluralistic with respect to values, and since there are so many religious plausibility structures competing for social legitimacy, how am I to know if my religion and values are worthy of my commitment? If I were raised by Hindu parents, would I not also be a Hindu and just as satisfied with my life? In America, we believe in value pluralism—everyone has the right to personal beliefs and values. However, if there is a certain inherent degree of validity to another's values (which may be contrary to one's own values), then everyone's value commitments are necessarily precarious.

This theme relates directly to Peter Berger's (1969:133) discussion of religion and the secularization of society:

> Religion is located in the private sphere of everyday social life and is marked by the very peculiar traits of this sphere in modern society. One of the essential traits is that of "individualization." This means that privatized religion is a matter of the "choice" or "preference" of the individual or of the nuclear family, *ipso facto* lacking in common, binding quality. Such private religiosity, however "real" it may be to the individual who adopts it, cannot any longer fulfill the classical task of religion, that of a common world within which all of social life receives ultimate meaning binding on everybody. Instead, this religiosity is limited to specific enclaves of social life that may be effectively segregated from the secularized sectors of modern society. The over-all effect of this process is that religion will only manifest itself as public rhetoric and private virtue.

I believe that Berger has done an excellent job in capturing the dilemma of the modern American individual who has made personal value commitments. He or she can privately live a life that reflects a strong commitment to a world view or to a set of personal values. These value commitments will most likely be supported by groups of individuals who share the world view (e.g., a spouse, a friendship network, or a local church). But given the larger society, which is extremely pluralistic with respect to values, he or she cannot assume a world view, or set of values, that has "an objective, taken-for-granted status."

In public discourse, Americans find it very difficult to discuss things at the core of their personal values. Furthermore, they are extremely suspicious of people who are able to openly speak of such personal commitments. In a 1987 Gallup poll, as reported by the *Minneapolis Star and Tribune* (March 8, 1987:13A), when a random sample of Americans were asked the question: "Which group of people would you *not* like to have as neighbors?" 44 percent listed members of religious sects or cults and 13 percent listed "religious fundamentalists."

What we find is that Americans are more comfortable in keeping their deeply held beliefs to themselves. When they do discuss these beliefs, it is typically only with individuals who share their commitments. Consequently, religion and politics are thought to be topics that polite people appropriately avoid in most social settings. This has led Berger (1969:151) to conclude that religious beliefs in American society have become "deobjectified"—deprived of their status of a taken-for-granted, objective reality. As a result, Berger (1969:152) would contend that value commitments have become "subjectivized" in a double sense: Their "reality" becomes a "private" affair of individuals—they cannot talk with others about it. And their "reality" is believed to be rooted in their personal consciousness and not in the objective realities of the external world—there is not an objective source of *truth* to which all Americans refer.

Yet, personal values are very salient in the daily lives of Americans—so important and personally relevant that they cannot talk about them. This is not unlike my Swedish father-in-law who loved his wife so much that he almost told her once. How are we to deal with this irony? Are we condemned to be silent regarding our faith and value commitments? Furthermore, how can we even make value commitments in the face of social relativism?

The solution to this dilemma will not come easily, but it will be discovered with patience, intelligence, tolerance, and diligence. As a student, you are already becoming aware of the complexity and abstractness of human wisdom. It is important for you to gain an appreciation for the diversity of human cultures and value systems. However, this appreciation may lead you into a journey of cynicism and relativity. This is a difficult journey, but one you are wise to take—"the life which is unexamined is not worth living" (Socrates). For many students, this experience coincides with the sophomore year and is referred to as the "sophomore slump." During this period of your life, I would encourage you to claim the promise that God will reward those who diligently seek him and live by the words of 1 Corinthians 13:12: "For now we see in a mirror dimly, but then face to face. Now I know in part; then I shall understand fully, even as I have been fully understood."

Toward the end of your journey you will find that your cynicism and relativism will begin to turn on yourself—you will find it necessary to "relativize the relativizers." The statement "All truth is relative" cannot be true by definition, and if the search for truth is absurd, then why bother with this useless activity? Like the preacher in Ecclesiastes, you, too, will conclude that "all is vanity." But this understanding is the beginning of true wisdom. After having considered all ways of living and finding them lacking, the writer of Ecclesiastes penned these words: "Let us hear the conclusion of the whole matter: Fear God, and keep his commandments: for this is the whole duty of man. For God shall bring every work into judgment, with every secret thing, whether it be good, or whether it be evil (Ecclesiastes 12:13–14 KJV). Now you are ready to move beyond relativism to a position of "committed relativism." A committed relativist realizes that there are other points of view, but is still able to make a commitment to a course of action or value perspective.

An analogy might help at this point. When I was young, I believed that there was one "right" person in the universe who was destined to become my wife—if I could find her. After having dated a number of young women, I discovered that there might be several women who were equally suitable as marriage partners. I soon discovered that I had to give up the idea of a Princess Charming, commit myself to the person with whom I was in love, and share my life with her *as if* she were the ideal spouse for me.

In some ways, faith commitments are similar to marriage choices. We invest our heads, hearts, and souls in our faith commitments—realizing that many other people have made different choices. Through faith, and in spite of our doubts, we invest our lives and act *as if* we had no other choice. In the "real world," we must make choices among value commitments. If we choose not to honor God and do his will, we will do the will of another. The Christian gospel requires a response from us. In the words of Joshua (24:15): "Choose you this day whom ye will serve; whether the gods which your fathers served that were on the other side of the flood, or the gods of the Amorites, in whose land ye dwell: but as for me and my house, we will serve the LORD." (KJV).

Once we make a choice, it is important to find a plausibility structure that will encourage us in our choice. For the Christian, this means entering into relationships with other Christians. Fellowship groups, churches, and prayer meetings all assist believers in honoring faith commitments. As we act on our religious convictions, being supported by other Christians who share our value commitments, our faith will grow. As we mature in our faith, our world views will reflect more fully our intellectual pursuits, value commitments, and religious beliefs. As a matter of intellectual integrity, we have the responsibility to reveal and explicitly state our value commitments, philosophical assumptions, and world views to others. In doing this, we should guard ourselves against intolerance of people who do not share our beliefs. We must critically evaluate all ideas—including our own—but never use this as a rationale for being unable to make value commitments.

GOD'S ACTIVITY AND SOCIOLOGICAL PROCESSES

Before we conclude, we must deal with some issues that have been in the background of the concerns addressed in this chapter. Is there a complementary relationship between religious and social scientific explanations? Should we assume that God's activity is the cause of any religious behavior not accounted for by scientific explanations? How much of religious phenomena can be explained by "normal sociological processes," and how much can be accounted for only by divine intervention?

These questions come out of an orientation where reality is neatly divided into two mutually exclusive categories—empirical phenomena and supernatural phenomena. From this perspective, scientific investigations deal with the former, and the latter is the exclusive domain of theology. Some have called this the "God of the gaps" orientation to knowledge—anything that cannot be explained by human wisdom is God's domain. As a consequence, there is an inverse relationship between human knowledge and God's influence.

Of course there is an alternative perspective to this commonly held view. It is possible that God's influence is present in both sociological processes and supernatural events. I would contend that in Scripture God's activity is more frequently observed in nonmiraculous situations. The men and women through whom God reveals his message are in most ways just like us. Even such "heroes" of our faith as Moses, David, Rahab, Ruth, Nathan, Esther, Samuel, Isaiah, Sarah, Jonah, Jonathan, Peter, Paul, James, and Matthew share our human condition. Yet, the best example is found in the person of Jesus, who though he was God was also fully human. Like us, he was tempted by Satan, was ridiculed by the masses, experienced rejection from his closest friends, endured physical and psychological pain, and finally died an agonizing death. However, through his obedience to God, he was also miraculously raised from the dead and had his rightful divine status restored (*see* Philippians 2:6–11).

The Christian church is the body of Christ and an institution subject to sociological processes. Like other social institutions, within the church we find evidence of the socialization process, stratification systems, and the tendency for structural differentiation and primary group formation. I can only assume that God is using the social order for his purposes in the same way that he has used other human institutions in biblical times—the extended family of Abraham, the Babylonian conquest, and the extensive system of roads of the Roman Empire, for example.

I believe that Christian sociologists should not compartmentalize sociological knowledge and theological understanding. Rather, we should attempt to facilitate our Christian growth through the insights gained from our sociological studies. There is much that sociology can contribute to the church and its mission in the world. A sociological perspective can serve a prophetic role in the church as well as improve the institutional effectiveness of religious groups. For these reasons, it is important that I do not check my sociological thoughts at the door when I enter my church to worship. Many times I will experience tension as I "bring" Durkheim, Marx, and Weber to church as my guests. Furthermore, some of my fellow worshipers would rather have me leave these friends at home. But my life and the church are enriched by the perspective that they can contribute to the body of Christ.

REFERENCES IN CHAPTER

Berger, Peter L. 1969. *The Sacred Canopy: Elements of a Sociological Theory of Religion*. New York: Doubleday, Anchor Books.

Clark, Robert A., and S. D. Gaede. 1981. "Where Your Treasure Is: A Christian Exploration of the Sociology of Knowledge." Paper presented at the annual conference of Sociologists Teaching at Christian Colleges at Calvin College, June 18.

Durkheim, Emile. 1915. *Elementary Forms of the Religious Life*. New York: Free Press.

Gallup, George. 1987. Gallup poll in *Minneapolis Star and Tribune*, March 8.

McGuire, Meredith B. 1987. *Religion: The Social Context*. Belmont, Calif.: Wadsworth.

O'Dea, Thomas F. 1983. *The Sociology of Religion*. 2d ed. Englewood Cliffs, N.J.: Prentice Hall.

Parsons, Talcott. 1968. "Emile Durkheim." In The *International Encyclopedia of the Social Sciences*, vol 4, edited by David L. Sills. New York: Free Press

CHRISTIANS AND DEVIANCE / CHRISTIANS AS DEVIANTS?

Zondra G. Lindblade

While involved in criminal conduct that permeated the securities industry in the 1980s, Ivan Boesky and his coconspirators said they were too big, too smart, and too powerful to be governed by the rules (Widder, 1987). Most of us are not Boeskys. We follow the rules and do not think of ourselves as deviant.

But we know what deviance is and who the deviants are. They are the ones who end up in prison—the inside traders who defraud, the murderers, the rapists, those who assault and physically batter others. We read about them daily in our newspapers; we see the poignant victim vignettes on eyewitness television; and we watch fictional deviants get what they deserve on "Miami Vice" and "Hill Street Blues."

Over and over again the perception is reinforced—*us* and *them*. They are different from *us*. Deviants are irrational, out of control, and evil. We fund humane state and federal correctional systems costing millions, lock them up, and throw away the key. Given their same situation, we believe we would choose to live rightly.

But nagging thoughts tug at the edge of this perspective. There, but for the grace of God, I might be (maybe even should be). And the prisons are not humane, but awful expressions of anger—perhaps revenge. In addition to isolating delinquents and criminals by imprisoning them, we tend to estrange ourselves from other groups that are different from us—the handicapped, the eccentric, the mentally retarded, the poor. These, too, are defined as deviant.

If I come to know a "deviant," I am surprised to find the person is a lot like me with hopes, dreams, hurts, and sorrows. The Bible reminds us not to forget that "such were some of you"

(1 Corinthians 6:11). Perhaps the separation into *us* and *them* is simplistic and inaccurate. We need to ask and find answers to some questions about deviant behavior. Where do we draw the line between social normalcy and deviance? Why do some but not others break the rules? How should Christians respond to deviance? What about Christians as "deviants?"

WHAT IS "DEVIANCE"?

I would like to explore three definitions of deviant behavior. The *normative* definition focuses on the basic social rules that every culture develops. These norms come from important values held by the group. They are informally decided and subtly communicated. Appropriate language, dress, attitude, and actions are learned. Normative deviance is any behavior that does *not* fit commonly accepted standards, and which is negatively perceived. Those who do not live by the standards are "outsiders," socially and sometimes physically isolated from the others. Even unintended violations of the "rules" arouse response, with wayward members quickly instructed into "more suitable" behavior.

Let's imagine you are invited, along with others, to a faculty member's home for supper. The dining room is comfortable and carpeted in light beige. Spaghetti is served. Although the silverware is alongside your plate, you begin to eat the meal with your fingers. Silence reigns, then nervous laughter begins as the physical consequences drip from your fingers and chin to the tablecloth and onto the carpet! You are never invited back.

This is an example of a broken social rule expressing good manners and courtesy—a **folkway**. Such rules do not reflect moral right and wrong. They may differ widely from group to group and from culture to culture. Folkway deviance may bring some ostracism, perhaps ridicule, but does not define the offender as immoral.

Long-lasting, stronger rules that protect individual property, freedom, rights, and life are called **mores**. These rules prohibit such things as murder, rape, arson, and fraud; they are the bases for social morality. Without such rules all social relationships would be uncertain and risky. Some mores come from "natural law"—that is, they are rules against acts considered inherently evil in all human cultures. Others are specific to a particular time and place. In the United States, most mores are written in state and federal criminal codes. Violations of the law demonstrate immoral or evil character. The "normals" (those who have followed the normative standards) swiftly respond and socially isolate the deviants. Other consequences may include punishment, incapacitation, revenge, and sometimes permanent social stigma.

Social role expectations represent a third type of norm. For example, specific behaviors are expected of students and teachers when they are in an educational setting. Students are learners and expected to bring the learning props with them—willing and inquisitive minds, writing tools, and paper. Teachers are also learners but with more advanced props—organized information, examples, questions to guide the students' thinking, and an understanding of the goals toward which learning is directed. Students are not to cheat, and teachers are not to come to class unprepared. Failure to fulfill role expectations brings external and internal consequences—teachers get fired, students don't graduate, and a sense of personal failure results.

Each of these norms fills a social need for guidelines. We could not live without them. They help us know what to expect of ourselves and others. When violators are punished, the boundaries for acceptable behavior are reinforced, the sense of belonging is confirmed for those living by the rules, and social predictability is strengthened.

Most of the folkways, mores, and role expectations are humanly created and are therefore limited. In contrast, God's standards fit the human character perfectly, are consistent, and always benefit our immediate and long-term living. **Scriptural norms** give clear instructions about how to live together in peace and love and how to satisfy our deepest personal longings. For example, God asks us to treat others as we would like to be treated; to accept his forgiveness and love, to love him in return; to be humble, do justice, and love mercy. The scriptural norms reflect God's omniscience and care for us—they are illustrations of his grace. Violations of God's norms are sin.

Statistical deviance represents a second definition. A silent but powerful revolution in morality is taking place in post-industrial societies. Many persons have moved away from using norms (social or spiritual) in defining acceptable behavior. The statistical definition is in vogue. If everybody is doing it, then that behavior must not be deviant.

One American use of this definition is illustrated by the fact that the single largest segment of the "underground economy" (that income not reported to the government) is legal *cash* income *unreported on income tax forms* (Simon and Witte, 1982). It is estimated that 60 percent of all personal tax returns underreport economic transactions. If "everybody" is doing it, aren't you foolish to include every penny, nickel, and dime on your IRS form? (Here you are "deviant" if you do NOT follow the crowd.)

The statistical definition also has crept into the rules for intimate behavior. A recent Harris poll shows that 57 percent of all American seventeen-year-olds have had sexual intercourse (released by Planned Parenthood, 1987). One official said respondents indicated that sexual activity is expected and "everyone does it." The implication is clear—something is wrong if a person leaves the teen years still a virgin.

Although the statistical view of deviance justifies much of today's behavior, a close look exposes its deceit. For income tax evaders, "everybody is doing it" is not a defense when caught. Premarital sex still is disapproved—consider the response to an illegitimate pregnancy. Here the normative standards against sexual immorality function with surprising strength. The "everybody is doing it" morality is dangerously foolish.

A third view of deviant behavior is another well-used substitute for normative standards. The *pathological definition* says behavior is deviant only if obvious guilt, hurt, or injury results. We use this perspective when we rely on comments like these: "No one is going to get hurt" or "It's nobody's business—this is just between the two of us" or "How could anything be wrong if it feels so good?" or "I don't feel guilty—it must be okay."

The pathological definition is also a fraud; it is presumptuous and impossible. Humans are finite, not omniscient. We have no way of knowing how long or in what ways an experience will affect us. We cannot accurately foresee the ripple effects of our behavior on others. It is arrogant to think we can see the end from the beginning.

THE NORMATIVE VIEW RECONSIDERED

Having rejected the statistical and the pathological definitions for behavior, let's look again at the normative definition. A simple diagram illustrates the relationship between the norms and deviance.

Figure 1. The Normal—Deviant Continuum

Deviants	Normals	Variants
1. impaired	(Live according to norm)	(Live by "super-norms")
2. rebellious		

Normals are persons who live by the group rules. The *deviants* and *variants* are those who do not—they live "outside" the rules. The vertical lines on the diagram reflect the estrangement of the normals who feel uncomfortable, insecure, and perhaps even afraid in the presence of outsiders. To reduce the discomfort and fear, the normals attempt in various ways to turn those "outside" toward more acceptable behavior. In this analysis it is important to understand that both the deviants and the variants deviate from expected normative standards.

Within the deviant group are the *impaired*—those who do not follow the rules because they cannot. They are persons with handicapping conditions: the physically disabled, the mentally retarded, the poor, or the chronically ill. They do not choose to be deviant, but the normals nonetheless ostracize them. Erving Goffman (1963) has written extensively about the interaction between the normals and the impaired. He pointed out that normals display their discomfort by simple avoidance, psychological distance, and inability to recognize human capabilities in disabled persons. If you doubt Goffman's observations, think about your own uncertainty in the presence of a blind or handicapped person. The normals also physically separate impaired persons into rehabilitative institutions. In recent years good intentions have legislated the early release of the mentally ill and retarded from these institutions. For many, however, such releases have meant a different kind of confinement in segregated areas of our cities without supervision or rehabilitative care.

The *rebellious* are deviants who know the rules and could live by them, but choose not to. Eccentrics, punks, and others who violate folkways would be included in this group. So also are individuals who violate mores—adult offenders such as burglars, auto thieves, and those involved in sexual assaults. The normals ostracize the folkway violators; but they try to incapacitate and punish those involved in immoral behavior.

Definitions of *impaired* and *rebellious* are not static. Several criminal groups recently have been recategorized, and confusion exists over the appropriate designation for others.

— In the state of Illinois public drunkenness had been defined as illegal behavior—with jail and/or punishment the appropriate response. This behavior has now been removed from the criminal code, and the violators are defined as impaired. The appropriate response is rehabilitation in detoxification centers.

— Criminal insanity is an example of behavior defined as impaired *and* rebellious. Several states have instituted a category for convicted criminals "guilty, but insane." For these offenders, impairment and the need for rehabilitation are recognized; at the same time the behavior is defined as rebellious—requiring punishment. The convicted offender is first sent to a mental institution for care; upon release the individual is incarcerated to serve out the prison term.

— Is a fatality caused by DUI (Driving while Under the Influence), an accident or murder? Was the offender drunk and therefore impaired, or rebellious and therefore drunk? Should the response be rehabilitation or retribution?

— Juveniles are young and immature—they are considered not fully responsible under the law. Their rule violations are considered the result of this "impairment." The goal of the U.S. Juvenile Court, therefore, is rehabilitation. However, if the offense is habitual, heinous, or capital, the juvenile can be defined as rebellious and tried in criminal court where the appropriate response is retribution and punishment.

WHAT MAKES THE REBELLIOUS DO IT?

Sin is the ultimate explanation for deviance. We all have sinned and fallen short of God's glory (Romans 3:23). But "sin" does not explain why some persons flagrantly violate the law while others do not; nor why some ethnic/racial groups are overrepresented in correctional institutions; nor why more males than females are considered criminally deviant. Looking at immediate circumstances may explain rebellious deviance.

Early criminologists thought deviants were biologically flawed. The person who "looks like" a criminal must be one. Chuck Colson (cited by Stott and Miller, 1980) refutes this view with the following story: "The inmates joined those who were at the house for lunch, perhaps thirty in all. The prisoners were dressed in ordinary clothes with which we had provided them. I stood in the doorway of the dining room with some of the dissident neighbors and suggested they pick out those in the room who were convicts—nine of the ten picked a congressman!"

Inadequate learning of the rules may explain deviance. Norms have been learned which are not appropriate to the situation. Immigrants may deviate from the rules because they are following norms from their old culture and do not see conflicts with the new. For example, Indo-Chinese refugees who moved to California after the Viet Nam War were catching and eating stray dogs; this practice was acceptable in their former culture where pets are not prized and food is scarce. In California, this behavior is illegal.

The norms may not be well-taught. In the midst of a frenetic lifestyle, a disintegrating marriage, or a struggle to put food on the table, parents may not carefully teach right and wrong. When asked about her promiscuous lifestyle, a recent graduate of a Christian college who had been raised in a very religious home said that she had learned how to keep her checkbook, set a fine table, and be dependable on the job, but she had never learned reasons to say no.

Differential association theory adds another perspective to learned deviance. Friendship groups may both teach and reinforce rebellion. Twelve-year-olds from the same neighborhood talk about how much fun it would be to shoot out streetlights with BB guns. Their sense of "adventure" is contagious; they communicate to one another many reasons why the mischief is okay and how to do it without getting caught. Although they know vandalism is wrong, the momentum of the group moves them toward deviant behavior.

For many of us, lack of opportunity is all that has prevented us from getting into trouble. For others the overwhelming presence of opportunity encourages deviance. At twilight, an unattended sports car with windows open and keys in the ignition is opportunity. One study has connected the increase in property crime with the increase in the number of homes empty during the day because wife and husband both work. Opportunity knocks, then breaks and enters.

Most Americans adopt the media's definition of the "good life." Wealth, comfort, happiness, and a little prestige are all part of the "American Dream." Obtaining an education, a job, and a big break, which would make the dream possible, is another story. However, for many, the deprivations and contradictions of the culture set the stage for deviant behavior. Robert K. Merton (1968) explains this by suggesting that persons who cannot get a good education or a steady job find alternate (illegal) ways to finance the dream. Poverty, discrimination, and unemployment are possible explanations for criminal behavior. A student with a medical school dream perhaps is an example closer to our experience. The student finds GPA competition tough and decides to use an alternate means (cheating) to accomplish the goal.

When social bonds are strong, group members conform to the norms. When the bonds are weak and the norms problematic, deviance is a likely outcome. A post-industrial society is geographically mobile, split off from extended family, and secularized. Secondary relationships typify our neighborhoods, the fragile nuclear family is fending for itself, and religious roots have disintegrated for many persons. Each of these factors weakens the social bonds and lessens commitment to the community. Rebellious deviance is nurtured in such a climate.

Connected with the social-moral disintegration is the view that the United States has become a criminogenic society—creating the deviance it pretends to abhor. A Canadian observer suggested that our national symbol is not the eagle, but the gun. Television violence (shooting, stabbing, strangling, and torture murders) is approved as public entertainment while sex and nudity (which in his country are considered "natural") are defined as obscene.

The enormous number of lethal weapons and the ever-expanding national defense budget set models for "first use" of violence rather than negotiation or other modes of conflict resolution. Advertisers stimulate sales through the use of children as sex objects and sensational "sick" store windows. Such advertising has been found in store windows in many different parts of the country: Harvard Square, Massachusetts; a suburban shopping mall near Wheaton, Illinois; San Francisco. Usually a mutilated, murdered female corpse' (mannequin) is front and center along with the product for sale and a caption similar to "we'd kill for these." Such methods can only add to violence and exploitation of others.

In addition, corporate crime is escalating. Business organizations and even entire industries are engaging in deviant, illegal practices. For example, a public relations director in the food industry said, "The ethics of my own corporation, like the industry in general, was 'dog eat dog.' Problems grew out of government regulations to control certain accepted unethical industry practices and also excessive competition. Payoffs, kickbacks, etc., were all part of the business" (Clinard, 1983).

Each deviant act is multicaused. Any explanation of rebellion must consider the possibility of inadequate socialization and the support for deviance that friendship groups can give. We also should be aware that opportunity, deprivation, and the disintegration of cultural morality contribute to deviance. When an entire society—media, economic structures, and national mood—depicts high proportions of deviance, asking the question, "Why deviance?" seems almost irrelevant.

BIBLICAL NONCONFORMITY: CHRISTIANS AS VARIANTS

When we measure ourselves by God's standards, we find that each of us is deviant. We are impaired and handicapped by sin and intentionally rebellious. Studies of self-reported deviance show almost 99 percent of all Americans sometime in life violate criminal laws—with a percentage of this deviance serious enough to warrant imprisonment if caught. Knowing the reality of sinful human nature and the propensity to live out the rebellion, Christians of all people should be humbled, show mercy, and extend forgiveness.

It is exactly this call to live by "supernorms" (*see* figure 1, p. 172) that makes Christians variants. We are to not live under the law as normals live, but beyond the law. We are to forgive seventy times seven—without limit. We are to love our enemies (and even deviants), do good to those who persecute us, and show mercy. Each of these activities is a way to love and serve God, but they certainly deviate from conventional American norms.

Other groups also are variant. The wealthy, the genius, the world-renowned composer, and the artist—each lives out a supernorm and deviates from conventional standards. The normals are uncomfortable around the variants; they feel inadequate and may even be in awe of the variants. The normals respond by distancing themselves from these unusual persons. At the same time they try to bring the variants back into conventional behavior by finding closet skeletons or less-than-admirable personal qualities, or by encouraging rejection of the supernorm itself.

Variants are uncomfortable, too. Estrangement is lonely and doesn't feel good. Peer acceptance and approval are powerful temptations for Christians. Mentioning Jesus Christ as someone we love and serve can stop conversation, arouse ridicule, or stimulate the response, "Why take religion so seriously?"

We may agree and forego the scriptural norms. As a result, the culture again squeezes us into its mold. Romans 12:2 reminds us not to be conformed to this world, but to be transformed so that we may do the will of God which is good, acceptable, and perfect. Sounds like variants, doesn't it?

Or we may put on a superficial "saintliness." Hector Timourian wrote a parable about people who once were authentic Christ-ones, but then drifted to become modern-day "whited sepulchres"—variants on the outside, but empty on the inside.

> In the parable the Christ-ones were called "Shadowless People"—as they fed on light invisible to others their bodies became translucent and they cast no shadow. They received much notoriety, attention, and even respect in their city. Until the Calamitous Event. As the city population grew, so did smog. Eventually, no one cast a shadow since every day was sunless.

> The Shadowless People were upset and missed the attention their former variant status had brought them. They decided to put on colorful arm bands to distinguish themselves and began to fight over what color the arm bands should be. The strongest voices for each color gained followers and the groups competed by parading up and down the streets. They were eager to regain the attention they had lost. Their efforts were exhausting but even worse, the city population began to shun and ridicule them.

> One group of Shadowless People did not have these frustrating experiences; they were too busy to bother with arm bands. They were occupied with teaching others how to feed on the light. (Paraphrased from HIS magazine, March 1958)

Authentic Christian living draws others to Christ. "For we do not preach ourselves, but Christ Jesus as Lord, with ourselves your bond-servants for Jesus' sake. For God, who said, 'Light shall shine out of darkness,' is the One who has shone in our hearts to give the light of the knowledge of the glory of God in the face of Christ" (2 Corinthians 4:5–6 NASB).

HOW SHOULD CHRISTIANS RESPOND?

Since we are "in the world," the immediate circumstances that encourage rebellion are also part of our lives. The first response should be to handle our own rebellion against God.

— Do we know "normal" life best, but are relatively untaught about God's norms?
— Are friendships that will encourage love for God the ones we search out?
— Service for God means fewer opportunities for rebellion.
— God's faithfulness and provisions are constantly available, even when living by supernorms seems beyond our reach.
— Believe the strong warning God gives us about the criminogenic nature of the world—run from temptation.
— Follow Christ's example. He came to preach good news to the poor, to release the captives, to recover sight to the blind, to set at liberty the oppressed, and to proclaim the year of the Lord (Luke 4:18–19).

Since deviance is multicaused, the response to it and control of it must be also. The passage from Luke (Jesus was quoting Isaiah 61) suggests two beneficial responses to normals and deviants—prevention and restoration. *Prevention at the micro level* changes the amount and type of resource possessed by the individual. Careful teaching of mores and folkway expectations provides a good beginning; for some, this instruction is most effective in a therapy setting since remedial learning is required. Parents and teachers occasionally intervene to redirect a person's peer associations—recognizing the negative influence of shared mischief. Street workers, counselors, and church leaders work to build close, personal relationships with predelinquents that create bonds of affection, commitment, and motivation toward normative behaviors. In order to be effective, such persons must be authentic and accountable to the rules themselves.

Prevention at the macro level alters the deprivations and affects the opportunities of the culture. Christians can make a difference in the world. Many are active in deviance prevention at the micro level, but this is only half the task. Job and educational opportunities need to be opened to those now disenfranchised because of race, religious background, gender, or age. Our collective voice can be raised against the use of violence for entertainment. We can join those trying to control the exploitation of children, women, or the elderly for personal pleasure or gain.

Restoration of the deviant has typically focused on methods of rehabilitation. Punishment intends to rehabilitate in the sense that it may function to deter further rebellion. Counseling and therapy for prison inmates are *rehabilitation* methods which have been used for decades. For a captive group, however, therapy may be coercive, and few seem to benefit permanently. Making the offender "pay the consequences" (retribution) recognizes individual responsibility and is now the most frequent response of the law to illegal behavior (Reid, 1988).

Much deviant behavior victimizes, but methods of restoration have generally overlooked victim needs. The Christian perspective can add two methods of restoration that relate to both the offender and the victim. Van Ness (1986) gives convincing scriptural support for *restitution* as one of these methods. In the process of repaying the victim, the offender has a chance to make things right, and the broken *shalom* is restored. *Shalom* is a Hebrew word that means community well-being and peace. It defines the reconciliation between offender and victim and the restoration of harmony and health in the entire community, which was broken by the rebellion of individuals or groups. Restitution takes a giant step toward healing the brokenness between offender and community.

Reconciliation goes beyond this to heal the broken relationship between the rebellious and God. No substitute exists for believing and accepting Christ's work on the cross. This restoration heals; it is permanent and life-changing. We don't need to take this on faith. Many illustrations demonstrate the power of God's work. Perhaps the best example is Chuck Colson's Prison Fellowship organization—a group centered on the restorative work of Jesus Christ in the lives of criminal offenders. Both *Jubilee*, the newsletter of the organization, and Mr. Colson's writings give evidence of the power of God to change lives. Working toward reconciliation provides a model of Christian variant action and a source of hope for deviants.

REFERENCES IN CHAPTER

Clinard, Marshall B. 1983. *Corporate Ethics and Crime.* Beverly Hills, Calif.: Sage.

Goffman, Erving. 1963. *Stigma: Notes on the Management of Spoiled Identity.* Englewood Cliffs, N.J.: Prentice Hall.

Merton, Robert K. 1968. *Social Theory and Social Structure.* New York: Free Press.

Planned Parenthood Review. 1987. Published by Planned Parenthood Federation of N.Y.: America, Inc.

Reid, S. T. 1988. *Crime and Criminology.* New York: Holt, Rinehart & Winston.

Simon, Carl P., and Ann D. Witte. 1982. *Beating the System: The Underground Economy.* Boston, Mass.: Auburn House.

Stott, John, and Nick Miller. 1980. *Crime and the Responsible Community.* London: Hodder & Stoughton.

Timourian, Hector. 1958. "The Shadowless People." *HIS* magazine, March.

Van Ness, Daniel W. 1986. *Crime and Its Victims.* Downers Grove, Ill.: InterVarsity.

Widder, Pat. 1987. "Boesky Gets 3 Years for Insider Trading." *Chicago Tribune,* December 19.

SOCIAL CHANGE:
THEORY AND PRACTICE

Ronald J. Burwell

I am writing this introduction in my office at Messiah College. As I sit here, I am struck by the fact that most of the things in my office—books, paper, pens—have been around for a long time. Yet, even here, I find evidence of a changing society. A computer terminal sits on my desk. It is hooked up to the campus computer—a machine that is fast becoming obsolete, even though it is only three years old. On another corner of my desk is a sophisticated phone that takes and sends messages and simultaneously transmits computer signals. Next to my phone is a plastic box filled with things called "floppy disks" that contain my lecture notes, tests, and letters. None of these things would have been on my desk ten years ago. These items remind me that change is ubiquitous—it is everywhere. How can sociology and Christian faith help me to understand *and* participate in social change?

The study of social change is a difficult but necessary part of sociology. The founders of the discipline, including Auguste Comte, Karl Marx, Emile Durkheim, and Max Weber, recognized that all societies change. They wanted to understand why change occurred and how change influenced the society and its people. But like all would-be analysts of social change, they discovered that the task is complicated. First of all, change can be studied at several different levels, including total civilizations, cultures, social systems, communities, social institutions, organizations, interpersonal relationships, and the individual. Hence, theories of social change must be level specific—that is, some theories are applicable to one level but not necessarily to other levels.

Furthermore, it is not easy to pinpoint the causes of change. Typically, change is neither wholly external nor wholly internal to a society. Change is caused by factors outside the social system and within the social system (Moore, 1974:11).

My exploration of the topic of social change begins with the same simple question faced by the sociological masters: Why do societies change? To answer this question, I compare two alternative theories of change—the materialistic and the idealistic—as they apply to the test cases of changing gender roles in the United States and the rise of modernity in Japan. I also pursue a practical application of Christianity in the area of social change. Here I am interested in another question: How should one who is a change agent, and a Christian, think about the task of introducing social change? To help answer this question, I consider a fictional case study—the case of the Melrec and the conflict between beer bashes and chain saws.

THINKING CHRISTIANLY ABOUT SOCIAL CHANGE

Since the 1960s, sociologists have become more concerned about the relationship between their religious and philosophical commitments and their task as sociologists. One part of this movement has been a growing awareness of the need for those who are Christians and sociologists to somehow bring these two commitments together. It has helped that other committed people (antiwar, antiracist, Marxist, feminist, pro–gay rights) are also struggling to know how their commitments should be related to their practice of sociology. If one can ask, "Can there be a Marxist sociology?" one can also ask, "Can there be a Christian sociology?"

Prior to this time, Christian sociologists were content with some compartmentalization of their lives. Christianity and sociology were kept distinct and separate. This stance was supported by a strong heritage of Weberian value-free sociology. And although some still hold out for a compartmentalized approach (for example, Berger and Kellner, 1981), a growing number of sociologists feel it is appropriate to struggle with the relationship of Christianity and the substantive and theoretical issues in sociology.

To understand the following discussion, the reader needs to know how I connect my faith with the practice of sociology. In chapter 13 Rich Perkins outlines three options: value-free sociology, value-aware sociology, and value-committed sociology. To some extent, I am comfortable with a value-aware sociology. That is, I believe we cannot set aside our values in the midst of doing sociology, and so we must be clear and explicit about the values that will influence our work (Burwell, 1981). But I also share some sympathies with the value-committed approach. I believe some values are foundational and operate as controls in weighing and devising theories in sociology (Wolterstorff, 1976). I am committed, because of my Christian world view, to certain beliefs about the nature of the world and the nature of human beings. These beliefs operate when I consider different issues in sociology, including theories of social change.

In addition to clarifying my position on the place of Christian faith in sociology, I should spell out some of my assumptions about sociological theories. First, I believe that an adequate theory must generate concepts and propositions that may be tested objectively. I am willing for the testing process to involve a variety of observational and data-gathering techniques, including historical studies. Some would define an acceptable theory more narrowly than this (such as restricting tests to experiments). Second, I do not believe that a single theory of social change is adequate for all purposes (Burwell, 1982). Various levels of analysis may demand different kinds of theory. Finally, I prefer theories that offer, as part of their framework, a view of human beings as not totally determined. I opt for theories that view humans as rational and deliberative creatures. This does not rule out the fact that on occasion human actions may be largely nonrational and determined.

You will be able to see my values at work in the following extended examples of the analysis of social change. I hope to show how one might analyze social change, given specific commitments to a Christian world view.

Example #1: Changing Gender Role Stereotypes

Ideas of what men and women are like are in the process of significant change. Every society has gender role expectations and places strong pressures on men and women to conform to expected roles. Traditionally, in the United States, women were to focus their energies around the home and concentrate on child rearing and housework. Men, in contrast, were to work outside the home and provide economic support for the family. Furthermore, women have been characterized as more moral, more sensitive and emotional, less rational and aggressive, nurturing, religious, and weak. Men have been characterized as achievement oriented, objective and rational, sexually experienced, authoritative, decisive, and natural leaders.

Although elements of traditional American gender role stereotypes still operate, significant changes are taking place. Women are viewed as having the potential for manifesting characteristics traditionally attributed only to males, such as leadership, rational thought, achievement orientation, heightened interest in sex, and aggression. Likewise, men are seen as capable of nurturing, being sensitive, emotional, and interested in child rearing.

Changes in gender role stereotypes seem to be leading to actual changes in the division of labor between men and women. Women are working outside the home and providing economic support for the family. Men are sharing greater responsibility for child rearing and housework (although women still do a larger share of these tasks—even when both spouses work outside the home). How did these changes occur?

One of the more persuasive attempts to answer this question is based on "structural-functional" theory that identifies external factors as precipitating the changes. This theory locates the basis for the fundamental shift in gender role stereotypes in the movement of women to work in settings outside the home. In particular, this transition is linked to the historical events of World War II. Prior to World War II, the vast majority of American women worked in the home (unless they were poor or black) as housewives and mothers. However, the crisis of the war drew great numbers of men from the work force and placed them in the armed services. This created a vacuum, a severe shortage of workers in many industries. The only option was to recruit women to fill jobs. The emergency justified a violation of the cultural patterns and the gender role stereotypes.

In writing a brief history of women and equality, William H. Chafe (1977:41) adopts an explicitly functional theory of change to explain the changes in women's roles. He states:

> By definition, organisms tend to maintain themselves and to provide means of self-regulation that discourage dislocation and change. As social and economic structures become more established they afford less and less room for fundamental alterations. Thus, in most cases it takes a transformation from without to create the possibility of major change within.

Operating from this perspective, Chafe looks at the events of World War II as they apply to changing roles for women. He observes that the war caused over six million women to take jobs outside the home increasing the female labor force by 50 percent. This had significant consequences. He notes:

> Most important, public attitudes appeared to change. Instead of frowning on women who worked, government and the mass media embarked on an all-out effort to encourage them [women] to enter the labor force. The war marked a watershed in the history of women at work, and, temporarily at least, caused a greater change in women's status than half a century of feminist rhetoric and agitation had been able to achieve. (Chafe, 1972:136)

One of the most interesting results of this was the discovery that women could function in jobs previously reserved for men (e.g., jobs that involved strength, manual dexterity, and danger).

When the war ended, it was assumed that women would return to their homes to resume work as housewives and mothers. However, something had happened—women discovered that they liked working outside the home, and great numbers remained in the work force. Although in the early postwar era strong pressures toward traditional gender role stereotypes persisted, a process of change had begun. Now over half of all mothers with children one year old or younger are in the work force. The married mother with small children who fits the traditional stereotype by staying at home is in the minority in the United States.

This functionalist view argues that the current changing notions about women's roles find their root in the changes brought on by World War II. Without the war, women's roles would be largely unchanged. However, the war disturbed the equilibrium of society, and now we are creating a new equilibrium in response to those experiences. Changes in our ideas, beliefs, and attitudes about women were caused by external changes in the economic and vocational experiences of American women. This theory does not see change as a deliberate, rational process that begins with a change in ideas and then a change in behavior. Changing images of women's roles existed prior to World War II in such social events as the women's suffrage movement, but these ideas were not effective in bringing about far-reaching social change. Perhaps in this case the structural-functional explanation of change is valid. However, does this mean that all social change can be explained by this theoretical model? Let's consider another case study.

Example #2: Japan and Modernization

One of the great debates in modern social theory is about the reasons why modern, industrial, capitalistic societies have emerged in the last two centuries. Karl Marx believed economic factors are foundational to all of society. He saw human history as an inevitable process involving transition from one economic form to another. In his view, capitalism is one form of economic organization that evolved out of an evolutionary law of human history. However, he also believed that certain innate flaws would eventually cause capitalism's self-destruction. Nevertheless, given his view of history and the evolution of societies, he would predict a capitalist phase to be found in the history of most societies (Marx and Engels, 1987). We often refer to Marx's theory of change as based on material (that is, economic) factors.

Max Weber disagreed with Marx about the rise of capitalism in Europe. Weber saw a set of ideas as having a formative effect in creating the conditions for the emergence of capitalism. In a famous essay Weber developed the idea that certain elements in the Protestant Reformation created an "ethic" that encouraged people to live lives characterized by the "spirit of capitalism" (Weber, 1958). The irony was that this was an *unintended* consequence of the Protestant Reformation.

Weber identified the idea of a "calling" and concern over one's eternal destiny (election) as leading to a frugal, monastic, and self-denying lifestyle. Wealth was not consumed; it was used in a responsible way to create evidence that one was part of God's elect. Weber concluded that a set of theological beliefs, when translated into maxims about lifestyle, inadvertently had profound economic consequences.

The major point of disagreement between Marx and Weber concerns the role of ideas in the development of capitalism. Marx saw the so-called spirit of capitalism as coming *after* capitalism was already established; Weber saw it as coming *before* the rise of capitalism. These two great sociologists show us two approaches to the role of ideas in social change.

Today most students of social change raise questions about the specific connections that Weber made between Calvinistic theology and capitalism (Eisenstadt, 1968). However, many agree that the basic idea is still accurate, even though the details are debatable. In other words, many believe that a change in ideas fostered by the Protestant Reformation served as a catalyst to facilitate the emergence of modern capitalism. But what about non-Western societies? Does Weber's idea hold true in non-Western contexts?

A fascinating example of social change is the phenomenal rise of Japan from a largely rural peasant society in the 1800s to an economic and industrial giant in the present world. How and why did Japan make this transition? Let's weigh the merits of Marx's and Weber's theories in this case.

Marx, if he were alive to see present-day Japan, would see it as merely responding to the inevitable laws of history that dictate the move from a feudal society to a capitalistic one. He would also predict that the capitalistic phase will be only a temporary one for Japan because it is doomed from the start. However, it is difficult to use a Marxian perspective to explain why this change came when it did and why the change was accomplished so quickly and without significant social trauma and upheaval.

An alternative view is presented by Robert N. Bellah, one of the most perceptive writers on the emergence of modern Japan. Bellah, basing his theory on Max Weber, argued that a series of changes in the culture of Japan—particularly in the realm of religion—paved the way for the emergence of modern capitalist Japan. In his work *Tokugawa Religion* (1957), he explicitly developed a theory modeled on Weber's ideas. In his view, during the Tokugawa Regime (1600–1868) changes were taking place; gradually Buddhism was de-emphasized, and a revived Shintoism emerged. By appealing to loyalty to the emperor, those wishing to promote change used Shintoism's veneration of the emperor. Bellah (1958:5) summarized his view this way:

> The young samurai who put through the Meiji Restoration used the central value of loyalty to the emperor to legitimize the immense changes they were making in all spheres of social life and to justify the abandoning of many apparently sacred prescriptions of the traditional order. No other sacredness could challenge the sacredness inherent in the emperor's person.

According to Bellah, if religion rigidly prescribes how things are to be, it will be very difficult to change society. However, if religious ideas are stated in terms of general principles, and if there is leeway in how those principles are to be worked out, then society will be able to change. This seems to be what happened in Japan by 1868. Changes in religious ideas freed Japanese culture to change in the direction of more modern, Western patterns. Unlike Weber, who saw religion as providing the motivation for capitalism, Bellah believed religion stimulates and justifies changes in the institutions of society. In his later work Bellah saw an even broader role for religion, suggesting that it simply legitimates change in general.

We have looked briefly at two different cases of social change. In one case, a structural-functional theory has merit. In the other case, a Weberian idealistic theory is persuasive. It is tempting to think that there is not much more to be learned from these two cases. However, deeper issues are involved.

Our theories of change presuppose different ideas about human nature. In order to understand this we need to use Martin Hollis's two "models of man"—"autonomous man" and "plastic man" (1977). Plastic man is essentially determined by factors external to the person and is passive, reacting only to external stimuli. Plastic man brings nothing additional to the action. Autonomous man is an active person who contributes some part to the action that is performed. Autonomous man is not merely controlled by external factors but may on occasion choose between alternative actions, regardless of identical external conditions.

Applying Hollis's models to our cases of social change, we find some interesting parallels. The functional theory of changing female gender roles regards the stimulus for change as external. People are depicted as acting passively in routine patterns with no incentive to change. Similarly, Marx's notion of the rise of capitalism occurs largely beyond the conscious involvement or action of persons. In contrast, Bellah depicts human beings actively choosing goals and using a set of ideas to bring about a new state of affairs.

But should we allow our Christian biases to influence which theories we choose? As a Christian, I am attracted to Bellah's and Weber's ideas. However, the functional explanation of changing gender roles is supported by the historical data. Perhaps we should accept the functional theory, even though it raises questions about human nature. By accepting this theory, we may gain a valuable corrective to our views of human nature and social change. It is hard to deny that we do change because of externally precipitated, nonrational factors (like war). Human beings do create and use abstract ideas, but these do not always govern our actions. Hence, we must allow what we find in our study of the world through a discipline like sociology to reform and improve our assumptions about human nature.

In reflecting on these two cases, we also see that it is quite possible to adopt two rather different explanations of social change. Our theoretical choices are influenced by the particular case and the particular level of analysis. Furthermore, data plays a central role in sorting out our options. If a theory fits our control beliefs but is not supported by observations or data, we should reject it as inadequate.

It is apparent from our discussion that there are numerous answers to the question of why societies change. In some cases, change is created by largely uncontrolled alterations in the external environment. In other cases, deliberate human reflection and choice of action may result in social change. Rather than arbitrarily adopt one answer to this question, we might better look at the specific change and then ask why that change has occurred.

We also discovered that our answer to the question about why social change occurs may have deeper philosophical implications about our understanding of human nature. On occasion we may opt for an explanation of social change because it fits with our Christian ideas about persons. At other times we may find that study of particular cases causes us to revise and reconsider what persons are like.

A Christian view of social change is not simply an idealist view rather than a materialist view, or an evolutionary view rather than a structural-functional view. Within the limits of one's Christian world view all these options may be acceptable. Instead, we must ask if the theory corresponds to the facts observed and if it fits our assumptions about human nature.

THE CHRISTIAN AS AN AGENT OF CHANGE

The issue of how a Christian looks at different theories of change is an important intellectual puzzle. However, this question can be far removed from the real and immediate implications of social change. As Christians, we need also to consider how an individual might function as an agent of change.

For a number of years social scientists have debated the merits of actively seeking to change society. It is part of a larger question of scholarly detachment versus commitment: Should scholars stand back and observe society objectively? Or should they be involved in the things they study? Should a Christian social scientist consciously seek to bring about change in a society?

I will approach this dilemma by considering a scenario that will help us to see the dimensions of this issue. Specifically, I want you to imagine yourself a missionary in a culture different from our own—a missionary struggling with whether or not to introduce a certain technological change. However, before we turn to this case study, let me sketch some of the reasons why one might question the legitimacy of trying to introduce change.

Traditionally anthropologists, who have been very interested in change in other cultures, have been critical of attempts to consciously introduce change. The underlying reason for this is their commitment to cultural relativism. The principle of cultural relativism suggests that various sociocultural practices must be evaluated in terms of the values of the culture in which they exist (see chapter 4 by Robert Clark). Typically change agents seek to bring about change based on their values that may be very different from the values of the culture experiencing change. Hence, anthropologists often argue for a noninterventionist stance. The proper role of outsiders is to observe and gain appreciation for the culture, but not to seek to change the culture.

A second reason for avoiding change is found in the use of structural-functional models of society by sociologists and anthropologists. These models stress the interrelatedness of various aspects of societies, an interrelatedness that means any change will have far-reaching, "ripple" effects on the social system. The possibility of harmful, unintended consequences from change is thus increased.

Social scientists are suspicious that the typical change agent is ethnocentric and will try to remold another culture in the image of his or her own culture. Social scientists are especially suspicious of missionaries who, as part of their role, are trying to induce another group of people to adopt their religious views.

What response can we offer to this generally negative view of the role of the individual seeking to change another culture? One response is to point out that change, particularly technological change, is likely to take place anytime there is contact between a person from a technologically more sophisticated culture and people who lack advanced technology. In fact, the mere presence of a social scientist (like an anthropologist) will probably cause change in a traditional culture. So the issue is not about change or no change, but about what type of change, how it will be introduced, and its ramifications.

Another response is that the structural-functional model overemphasizes the stability and harmonious balance of a society. In fact, it is often the case that existing cultural and social patterns are dysfunctional to a given society and might well be changed or dropped to benefit that society. This judgment can be defended by appeal to the internal values of a society and need not be automatically assumed as ethnocentric.

A final response can be made on ethical or humanitarian grounds. If a change agent contemplates a change that will possibly alleviate suffering or increase the quality of life, would it not be immoral to withhold such changes merely because of the principle of cultural relativity? For example, if I have access to an antibiotic that can miraculously cure a life-threatening illness, should I withhold such medical aid for fear of unexpected negative consequences to the social system? Most people would find it immoral to prevent such a change.

Beer Bashes and Chain Saws

The test case that I propose is fictional but based on real ethnographic facts (Nida, 1954; Kennedy, 1978). I could propose this case in connection with other possible individual change agents such as Peace Corps workers, UNESCO (United Nations Educational, Scientific and Cultural Organization) advisors, and government experts, but I believe that the missionary—a distinctively Christian change agent—is more relevant and interesting for our consideration.

Suppose you are a missionary to the Melrec people. You have been living in a Melrec village for three years and have reached a fairly fluent level in the language. Furthermore, you have been able to gain an understanding of the Melrec culture. Your task as defined by you and your mission is to do linguistic work and develop a base for planting churches in the culture. Although you are the first missionary to this group, other missionaries are working in neighboring cultures that share similar customs but different languages.

You know that the Melrec people pursue a way of life characterized by simple slash-and-burn agriculture. They are what sociologists call an "incipient peasant society" with very modest technology and fairly simple material culture. Their staple crop is corn, and they also plant beans, squash, and other vegetables that can be grown in small gardens. The Melrec have a longstanding traditional pattern for developing their fields and raising a corn crop. Because they practice slash-and-burn agriculture, it is necessary periodically to cut down new areas of the forest in order to plant a corn crop. Fields can be used only a few years before the soil is depleted and new areas have to be cleared.

Since the Melrec have only simple tools such as hand saws and axes, they need help in cutting down the forest and burning off the underbrush. Typically a man gets help in this task by brewing a large quantity of the native beer and inviting many friends and neighbors to clear the fields. Assistance is given in exchange for beer and the expectation that the man will help clear his neighbors' fields. The key factor, however, is the amount of beer. The more beer that is brewed, the more people who will come to help and the larger an area that can be cleared. In turn, a larger corn crop can be planted, which in the next year can be turned into even larger quantities of beer (the beer is made from fermented corn).

Figure 1. Ecological Model of the Beer Bash—Field-Clearing Cycle

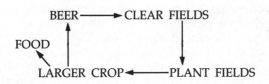

As an observer, you now understand the importance of the beer bash–field-clearing ecological cycle. However, you are aware of some serious problems as well. During these beer bashes, there are cases of adultery, many violent fights, and occasionally fatalities. Furthermore, some of the men return home from these events only to beat their wives and children. In the meantime, a small group of new Christians has come into being through your work with the Melrec. They ask your advice: Should they continue to participate in this pattern of using beer to gain help in clearing fields? What do you say?

You have three possible responses to this question. You may suggest that they continue this pattern; you may refuse to give advice; or you may argue that they ought to withdraw from the activity. Let's look at each option.

As the scene is set, it seems unlikely that you would propose that they continue to engage in this practice. There are some clearly obvious harmful aspects to this practice. However, you may be concerned about pressing your value system on the Melrec, and you may fear disturbing the cultural balance of their way of life. Nevertheless, to say yes to this practice would mean to go against universal moral and ethical values.

A more modest option would be to refuse to give any advice. In a sense you would be saying to the Melrec that they have to work out their own answer. Yet, to do this would be particularly harsh to a group of new believers. They do not have your knowledge of the Scriptures, and they are only beginning to understand the implications of the gospel in their lives. You are in a position to give them advice. They have already looked to you for help, and they responded when you presented the gospel. You set a precedent by encouraging them to make certain changes. To stop at this point would be inconsistent. Besides, to avoid a direct answer infers negative evaluation of this cultural pattern.

The remaining, and most consistent, position would be for you to give them advice—explain why you feel this cultural pattern is dysfunctional and why you believe it would be good for Christians to avoid this practice. At this point it would be up to the Melrec to decide for themselves. They might well decide that your advice is faulty and continue in their traditional patterns. You must accept their decision and not try to force them into adopting your view. Unfortunately, missionaries are prone to use their considerable power to force changes that are not clearly supported by believers in the culture they are serving.

Let's assume, however, that the Melrec accept your advice and decide to withdraw from the beer bash–field-clearing cycle. It is extremely important for you as a change agent to understand the social and cultural implications of this decision. Several problems remain to be resolved. First, how will the Melrec get their fields cleared? Second, how will they remain in social contact with their nonbelieving friends, neighbors, and relatives? And third, how will their refusal to be a part of this cultural practice influence the future spread of the gospel among the Melrec?

Generally, in this situation, a change agent seeks a functional substitute for the cultural pattern that is being changed. This substitute should fit into the existing system with a minimum of disruption of the rest of the culture (Nida, 1954:265), but even seemingly simple substitutions can be fraught with dangerous, unintended consequences (Sharp, 1952). What might the Christian Melrec do to substitute for the beer bash? One possibility is to offer alternative refreshments. Some other food or drink may be equally valued by the Melrec. But it is probable that it would not be directly related to the previous corn crop, and it would be necessary to exchange corn for money to buy the substitute refreshments. This may or may not be economically feasible. And the substitute may not function as well if it does not loosen the inhibitions of the Melrec—perhaps the whole point of the beer bash.

Another option is to find a functional substitute for the way the fields are cleared. Cutting down the forest with axes, machetes, and hand saws is relatively inefficient. Perhaps you as a change agent might import a chain saw. One Melrec with a chain saw could be as efficient as a large group of Melrec using traditional tools while partying on the native beer.

On the surface this suggestion seems to be ideal, but it has some definite disadvantages. For one thing, the Melrec Christians would become more dependent on you for support. You would need to help in supplying gasoline, parts, and repair for the chain saw. Furthermore, this plan would create distance between the Christians and the non-Christians since they would no longer work side by side in clearing the forest. Another unknown possibility is that non-Christian Melrec may see the efficiency of the chain saw and go through the motions of becoming Christian just to get access to the new technology. Other disadvantages include the greater risk of injury and a damaging impact on the environment given the possibility of clearing larger areas of the forest.

ON BEING AN AGENT OF CHANGE
AND AN AGENT OF GOD

With reflection you could see other dimensions of this case. However, let me summarize what I believe this case teaches us about being a change agent. First, if a change is proposed, there must be a good and sufficient set of reasons for implementing the change. In the Melrec case we must be sure that the negative aspects of the beer bash–field-clearing cycle are severe enough to cause us to intervene, and we must have support from believers in that culture who have come to the same conclusion.

Second, when seeking a functional substitute, we must assume that any change will have both intended and unintended consequences. We should try to anticipate, as much as possible, what those consequences might be. We can benefit from other case studies and the experiences of change agents who have introduced similar change elsewhere. We can also enlist the help of knowledgeable people in the culture who can suggest some likely consequences.

Third, any proposed functional substitute should be chosen in consultation with members of the culture who may be able to select from a list of alternative plans the one that seems best suited to their situation. Missionaries and other change agents need to study the theory and practice of applied social change. A considerable body of literature on introducing change includes many case studies that provide parallel examples. In the case of the Melrec and the chain saw we can learn from other settings where similar technological innovations were introduced. For example, Pertti J. Pelto (1973) systematically studied what happened in the Arctic when the snowmobile was introduced in place of dog or reindeer sleds. He found certain general outcomes accompanied these changes.

The same kinds of outcomes would accompany the introduction of a chain saw among the fictional Melrec. First, such a change would increase the need for cash to purchase more of these devices as well as parts and supplies. This would shift production and work toward pursuits that could raise cash, stimulating migration in search of wage-earning jobs in urban centers. No doubt contact with a wider world would be increased and acculturation would accelerate. Pelto called this process "delocalization" (1973:166).

Second, the likelihood of stratification would be increased. A contrast between the "haves" and the "have nots" would arise; some Melrec would possess chain saws, and others would be unable to possess such technology but would depend on it.

Having thought about the case of the Melrec, many readers might believe that no one in his or her right mind should ever decide to be a change agent. Such a response is understandable given the complexities and dangers of such a role, but I would offer this rejoinder. Remember that change is ubiquitous; it will occur with or without our conscious intervention. Granted, our involvement will hasten change, but it might also eliminate some of the serious negative consequences of change. If change is introduced with a sensitivity to the values and existing patterns of a culture, it will be infinitely preferable to ignoring change and trying to avoid the role of a change agent.

In this area, like others, Christian faith has implications for social theory and practice. Our faith influences our view of persons and our view of responsible action toward others. But we must also remember that sociological knowledge is useful for the exercise of our faith. The disciplined study of human behavior helps us to be more effective and compassionate agents of God's kingdom.

REFERENCES IN CHAPTER

Bellah, Robert N. 1957. *Tokugawa Religion*. New York: Free Press.
_____. 1958. "Religious Aspects of Modernization in Turkey and Japan." *American Journal of Sociology* 64:1–5.
Berger, Peter, and Hansfried Kellner. 1981. *Sociology Reinterpreted: An Essay on Method and Vocation*. New York: Doubleday, Anchor.
Burwell, Ronald J. 1981. "Sleeping with an Elephant: The Uneasy Alliance Between Sociology and Christianity." *Christian Scholar's Review* 10, no. 3 (Spring, 1981): 195–205.
_____. 1982. "Social Change." In *Christian Perspectives in Sociology*, edited by Stephen Grunlan and Milton Reimer. Grand Rapids, Mich.: Zondervan.

Chafe, William H. 1972. *The American Woman: Her Changing Social, Economic and Political Roles: 1920–1970*. New York: Oxford University Press.

————. 1977. *Woman and Equity: Changing Patterns in American Culture*. New York: Oxford University Press.

Eisenstadt, S. N. 1968. *The Protestant Ethic and Moderization*. New York: Basic Books.

Hollis, Martin. 1977. *Models of Man*. Cambridge: Cambridge University Press.

Kennedy, John G. 1978. *The Tarahumara of the Sierra Madre*. Arlington Heights, Ill.: AHM.

Lauer, Robert H. 1977. *Perspectives in Social Change*. 2d. ed. Boston: Allyn & Bacon.

Marx, Karl., and Friedrich Engels. 1987 [1890]. *The Communist Manifesto*. New York: Pathfinder.

Moore, Wilbert E. 1974. *Social Change*. 2d. ed. Englewood Cliffs, N.J.: Prentice Hall.

Nida, Eugene. 1954. *Customs and Cultures*. New York: Harper & Row.

Pelto, Pertti J. 1973. *The Snowmobile Revolution: Technology and Social Change in the Artic*. Menlo Park, Calif.: Benjamin-Cummings.

Sharp, Laurston. 1952. "Steel Axes for Stone Age Australians." In *Exploring Human Problems in Technological Change: A Casebook*, edited by E. H. Spicer. New York: Russell Sage Foundation.

Stipe, Claude. 1980. "Anthropologists versus Missionaries: The Influence of Presuppositions." *Current Anthrpology* 21: (April): 165–79.

Toffler, Alvin. 1970. *Future Shock*. New York: Random House.

Weber, Max. 1958. *The Protestant Ethic and the Spirit of Capitalism*. New York: Charles Scribner's Sons.

Wolterstorff, Nicholas. 1976. *Reason Within the Bounds of Religion*. Grand Rapids, Mich.: Eerdmans.

WHY STUDY SOCIOLOGY?

Richard Perkins

Several years ago, while I was delivering a lecture, a student interrupted me and asked, "Why should I study this stuff?" I was stumped. I had never been asked this question before (at least not so directly). My halting response was due as much to the audacity of the questioner as to the question itself.

Later, as I searched for an answer to the student's question, I reflected back on my graduate education. I realized that I had encountered two strikingly different rationales for studying sociology. The first was based on the general approach used in the natural sciences. Ask physicists, biologists, or chemists why they study the natural world, and most will say they want to find out how it works—to discover the natural laws that explain its regularity. And they'll be able to give you some examples of natural laws—laws governing heat transfer, gravity, chemical reactions, and so forth.

Many sociologists give the same sort of answer. Of course, they recognize that there are differences between the natural and social sciences (for example, the methods used), but the aim is the same—to discover the laws that account for the patterns we observe in social life. However, if you were to ask these sociologists for examples of such laws, they would say it all depends on the theoretical perspective employed. For example, sociologists following the lead of Karl Marx claim that social change is generated by class struggle. Social order, they say, is imposed—an artificial creation maintained through political power and the force of dominant ideologies.

By contrast, sociologists following the lead of Emile Durkheim claim that social order is an inherent feature of all social systems— that cohesion is naturally generated by the ritualistic nature of social interaction. Social rituals underscore the moral consensus on which role integration is based. So, depending on the theoretical perspective, society exists either as an ongoing struggle between contesting classes or as a self-balancing system. It would be difficult to imagine two more different—perhaps even contradictory—answers.

Which approach gives us the truth? Both groups can present considerable evidence supporting their claims. Both claims represent what their advocates hope will eventually lead to full-fledged scientific laws.

Scientists who have these hopes are called "positivists." Positivists proceed on the expectation that there are natural laws governing all empirical phenomena. However, the search for universal scientific laws is undercut by the realization that different theories yield different interpretations as to what laws can be discovered. Since theoretical interpretations vary, the universality of scientific law is brought into grave doubt. Even so, the positivists press on toward their goal. Like other scientists, they assume knowledge of laws is inherently valuable. No other justification need be given. So, when someone asks, "Why do we study sociology?" they respond, "In order to know the answer." Scientific knowledge of the truth is enough. I could have given this as the answer to the student's question, but I didn't. I'm not a positivist.

A very different type of answer is given by those representing "humanistic sociology." Humanistic sociologists assume that physics and sociology represent fundamentally different scientific disciplines. It's not just their methodological approaches that are different; their scientific goals are different, too. Natural scientists study planets, birds, rocks, and such; social scientists study people and the societies they create. Of course, there are plenty of differences between rocks and people, and the primary one is that rocks do not create a symbolic world in which to live—but humans do.

Thus, positivists search for laws explaining the patterns of society. By contrast, humanists disclaim even the possibility of such laws. Instead, they search for regularities and insights into ways people create and sustain their social situations.

The purpose of humanistic sociology is found in the application of these insights for how we choose to live our lives. Knowing the "facts" is never enough. Humanistic sociologists defend the study of sociology in terms of what has become known as "praxis"—that is, learning about social life by becoming involved in it.

That sounds simple enough—learning through involvement—but it's not. Involvement by scientists in what they study raises the thorny issue of the relationship between facts and values, between the objectivity and the subjectivity of scientific truth.

Not that positivists and humanists have no common ground. They all agree, for example, that anyone called to the role of social scientist is primarily committed to generating reliable and valid scientific knowledge, not subjective opinion. Scientists presumably seek the truth about the natural and social world as it really is, not as they wish it were. "Good sociologists" must maintain a sharp distinction between opinion and fact. Both naturalistic and humanistic sociologists revere careful, disciplined study of empirical phenomena. Both employ versions of the scientific method in their research studies and require that sociological theories must be testable to be considered valid. Although there is much disagreement over just what "objective knowledge" looks like, and how it ought to be generated and used, all sociologists acknowledge the crucial difference between analysis and advocacy. Whatever one's commitment to scientific involvement, the true scientist's job is to find out what *is*, not what *ought to* be.

However, apart from this agreement, the relationship between fact and value continues to create debate within social scientific circles. Positivists seek to keep the two realms strictly separated, claiming sociologists have no business dealing with values at all, except as data. Of course the subjects of sociological research have values, and sociologists want to know why they do. They also want to know the social consequences of these value commitments. Apart from those values that may influence the choice of the topics for sociological investigation, the personal values of positivist sociologists presumably have no other significance in their *objective study of social facts*.

This view isn't supported by humanistic sociologists. They regard values (their own included) as intrinsic to the study of society. To them, social reality is a "value-laden" enterprise. A shared sense of how reality ought to be defined is socially constructed out of on-going social interaction. Moreover, a part of this socially constructed reality is sociology itself. Sociologists, say the humanists, do not stand outside social reality—they are not immune to values, as the positivists suggest. Consequently, what can be said about the relativity of definitions of reality can also be said about sociology and its theories. Since social reality is relative, it is useless, say the humanists, to search for universal laws. Since each social situation is defined into existence by its participants, each situation is at least somewhat unique.

Values can be ignored, as the positivists prefer, but in so doing, science is diminished, not enhanced. What's worse, instead of being acknowledged and taken into explicit account, ignored values are driven underground, so to speak, to become even more of a distorting influence.

From a Christian standpoint, there are a number of objection-able features to the positivistic approach to facts and values. First, positivism is overly deterministic—treating human beings as if they are nothing more than "role players" whose actions and thoughts are "structured" by their respective social locations. People are seen as cogs in a complicated social machine—their action determined by the structures of that system. Humans react; they do not create. This model leaves little or no room for the notion of humans being created in the divine image—an image that includes a measure of creativity and choice.

Second, to the committed Christian, the positivist's commit-ment to "value-free" sociology represents a clear and distinct challenge to the primacy of the gospel message. Giving value-free sociology primacy is a form of idolatry, and it is unacceptable for this reason. Our values as Christians must not be set aside. Nor should we define our religious values as mere products of social forces—as if by doing so we could explain them away. Our values are influenced by our social contexts, but this influence does not discredit the truth-claims of the values.

Third, the positivist's vision for social sciences is naive. People are not rocks. Sociologists cannot stand outside the world of symbols, interpretations, and values. Were they somehow able to do so, their understanding of social reality would be nil. To understand human action, symbolic as it is, sociologists have to interpret action as the people being studied interpret it. Setting aside values clouds this possibility. Indeed, it is unrealistic to think our values *can* be set aside, even if, for some reason, we wanted to. Does a cancer researcher stop believing that cancer is bad because "objective science" requires value-neutrality?

Once we recognize that values are intrinsic to social action, we confront the question, What are sociologists to do with their values? Some humanists argue that the sociologist's values ought to be kept strictly separated from the process of research (except, of course, values pertaining to choices regarding subject matter and research approach). According to humanist sociologists, good sociologists never confuse their personal values with those of the people they study. The sociologist's personal values are irrelevant to the research task; in fact, these values can easily corrupt the study. Our task as sociologists, they say, is to understand the point of view of the people being studied, not to confirm reality as we prefer to see it. But how is this done so as to advance, not retard, the cause of science?

It may not be easy to segregate one's values from those of the people being studied, but the good sociologist will always try. Values are crucial to the study of society, to be sure, but the sociologist's values must somehow be kept from biasing the interpretations. To prevent such bias, sociologists must be aware of their personal values and the effects these values have on their interpretation. For this reason, I will call this position the "value-aware" approach.

This humanistic approach is advocated by some of the most well-known and respected contemporary sociologists. Peter Berger, whose name has appeared many times in this book, is an outspoken value-aware sociologist. Berger and many other contemporary humanistic sociologists are disciples of the originator of this approach, Max Weber.

Sociologists committed to either the positivist's value-free approach or to the humanist's value-aware approach agree that the sociologist's personal values must be segregated from the research. (Taken together, these two groups represent the vast majority of all contemporary sociologists.) Even so, there are important differences between those committed to value-freedom and value-awareness. Value-aware sociologists regard values as an essential factor in the formation of social action; value-free sociologists do not. Moreover, unlike the positivists, value-aware sociologists deny that social action can be accounted for by universal laws.

There is, however, a third category of sociologists. A minority of humanistic sociologists, following the lead of Alvin Gouldner (1970), argue that sociologists should not attempt to segregate their personal values from their research. I will call the position advocated by Gouldner and his disciples the "value-committed" approach. Value-committed sociologists give several reasons in support of their position, but the most important one is that personal values cannot possibly be avoided. Any attempt to deny this fact, they say, makes the objective study of society less—not more—likely.

Sociological research, value-committed sociologists say, is always guided by theory. But sociological theory is not monolithic; as we have seen, there are always theoretical alternatives from which to choose. All theories are based, in turn, on a variety of theoretical models (sometimes called "paradigms"). A theoretical model is a verbal (sometimes mathematical) image of the essential nature of the phenomena to be studied. These images incorporate significant values, such as those pertaining to the definition of human nature and social organization. Are humans naturally altruistic, benign, or self-centered? Is the social order based primarily on normative agreement and cooperation, or on conflict and coercion? Do roles and institutions exist apart from human consciousness, or are they nothing more than mental constructs—constructs that cease to exist as soon as we change our ways of thinking about social reality?

No empirical methods can finally settle these matters. The answers depend on values, and scientists—no matter how sincere the effort to segregate personal values from research—cannot avoid making these choices. As Alvin Gouldner (1970) repeatedly insisted, the more we hide from this fact, the more biased our research becomes.

At this point we must add that this assertion is as applicable to the natural sciences as it is to sociology. Every science is based on a model of the phenomena studied in that science. These models imply a number of untestable claims or assumptions. In biology, for example, the dominant Darwinian paradigm implies numerous important values about nature and humanity's relationship to it. These assumptions are no less untestable simply because most reputable scholars accept them. (The classical Darwinian paradigm is now being increasingly called into question by many biologists. As this process continues, the value presuppositions of Darwinian evolution will increasingly come into focus.)

It seems to me that Gouldner has a good argument. Furthermore, as a Christian sociologist, I am committed to the goal of relating my religious faith to my work as a sociologist and vice versa. To be a value-committed Christian sociologist carries implications that run throughout sociology. For example, as a sociologist committed to the authority of the Bible, I have to consider carefully what it means to regard the Bible as "authoritative." What does it mean for a Christian to claim "biblical truth"? This question leads us to consider the ways the word "knowledge" is used by the writers of the Bible. In both Old and New Testaments, writers use the word knowledge primarily as a verb—to know something is to be in relationship with the source of knowledge. A wife knows her husband through the intimacy of married experience; Christ's disciples are known by the loving quality of their relationships; Christians know God insofar as they obey his commands; and on the Judgment Day, Christ will say to many who merely believed but did not faithfully act on these beliefs, "I never knew you" (Matthew 7:23). We act, we are transformed in the process, and thus we know.

By sharp contrast, the ancient Greeks and Romans used the word *knowledge* primarily as a noun. Knowledge of the truth was an external thing—to be discovered and possessed. By contrast, Jews thought of truth more intimately and subjectively—as something in which one invests oneself, as a process that transforms the knower (*see* Clark, 1983).

Thus, when Pilate asked Jesus, "What is truth?" two fundamentally different conceptions of knowing truth confronted each other. Pilate, the Roman, wanted Jesus to recite a universally true proposition. He wanted objective knowledge. Christ offered instead a relationship with the truth—a personal commitment. Jesus declared himself to be the way, the truth, and the life. He

did not offer a list of correct beliefs, he offered a relationship with
the truth. Praxis—fruitful, active commitment to the truth—is the
way of knowing Jesus offers (*see* Perkins, 1987).

Sadly, most modern Evangelicals appear to have either
ignored or rejected this biblically advocated way of knowing. Most
Evangelicals have chosen the Greek way, claiming a list of
propositions taken (presumably without interpretation) from an
"inerrant" Bible. In so doing, they attempt to banish all doubt so
as to attain utter certainty. By means of this sort of "spiritual
positivism," they hope to secure their salvation (*see* Hunter, 1983).

As a sociologist, I want to espouse a way of knowing more
consistent with Christ's way. Of course, this approach is hardly
the majority viewpoint in either modern sociology or contemporary Evangelicalism. If I needed to be classified, I guess I'd be most
comfortable with being called a "Christian humanist." (Some
conservative Christians think this is a contradiction in terms, but I
don't.) A Christian humanist is a person who is committed to the
following values:

— The first priority for the Christian is to obey God's will—a
  will expressed in the life of Jesus Christ.
— Humans are created in the image of God. We have the
  capability of developing aspects of our divine image, such
  as our capacity for rational thought, effective communication (and the creation of symbols), and supportive social
  relationships.
— Our task as disciples of Christ is to maximize these
  positive potentials for the purpose of glorifying God by
  means of building his kingdom here on earth. (Of course,
  humans have other "potentials," arising out of our sinful
  natures and the sinful structures of society [which we
  create] which we should not develop or promote.)

When we pray the Lord's Prayer, we repeat these words:
"Thy Kingdom come. Thy will be done in earth, as it is in heaven"
(Matt. 6:10 KJV). According to this prayer, our responsibility as
disciples of Christ is to do God's will here and now—to establish
on earth the kinds of conditions and relationships that already
exist in heaven. If we are to maximize our contribution in building
God's kingdom, we will need to develop our capabilities to solve
problems and communicate effectively. Anything that can be done
for the kingdom can be done better if Christians can think and talk
more clearly. So, this response—that the study of sociology
makes us more useful citizens of God's kingdom—is one answer I
could give to the student who asks, "Why should I study this
stuff?"

A second reason sociology is worth studying can be discussed only after surveying the underlying principles one learns from the study of humanistic sociology. The principles of a value-committed Christian sociology are as follows:

— The social world is humanly constructed and socially maintained. In other words, social reality must be written with quotation marks around the phrase, "social reality." From a human standpoint, it never ceases to be "reality" *according to some point of view.* This is the lesson every student of sociology needs to learn. Of course, there is an obvious challenge here—Christianity is part of the socially constructed world. For the spiritually positivistic Christian who defines *faith* in terms of a list of doctrines believed to be utterly correct, this lesson will be a direct threat. But it won't be threatening to those who understand faith as committed action— action in the face of doubt and in obedience to God's will.

— Our socially constructed world is, in part, shaped according to our collective experience of it. In short, "social reality" is a function of one's social location. Therefore, as our collective experience varies, so too does our sense of common "reality." This point introduces students to the problem of relativity, with which I think every Christian studying sociology needs to wrestle.

— The more our experience is limited to a confined social location, the more likely we are to take "reality" for granted (meaning we will also less likely realize "reality" is humanly constructed). This point brings us to the connection between taking the world for granted and the ethical consequences of such. It is with these subjects that we directly encounter the explicit value commitments of Christian humanist sociology. Should Christians take the world for granted, refusing to consider whether "reality" is socially constructed and thus reconstructable?

— The social system is what the writers of the New Testament call the *Cosmos.* These writers frequently warn the followers of Christ that the *Cosmos* can have dangerous and subtle influence on the thinking and behavior of Christians. They warn us to reconstruct new ways of living more conducive to God's will for our lives (Romans 12:1–2).

— Those who know the least about the *Cosmos* are most likely to be influenced by it. Those who know the most about how the *Cosmos* actually operates are in the best position to influence it, rather than be controlled by it.

The last point represents the link between studying sociology and helping to build the kingdom of God on earth—thus fulfilling the Great Commission. This is the major reason I give for studying sociology. One implication of the study of society from a Christian, value-committed perspective is that we must be willing to rethink everything from the ground up. The "ground" from which Christian sociologists work is the Word of God—which is Jesus Christ. The means we use to rethink conventional reality are the concepts and theories of humanistic sociology—those of a reflexive, value-committed sociology.

Reflexivity goes beyond self-reflection (awareness of personal values), although it begins there. To be reflexive is to be able to intellectually and experientially step outside one's social location and frame of reference, vicariously and/or directly experience other social locations, and consequently apply these alternate frames of reference. In other words, reflexive people are outsiders to their own position within the social system. They are marginal people—able to critique their own positions and situations according to theoretical and ethical perspectives that would not otherwise be theirs.

Reflexivity demands that we submit ourselves to a standard outside ourselves, such as the rules of logic. Reflexivity also involves disciplined observation: "Did I just give a full account of the facts, or did I recount only those that serve my interests?" In a similar manner, reflexive sociologists are able to bring to bear alternative theoretical perspectives on their research. Consequently, their understandings of social phenomena are informed by multiple perspectives, each potentially critical of the others. They see things from theoretically informed standpoints unavailable to those who cannot see the world from a sociological perspective. Reflexive Christians can do the same with Christian ethics: "Am I truly treating others as I would have them treat me, or am I making up reasons that conveniently legitimate choices I want to make?"

In summary, these are the two main reasons why I think sociology needs to be taught from a value-committed, Christian position. First, the study of sociology leads to greater analytical clarity. The ability to engage in comprehensive, complex analysis, coupled with effective communication of theoretical insights, is invaluable in realizing our potentials as being made in the image of God.

Second, we need to understand how social reality is constructed and how it can be reconstructed if we are to avoid the dangerous influences of the *Cosmos* as we help to build the kingdom of God. We need the reflexivity that the combination of Christian ethics and sociological theory provides.

Moreover, since sociology is itself an important aspect of the *Cosmos*, it represents, in some respects, the vanguard of modern "enlightened" thought. For this reason alone, we ought to become more aware of what a sociological perspective is, and which of its assumptions (e.g., relativity or determinism) are in tension with orthodox Christian ways of thinking.

Such reflexivity has no use insofar as it remains a detached analytical exercise. Rather, it needs to be put into regular practice. I want to illustrate the meaning of this statement by referring to the following important (but often ignored) biblical concepts: *shalom* and *koinonia*. Both words carry complex meanings that are not easily translated into modern English. *Shalom* refers mainly to "right relationship," and *koinonia* refers to a corporate lifestyle of intimate sharing. Both refer to proper ways of relating to one another as God's children. When Christ identified the most important of the divine laws, he said we are to love God and our neighbors as ourselves. Due to the unacknowledged influences of North American culture and social location, modern middle-class Evangelicals appear to focus on the first and largely ignore the latter. "Loving one's neighbor" is typically restricted to being polite to one another, praying for one another, and bringing in meals when someone is ill. As important as these activities are, a proper understanding of *shalom* and *koinonia* demands that we take these imperatives far more seriously.

Our task as sociologically-informed, value-aware Christians is to reflexively examine what *shalom* and *koinonia* demand of us. Whatever else they entail, both concepts carry significant social implications, and a reflexive Christian sociology can be of immeasurable value in exploring these social implications.

The combination of reflexive sociology and Christianity has sensitized me over the years to the ways in which the Christian gospel has been reinterpreted from its original collective sense to its present individualistic forms within contemporary evangelicalism. Thus, when my family and I moved to Houghton College, a small Christian liberal arts college in western New York, we searched for housing that could accommodate students. Starting ten years ago, we formed a house fellowship consisting of several couples, including college administrators and faculty, and several dozen men and women students. I have found that my understanding of *shalom* and *koinonia* has been significantly affected by both my understanding of small group sociological theory and my direct personal involvement in the fellowship. I have been fortunate enough to develop a value-committed Christian sociology centered on a deepening involvement in what it means to build the type of relationships required in the kingdom of God. To do so has required a willingness to suspend belief in a number of cultural forms that have been attached to Evangelical thought. The most important of these are the assumed primacy of nuclear family living, the necessity of familial privacy, and (most difficult of all) the centrality of individual freedom and the right to make one's own decisions without consultation. Until Christians are willing (and able) to rethink these sacred American middle-class beliefs, they will not be able to budge "fellowship" much beyond ordinary cordiality. As important as *shalom* and *koinonia* are for understanding the gospel, they will be largely ignored until reflexive sociologically-aware Christians are able to rethink the conventional ways we have understood biblical commands.

Neither abstracted sociological learning about group dynamics nor theoretically uninformed personal experience are sufficient if taken separately. The combination of value-committed sociology and reflexive awareness of the Christian gospel represents the type of learning I recommend to Christians studying sociology.

The next Christian who asks, "Why should I study sociology?" will get this as an answer.

REFERENCES IN CHAPTER

Clark, Robert A. 1983. "Praxis Makes Perfect: Beyond Conceptual Integration in Sociology." Paper presented to the ACTS (Association of Christians Teaching Sociology) Conference, Eastern College, June meeting.

Gouldner, Alvin. 1970. *The Coming Crises in Western Sociology*. New York: Basic Books.

Hunter, James D. 1983. *American Evangelicalism: Conservative Religion and the Quandary of Modernity*. New Brunswick, N.J.: Rutgers University Press.

Perkins, Richard. 1987. *Looking Both Ways: Exploring the Inter-Face Between Christianity and Sociology*. Grand Rapids, Mich: Baker Book House.

INDEX

The Sociological Perspective
was typeset by the Photocomposition Department
of Zondervan Publishing House, Grand Rapids, Michigan
on a Mergenthaler Linotron 202/N.
Compositor: Nancy Wilson
Editor: Dimples Kellogg

The text was set in 10 point Palatino,
a face designed by Hermann Zapf in Germany in 1948.
Palatino is probably one of the two most highly
regarded typefaces of this century.
This book was printed on 55-pound White Vellum paper
by Evangel Press of Nappanee, Indiana.